Dedicated to-
My wife Sophie, who was with me page by page and to my son Jonathan,
who took an active interest in this project

APPLE BLOSSOMS AND SATELLITE DISHES
Celebrating the golden jubilee of Applewood Acres

Published by:

David L. Cook,
1077 North Service Road, #39, Box 20014,
Mississauga, Ontario, L4Y 1A6

Production by:

Print Solutions Management Inc.,
2202 Breezy Brae Drive,
Mississauga, Ontario, L4Y 1N5

ISBN 0-9734265-0-0   June 2004

1

PREFACE

The idea for this book originated in a very romantic setting. My wife Sophie and I were attending the wedding of a friend's daughter on their farm about 50 miles east of Toronto. We were all seated inside a large white tent. Harold Shipp and his wife June were seated in front of us and while waiting for the wedding to start, I leaned forward and asked Harold when he built Applewood Acres. As it turned out, the 50th anniversary was near. I felt something should be done to commemorate the occasion and the idea for the book came to me soon after.

As a newspaper reporter and radio broadcaster by trade, one of the most difficult things for me to do throughout this book was to inject 'first person' writing. First person writing is something I am not comfortable with and, in a news story, it is just not done. However, this book is not a news article and from time to time, I hope the readers will forgive my first person writing. But then again, my writing this book, and my family's roots here going back to 1910 when my father, Norman Edward Cook, was born in a small house on the north side of Dundas, just east of Dixie Road and myself having been a part of the community since 1957, does tend to make first person writing a necessity.

Also, there may still be people who have lived in the area who have gone on to participate in sports, entertainment, or some other endeavor of note and who may not be mentioned or profiled in this book. I have tried not to miss anyone.

I must also thank Terry Butt, former member of Mississauga Council who represented this area at one time, for providing the funding so that one book could be given free to each household in Applewood Acres. His love for the community certainly is deep and genuine. And also, to Sean Wedlock of Wedlock Paper Converters Limited, 2327 Stanfield Road for providing the bags used to deliver the books to the area homes. And finally, I want to say thank you to Susan Dales of Port Credit who gave so much of her time in editing this book.

Dave Cook

2

TABLE OF CONTENTS

FOREWORD

The history of Mississauga is well documented in numerous books and also in papers prepared by various municipal and special interest groups and authors. However we would certainly be remiss if we didn't delve a little into pre-Applewood Acres history.

As author of *Apple Blossoms and Satellite Dishes*, I make no claim to the accuracy of any dates, names, places or events, but I have tried to be as exact as possible.

This book attempts to deal with the subdivision, Applewood Acres, but will from time to time wander beyond the physical and temporal boundaries.

One of the best accounts of early years for this area can be read in the book *Reflections from Yesterday*, written by Frederick M. Ketchen, 150th Anniversary Chairman, The Anglican Church of St. John The Baptist, Dixie.

While there are many names and dates mentioned, it is impossible to tie them all together without extensive research. As an example, it has been documented that in the 1840's people moved in and out of Peel County at an astonishing rate. The early Peel Census shows that twenty five percent of the people enumerated would not be here for the next enumeration. The Census was taken every 10 years in those days.

The late Col. T.L. Kennedy, Peel MPP and former Premier of Ontario, tells a delightful story of the earlier days in what became the western portion of Applewood Acres.

In an interview done on May 3, 1955 regarding the history of Applewood Acres, and found in the archives of the Westacres Public School, Col. Tom tells of the lands on Con. 1, lot 9, s.d.s. (south Dundas Street).

"The land was originally Crown Land. A family by the name of Church received land between the First and Second Lines from the Crown in approximately 1804. The Church family was American (as were many of the original settlers in the vicinity) but could not be classed as United

Empire Loyalists. The Churches held the land for some time. Then the Haines family bought 300 acres from the Churches. The Haines sold the property to the Grahams, who built the brick, two-story house on what is now the Service Road. The house is now owned by Dr. R. J. Thompson. The Hedges and Stewarts each bought property from the Grahams at $20 an acre. The Hedges and Stewarts only bought the land about 50 years ago.

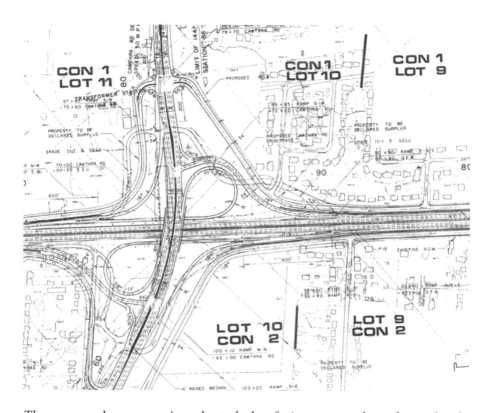

They were the ones who planted the fruit trees and apple orchards. Gordon Shipp bought the Hedge and Stewart farms, which he built up into the Westacres section of Applewood Acres.

The land in Applewood was once considered almost worthless. Since it is sandy soil it is not able to hold grain and hay crops. Only since the value of sandy soil for fruit trees has been discovered, have the acres proved valuable.

5

When the land was first obtained from the Crown, and for many years after that, all the homes were built along the Dundas Highway. The original Haines "homestead" is still standing at the corner of the Dundas Highway and Haines Road. It is built of stone, but a clapboard addition has been added. It is now owned by Van Erk Florists.

It is also interesting to note that when the land was given by the Crown to the original settlers, the latter had to live on the land for three years. After the three-year period had elapsed they were given the deed to the property. In Crown deed, however, it was stipulated that any gold or silver found on the land was the property of the Crown, as were any white pine trees. (White pine was used for the masts of sailing vessels, and was considered quite valuable). About seventy years ago the last white pine was removed from this area. It was about 200 feet tall, and twelve oxen were needed to pull it down to the north of the Etobicoke River.

The Churches, Haines and Grahams were all quite famous families. One of the Churches owned a distillery, one of the first in Ontario, on the Dundas Highway, where he made liquor and sold it legally, tax free.

The Graham family is also quite well known. A story is told about one of the Graham sons, which happened about seventy years ago. In those days medical students had to provide their own specimens for their studies. As a result, whenever there was an accident or sudden death, the students obtained the bodies. One of the Graham sons was working at the C.N.R. station in the area, when a man was killed by a train. Shortly afterwards two medical students came out from Toronto, with a hired grocery wagon and horse, to get the deceased. They managed to get the body, with Graham's help, and the three of them, their "specimen", and a bottle of whiskey started out for Toronto. Before they went very far they came to one of the old hotels then built along the Dundas, and feeling in need of liquid refreshment, the medical students (with their bottle) went inside. Graham was not invited, however. Not to be outdone, Graham removed the body from the back of the wagon, covering himself with the blanket formerly covering the corpse. The students came out and started on their way again, not realizing any change had taken place. Further down the road they came to another hotel, and an argument arose between the two students as to whether they should stop and have another drink. Suddenly Graham sat up in the back of the wagon and informed the others that he was thirsty, and could certainly do with a drink, too. The students immediately deserted the wagon and its contents, each going a different

6

direction. Graham was left with the horse and wagon and a corpse. He never did find out what happened to the students, or if they stopped running." Col. Thomas L. Kennedy.

Col. Kennedy refers to land grants given by the Crown as early as 1804 and of course there are many documented grants in books and papers written about Peel County, some of which will be dealt with in my book. But what I find curious about it all is that when the pioneers who had followed the military trail known as Dundas Street, which opened from York to Port Credit in 1793, the Crown was in the business of awarding these land grants at a time when Peel was still the preserve of the Mississaugas of The New Credit First Nation. The Crown didn't initiate an agreement with the Mississaugas until 1806. The Indians had resisted all attempts that the Crown made to purchase their lands until that time.

The war of 1812-14 brought immigration to a virtual halt in Peel. By 1818, however, the Crown and the Mississaugas Indians finally reached a settlement for the balance of the lands in what was known as the Mississauga Tract and the following year tenders were issued for the surveying of the new township. Today the Mississaugas occupy the New Credit Reserve which is located in Hagersville, Ontario. The reserve, which is more than 5,900 acres (2,392 ha), is home to about 650 aboriginal people. Almost the same number live off the reserve. Their native language is Ojibway.

It has been written that a tavern was opened in the Dundas /Cawthra Road area by Philip and Lydia Cody who came from New England around 1807. The Cody family ancestors were Huguenots who left France in the 1680's to escape religious persecution and had settled in Massachusetts by 1698.

According to history books of Peel Region, Mrs. Sarah Grant, from York, received a land patent issued in Toronto Township on May 19, 1807. Since she apparently had no intentions of moving onto the property, which is a requirement for accepting crown lands, Philip and Lydia Cody purchased the deed to the property the following week for $500. Cody built an inn on 200 acres on Lot 10, 1st Concession s.d.s. (South Dundas Street).

As a reference point today, Con. 1, Lot 10 s.d.s. would, according to all of the mappings of the area that I have seen, be placed on the east side of the first line (Cawthra Road) going south from Dundas Street to the Queen

Elizabeth Highway. Cody opened an inn for travelers, which he managed for some time before leasing it to others. In 1810 Philip Cody deeded a parcel of land in perpetuity so that a free church of the Protestant religion could be built. This is the building that stands on the north side of Dundas Street, east of Cawthra Road, beside St. John The Baptist Dixie Church and is known as the Dixie Union Chapel. The following year Philip and his wife had a son, Isaac, born September 15, 1811. Philip Cody held the rank of Ensign with the Second York Militia and fought in the War of 1812. He eventually sold the tavern in 1829 giving his time to surveying and the buying and selling of lands.

Among the first guests in Cody's inn were Joseph and Jane Silverthorn who stayed until their log cabin was built. This log cabin, which was substantially expanded, eventually became known as Cherry Hill House. It is now a restaurant and in 1972 was moved north of its original location. The Cherry Hill House actually stood in the green space inside the north-west loop of the interchange of Cawthra Road and Dundas Street.

The rest is well documented in the many books written about Peel. However, what has never been documented as being true, but makes wonderful folklore, is that Issac Cody returned to his place of birth to visit his older sister, Nancy (born 1805), who had stayed in the area having married Amos Marigold. While visiting in the Dixie area, Isaac's infant son became seriously ill causing them to have him baptized in the Dixie Union Chapel. The infant recovered and grew up to become Col. William Frederick Cody, who became known as Buffalo Bill Cody.

However, Fred H. Garlow, grandson of Buffalo Bill, is on record in the book *Reflections from Yesterday*, saying that W. F. Cody was born February 26, 1846 and that Isaac Cody and his wife, Mary Ann (Laycock), at the time were living at LeClaire, Iowa. The family moved to Kansas when Bill Cody was eight years of age. Mr. Garlow writes that in all of the history and family records he has read, he has never learned where and if Buffalo Bill was ever baptized. However, Mr.Garlow states in his letter that it would seem fairly logical that it was Isaac Cody, Buffalo Bill's father, who was baptized in the church. As mentioned, Isaac was born in Toronto Township, County of Peel in 1811. Again, I will leave that story for the historians, but as I said, it makes a great bit of folklore.

Isaac Cody had three wives. His first wife was Martha O'Connor and they had no children. Martha died in 1840 and Isaac soon married Mary Ann

8

Laycock. Together they had seven children, Martha, Samuel, Eliza, Julia, Laura, Mary and William Frederick. Isaac's wife died and he would marry for a third time to Rebecca Sumner and would have one child, Charles.

William Frederick Cody married on March 16, 1866 to Louise Fredwerici and raised four children, one of which was named after a famous western hero, Kit Carson.

Tracing original owners of land in the area of what is now Applewood Acres, is extremely time consuming. But briefly, the 1859 Tremaine's Map shows many new landowners south of Dundas and north of Middle Road (QEW). Going from east to west, starting at Dixie Road, we see William Orth, William Clarkson and Abe Death occupying the southeastern sector. To the north was a property listed as being owned by the heirs of A. Wilson. Next was Robert Church with a sizable chunk of land which was a narrow tract going from Dundas to Middle Road. His lands were approximately 75 X 12 chains, a chain being a measurement used by early surveyors of 66 feet (20m) to the chain, making his property just less than one mile (1.6 km) in length and about 825 feet (251m) in width. The Farr's, John and Joseph, had parcels along the east side of Con.1.s.d.s. and It was Joseph Farr who purchased the Cody lands and tavern in 1829.

The Walker and Miles Historical Atlas shows that by 1877 many of the earlier mentioned families still owned lands here. Again going east to west, familiar family names such as Clarkson, Death, Orth and the Wilson families are now joined by Thomas Stanfield. Stanfield arrived in Canada in the 1840's and apparently first settled near Streetsville. Eventually he purchased about 100 acres in this area. Jas.and John Hickie owned small parcels south of the Stanfield lands. Andrew Graham owned a very sizable parcel which would comprise most of the lands where Westacres is located, along with Jehoiada Haines, who also owned a very large parcel which stretched from Dundas south to Middle Road.

The Stewart family acquired property and a house from the Graham family and settled on 60 acres going north of what is now the North Service Road. The original Graham farmhouse is now 871 North Service Road. The Stewarts built a small cottage at what is now 835 North Service Road just to the west of the Stewart farmhouse for Carl Stewart, a cousin.

9

When the Shipp's decided to purchase lands north of the Queen Elizabeth Highway there were then about a dozen landowners between the First Line East (Cawthra Road), Second Line East (Stanfield Road) and Third Line East (Dixie Road). The Shipps, however, did not purchase all of the properties.

The establishment of Applewood Acres may have been the blueprint of how governments across Canada have come to deal with developers today. *Apple Blossoms and Satellite Dishes*, outlines the struggles not only of the developer, The Shipp Corporation, originally known as G.S. Shipp and Son, but also the struggles of the early residents with the school board and local municipality, and to an extent, higher levels of government. The approval process for Applewood Acres actually landed on the desk of the Premier of Ontario.

Dr. R.J. Thomson settled in the area just as the development of Applewood Acres began. He graduated from the University of Toronto Medical School in 1952 and interned at St. Joseph's Hospital in Toronto 1952-1953. He was no stranger to the area, having worked summer holidays from age 14 on a farm owned by Charles Grieg, a relative who emigrated from Scotland. Mr. Grieg originally worked for Garnett Goddard, who farmed the land on the southeast side of what is now Stanfield Road and The Queensway. Mr. Grieg eventually started his own farm, which is now the site of the Tiveron Apple Market at the corner of Camilla Road and The Queensway. Later, Mr. Grieg started a second farm in hopes that his sons would become farmers. However, when that didn't happen he sold the farm to Edmund Peachy for the development of Munden Park.

Dr. Thomson provides an insight into what life was like in the area during the earliest days of Applewood Acres. Many of the area residents became patients of Dr. Thomson.

"When I saw the Stewart farmhouse for sale I bought it to become my home and my office. Having my office in my house was a temporary arrangement that lasted for 20 years until I moved my office to a bungalow on Stanfield Road. My office was then located across the road from Mrs. Stanfield, one of three Stanfield families that had farms on Stanfield Road.

At the time I bought the Stewart farmhouse (871 North Service Road) from Howard Stewart in 1953, my street address was 889 Queen Elizabeth Highway, R.R. 1, Port Credit. To the west of me, at what is now 835 North Service Road, was the home of Carl Stewart. My entrance was directly off the highway. I was told by the Crown Life Real Estate agent that 60 feet of my frontage was designated to be a service road which the Department of Highways purchased from me.

The price of my home was $16,000 which was the same price as the Applewood homes at the time. They ranged from $16,000 to $18,000.

To my east was a bungalow belonging to Bill Hedge, his wife and two sons. Further east of that was the Hedge farm house (915 North Service Road) a gray stone building occupied by Mrs. Hedge and her other son, Fred.

My eastern boundary was the dividing line between the Stewart farm, which was 60 acres and the Hedge farm, also 60 acres. This boundary went all the way north to what is now Melton Drive. A farmer's lane existed which went to Melton and had orchards on each side. Some of the remaining large fir trees are remnants of what were once wind-breaks to protect the orchards from the north-west winds.

Behind my house was the barn of the Stewart farm, where 866 Ribston is now located. This barn was demolished and I have a picture of my son Robert and my wife Doris sitting amongst the rubble. Some of the blocks that line my driveway were acquired from this demolished barn.

When the houses on either side of me were being built, I could look out my bedroom windows and watch the bricklayers ply their trade. They would very quickly lay a row of bricks and then stop for a smoke. They were allowed to lay only so many bricks per hour.

In 1953, Mississauga, then known as South Peel, had a population of 50,000 people. We didn't have a hospital in the area. The closest hospitals were Oakville Trafalgar in Oakville and Peel Memorial in Brampton. The other one was St. Joseph's Hospital at Sunnyside in Toronto at Roncesvales and Queen Street.

When I started practicing medicine there were only nine general practitioners in South Peel. Dr. L.G. Brayley, who lived and had his office

11

in Port Credit, and I were on staff at St. Joseph's Hospital. I had interned at St. Joseph's and thus, had admitting privileges there. Most of my patients were admitted there for having babies, surgery and medical problems.

As the population of South Peel increased, hospitals became crowded to over capacity. St. Joseph's Hospital had patients in the halls until nurses very wisely refused to tend to patients in halls because there were inadequate facilities such as washrooms, sinks, etc.

Dr. Brayley was a member of the Rotary Club in Port Credit and suggested to the members that they embark on a project to build a hospital in South Peel. This they took up with enthusiasm. Mansel Ketchum, preisdent of the Toronto Stock Exchange was the first chairman of the hospital board but had to retire due to his many duties at the TSO. Gordon Jackson, a Port Credit lawyer, then became the chairman of the board.

The initial project was for a fifty bed hospital. At a meeting of 25 or so doctors in Clark Hall in Port Credit, chaired by Mr. Jackson, the question of how many beds should be The suggested number varied. Dr. J.D. Smith stunned the meeting by suggesting 200 beds. His suggestion was closest to the eventual number, which was 123 beds.

Meanwhile, Queensway Hospital was also in the planning phase and a meeting was held with the respective Boards of Directors of the two hospitals to consider the feasibility of building one hospital to serve both Etobicoke and South Peel areas. The chairman of the Board of Directors of the Queensway Hospital was Crawford Gordon, of the AVRO Arrow fame. The Queensway Hospital opened July 21, 1956.

From 1953 until the hospital opened with 123 beds in May 1958, I was on the Board of Directors of the South Peel Hospital. Dr. Brayley was the first Chief of Staff of the the South Peel Hospital, which became the Trillium Health Centre-Mississauga Site in October 1998. He performed the first surgery in the hospital (a tonsillectomy) and died shortly thereafter, not able to benefit from the hospital that he worked so hard to establish."

Dr. R.J. Thomson

12

Original doctors of the South Peel Hospital, now the Trillium Centre, back row, from left to right: Dr. Roman Sluzar, Dr. W.Kent, Dr. Eric Farkas, Dr. Ann Smith, Dr. J.D. Smith, Dr. Gordon Murphy, Dr. Getchel Williams, Dr. Welsh, front row, left to right: Dr. Terry Molony, Dr. Jas Brayley, Dr. Halina Solow, Dr. R.J. Thomson, Dr. Don Dunn. (Doctor Brayley is the son of the man who planted the seed for the hospital, Dr. A.E. Brayley.) Photo taken on May 3, 1993 at the 35th anniversary of the hospital's opening. Three doctors who were among the original hospital staff who lived in Applewood Acres were Dr. Getchel Williams, who lived on the northeast corner of Harvest Drive and Courtland Crescent and who became Chief of Staff, while Doctor Roman Sluzar, who was named the hospital's first Chief of Anaesthesia , lived at 2070 Annapolis Road Dr. Thomson lives on the North Service Road in the former Stewart home. *Photo by Bert Hoferichter, mpa.*

1 The Start

It could be said that the story of Applewood Acres started on the day Harold Shipp celebrated his 25th birthday, January 21, 1951 but the actual anniversary of the community might well be Mother's Day, May 11, 1952.

It was on Harold's birthday that lands south of the Queen Elizabeth Highway were purchased by G.S. Shipp and Son, a successful Toronto homebuilder. The land purchase was for 23 acres (9.3 ha.) at a total cost of $43,000. It was a piece of land 380 feet (115.8m) in width and 2,500 feet (762m) in depth and provided just room enough for a 66 foot (20 m) street which became Applewood Road. Interestingly, the Department of Transportation was quick to realize that a service road would be needed. At that time driveways emptied right onto the Queen Elizabeth Highway (QEW).

The plan was to construct 104 homes and then move north of the highway to begin a project that would become one of the largest single subdivision ever built in Canada by a family developer. There are some who would say it remains to this day the largest ever built. Without a doubt, Applewood Acres is one of the most unique communities built anywhere.

According to Harold Shipp, who 50 years later remains active in the community that he and his father Gordon S. Shipp built, lands for Applewood Acres were purchased in the summer of 1951 and sales of lots started May 11, 1952 on Mother's Day. When the final sales contract was written, G.S. Shipp and Son had constructed 836 homes above and below the Queen Elizabeth Highway.

The firm would continue to build north of Hwy. 5 (Dundas Street) creating communities known as Applewood Heights and Applewood Hills. But this story is primarily about the six Plans of Subdivision that constitute the first major community constructed on the western outskirts of the City of Toronto.

Situated north of the Queen Elizabeth Highway, south of what is now The Queensway and between Cawthra Road on the west and Dixie Road on the East, Applewood Acres became a celebrated community, which was covered extensively by the three daily Toronto newspapers, The Telegram, The Toronto Daily Star and The Globe and Mail. In addition, The

Financial Post, Daily Commercial News, and numerous trade publications, including the prestigious American Builder, hailed the coming of Canada's largest housing project.

Hardly a week would pass that a story of Applewood Acres or an advertisement wouldn't appear in one of the major daily newspapers. G.S. Shipp and Son were the first homebuilders to place full-page ads in the major dailies. They would also enjoy the fruits of advertisements placed by many of their construction suppliers and Harold was always coming up with promotional ideas to keep the name before the public. As an example, the Burroughes Furniture Company ran an advertisement in the Toronto Star announcing the winner of a lucky draw for a bedroom suite shown in the Shipp Shape model home- Mrs. L. Watson, 6, Rutherford Avenue, Mount Dennis, Ontario.

Harold's promotional events included utilizing airplanes to tow advertisement banners, displaying reindeer in a temporary habitat at the opening of the Applewood Village Shopping Centre, and tying a large bow around a house at Christmas. According to the Toronto Star at the time, the intensity of the publicity and promotion of Applewood Acres is believed to be the biggest ever by a home builder in the Toronto area.

The media treated the development west of Toronto as a major news happening. In fact, it actually was. The Toronto Daily Star, in its March 22, 1952 edition, carried a front page story by Paul L. Fox (reprinted with permission-Torstar Syndication Services) on the 'new town' being built 12 miles west of Toronto.

"A multi-million dollar construction boom, which is going to transform the rural area between Toronto and Oakville into a series of industrial and residential areas, started rolling with a $68,500,000 program planned for the next 18 months.

The present program is concentrated in a 20-square mile area from the Dixie Rd. to Oakville and from the Queen Elizabeth Way to Lake Ontario.

"The more than 200 acres to be subdivided on the Dixie Rd., near the Queen Elizabeth Way is expected to create a new town of more than 10,000 people and will include houses, apartments, schools and shopping areas. Its growth reflects the westward expansion of the residential area adjacent to the city.

In this area G.S. Shipp and Son have expanded their present subdivision by some 100 acres on which they plan to build 300 bungalows and storey-and-a-half houses, priced from $14,000 and $15,000 up. Most of the property is on the north side of the Queen Elizabeth Way."

The story was accompanied by a large drawing covering the entire top portion of the front page showing the location of the various developments along the QEW. It also made reference to the fact that a service road system would be installed, believed to be the first service road on provincial highways in Ontario.

Earlier, in a January 23, 1952 edition of The Telegram, a story was published which outlined a massive apartment complex being planned for the southwest corner of Dixie Rd. and QEW.

"It has been announced that apartment houses comprising from six hundred to nine hundred units valued at more than $5,000,000 are planned on the 28-acre property of Charles Hemstead at the southwest corner of the intersection."

The plan was to build one, two and three bedroom apartments, three stories high, eight units in each building. Meanwhile, George A. Rome and Son had purchased 115 acres for 350 homes to develop Orchard Heights (see chapter six) on the southeast corner. Plans, however, were vague. It seemed to call for a hospital, which was to be built on the northeast side of the intersection.

The council of the day, led by Reeve Sid Smith, was very vocal in its opposition to all but the Orchard Heights development. Their major concerns centered around the lack of school facilities, an issue which would play a major role in the plans for Applewood Acres.

The promise of schools was obviously a major draw for families making the decision to locate in what was the rural area west of Toronto. Shipp advertisements promised schools and no one, including G.S. Shipp and Son, had any reason to think differently.

In fact, the school board had announced plans for schools in March of 1952 and in a brief story in the Toronto Telegram newspaper, carried a mention that an "austerity" school would be constructed in Toronto

Township at a cost of $68,000 by G. S. Shipp and Son. The construction of the Applewood Public School would be of cement block and would slash the costs from $24,000 a room to about $13,000. The South Peel Board of Education, according to the article, instigated the move toward these "economy" schools.

However, establishing the first school in Applewood Acres was not a smooth road. The early purchasers soon found their children walking north on Dixie Road to attend school in temporary classrooms set up on the grounds of the Dixie Public School at Dundas and Dixie. In a little touch of irony, many of those children would, many years later as adults, be involved in an effort to keep the schools in Applewood Acres open.

Bruce MacDonald, Staff Reporter for The Toronto Daily Star reported on August 15, 1952, that due to substantial increases in property taxes the promise of a school in Applewood was placed on the back burner (reprinted with permission-Torstar Syndication Services).

"Residents of the 135 new homes in Toronto Township's Applewood Acres' subdivision, who see their property taxes jumping to almost three times what they anticipated when they began moving in only a few months ago, today were faced with another headache-the possibility of their youngsters will have to travel a mile and a half to public school.

Purchasers of houses in the new subdivision were told that taxes on their properties, ranging in price from $14,500 to $17,000, would be around $120 a year, and that a public school would be built in the area. It was on this assurance that many families decided to settle there.

Now they find their taxes will be $315 a year and more, and the proposed school has vanished. Instead of sending their youngsters to a public school within a stone's throw of their homes, it now appears likely they must pay the cost of transporting their children to and from temporary classrooms to be set up on the grounds of Dixie Public School, one and one half miles away. Instead of their children going back and forth to school along the quiet residential streets of Applewood Acres, they will likely have to travel along the narrow and dangerous Dixie Rd.

There is still a chance that the school board officials will agree to set up the temporary classrooms on a piece of property in the subdivision owned by the United Church but undeveloped. However, at a recent meeting between the residents and school officials, it was contended it would be more expensive to operate the classrooms there.   Leslie Hughes, chairman of the board, also argued that the board would not be permitted to install the necessary sanitary facilities since it did not own the land.

Although the provincial department of planning and development has approved use of the school site set aside by G. S. Shipp and Son, which developed the subdivision, school board officials have rejected it on the ground the land is too low and the soil unsuitable. Its use for temporary classrooms has also been discarded by the board."

Residents would argue that it would be too dangerous to continue to have their children walk up Dixie Road across the CPR tracks.   Henry Moxon, of 2072 Tolman Road, chairman of an emergency ratepayers' association, which was hurriedly established to fight for a school closer to home, pointed out that the plans to construct an overpass on Dixie Road over the Queen Elizabeth Highway added to those fears and would bring even more traffic into the area during the construction phase.

The lack of a permanent school site had been complicated by the refusal of the township to permit Shipp to proceed with further development because it was premature.

According to a provincial statute, five per cent of the land in a subdivision must be set aside for public use, that is for schools or parks. G.S. Shipp and Son planned to make a piece of land in the expanded area available, which adjoined that set aside for school purposes in Applewood Acres. Combined, the two sites provided 4.4 acres of land for a new public school. The school board, however, rejected this proposal and, instead, announced it had decided to buy land from Mr. Shipp in the middle of the easterly development.

The only trouble with that plan was that the land would have cost the school board more than $20,000 and it didn't have the money. Mr. Shipp contended the land which he set aside was suitable for school purposes and was the site desired by the parents in the area.

At the time, the township, wrestling with increased costs to deliver services to residents, imposed a tax on each building lot in the amount of $750. G. S. Shipp and Son challenged that levy and subsequently won.

The province refused to hear an appeal by Toronto Township on the Ontario Municipal Board's ruling, which permitted G.S. Shipp and Son Construction Company to build 230 homes in the municipality. The then Municipal Affairs Minister Dunbar informed the township that no useful purpose would be served in the hearing of such an appeal by the Ontario Cabinet. The municipal board also ruled that the company was not obligated to pay the $750 education tax on each building lot.

Angered by the decision, township officials met with the provincial government to seek answers to the problem not only of school costs, but of development growth. Residents angered by tax hikes caused overflowing meetings at numerous council meetings while at the same time developers were at odds with the township in efforts to win approvals to build.

G.S. Shipp and Son offered to loan the township $25,000 toward the construction of the Applewood Public School.

The offer was not accepted by the Toronto Township council. Instead, the council asked the Ontario Municipal Board to declare the new Shipp sub-division and 20 others planned for the township "premature" because there wasn't sufficient industrial assessment in the township to carry the tax load for services.

By October 1952 the municipality decided that it would take unprecedented action and appeal directly to the Premier of Ontario, who at this time was Premier Frost. This was the first time in the history of Ontario that a municipal council disregarded the ruling of a provincial board and appealed directly to the Premier and his Cabinet.

"We will go straight to the heads of the government," declared Reeve Sidney Smith. "We will disregard red tape, precedent and protocol." A resolution by Councillor Hugh Harrison and Deputy Reeve Lloyd Herridge instructed municipal staff to prepare the notice of appeal to take the matter to the Lieutenant-Governor In Council.

The ruling of the Ontario Municipal Board had granted approval to the 126-lot Shipp subdivision only, although 20 subdivisions had been sent to the board for ruling on a by-law asking sub-dividers to pay $750 a lot for educational purposes. The ruling provided that Shipp did not have to pay the $750 per lot or the hydro costs and emphatically stated the board's opinion that "any more residential subdivisions in the township are

19

premature, as the township should have time to consolidate its position. financially and otherwise."

The Premier's immediate response was that he tended to agree with the board's ruling saying that it seemed that Toronto Township has a very real problem.

"As a matter of fact it is a problem that confronts the whole metropolitan area. We will look at that matter carefully and consider it," said Premier Frost.

For many months the lawyers for both sides of the issue would meet, council would receive deputation after deputation on the issue and finally, in a marathon 17-hour council meeting held on April 1,1953, Council moved to end its stand on a housing ban and resolve the issue.

Toronto Township gave the green light for construction of 628 new homes valued at more than $10,000,000 and two shopping centers costing $3,000,000 on the Queen Elizabeth Way.

The meeting's unanimous decision was the first break in a home construction embargo imposed by council and the Ontario Municipal Board a year earlier following a tax row which led to a Government ordered investigation of township finances. Under the embargo all subdivisions had been declared premature and halted.

In contrast, some 50 years later, the City of Mississauga's financial situation became the envy of municipalities across the country. In the report "City of Mississauga-2002 Successes", it was revealed that the City experienced a very active construction year in 2002, issuing 6,952 permits with a prescribed construction value of $1.542 billion for all permits. This represents the sixth consecutive billion-dollar plus year. 2002 was the second year in which the residential prescribed construction value exceeded $1.0 billion.

The City of Mississauga, which boasted transit ridership in excess of 25 million passengers, also had been named one of Canada's top 100 employers for the third consecutive year.

The first Plan of Subdivision for Applewood Acres, marking the actual start of the process, was registered with the municipality on February 21,

1952 as Plan 439 for homes to be built on Greening Avenue, Melba Road, Tolman Road, Snow Crescent, Russett Road, MacIntosh Crescent and Second Line East (Bloomfield Road), which later became Stanfield Road.

Construction started with houses being built on Greening, Russett, Melba, Snow, Tolman and also on Stanfield Road. Photo courtesy Shipp Corporation

The land was purchased in the summer of 1951 and the surveyor was F.H. Mucklestone of Baird and Mucklestone who completed his survey on December 15, 1951. Two names shown as the mortgagees on the original copy of Plan 439 are Stanley Josiac and Charles Watson.

The Plan of Subdivision originally called for homes to be built on both sides of MacIntosh Crescent as Stanfield Road went straight down to meet the North Service Road thus creating 3.3 acres of green space between MacIntosh and Stanfield Road. Eventually the shopping centre was extended utilizing that green space. The original plans did not include a church site. However, a later sales brochure did show the location for the church. Another difference in the Plan of Subdivision and what finally happened is that a parcel of land was originally reserved for a school site at the north end of Russett Road, where Halliday Park is now located.

Next came Plan 463 registered on October 14, 1952, again surveyed by F.H. Mucklestone. This plan had homes to be constructed on the North

21

Service Road, Courtland Crescent, Melba Road, Harvest Drive, Rambo Road, Kendall Road and Melton Drive. Mortgagees were Hazel Death and Beverly Death, Executors of the Death Estate.

Originally, the plan had homes on a portion of Kendall Road which were intended to travel south from Melton Drive, parallel to Rambo Road, through the lands where Applewood Public School now stands, and then turn easterly. Also, the plan called for Melba Road to continue easterly across Harvest Drive terminating at Courtland Crescent. Plan 463 was later amended by Plan 466 and surveyed in December of 1952, providing for its present configuration. (As a result of this amendment the final tally of homes built north of the QEW is 732).

Plan 473 dated May 28, 1953, showed Wealthy Place and Primate Road taking its present configuration.

On August 17, 1953 Plan 481 opened up the western section of Applewood Acres below the hydro corridor with homes constructed on Whitney Drive, Annapolis Avenue, Breezy Brae Drive, Henley Road, Hedge Drive, Ribston Road, Redan Drive and Stewart Crescent.

Mortgagees who signed this document were Carl Stewart, H.B. Stewart, Sarah Mabel Hedge, Frederick McNally Hedge and William L. Hedge. One signature, which could not be positively identified on the original document, most likely would have been that of the Gentleman Farmer, Harry Whitehead, who owned the Breezy Brae Farm.

On December 4, 1953, Shipp registered Plan 493 for lands north of the hydro corridor for homes on Guthrie Lane, Baldwin Road, Johnathan Drive, Melton Road, Westfield Drive, Breezy Brae Drive, Harcourt Crescent, Wedgewood Road, Duchess Drive, Bartlett Lane, Candish Lane and Haynes (Haines) Road. The sales brochure interestingly showed this area to include a Junior School to be located on the eastern part of the lands west of Westfield Drive, opposite Baldwin Road. Westacres School was shown in its present location.

22

No roads, ditches or lawns, just a dirt road and houses in various states of completion. Looking along Duchess Road in 1954. Photo courtesy of Herbert W. Jarand, an original owner on Duchess Drive

Again, mortgagees were Sarah Mabel Hedge, Frederick McNally Hedge, William Lloyd Hedge, Carl Stewart, Harvey B. Stewart and James Guthrie.

A little over three years from the date of the first survey in Applewood Acres the final Registered Plan of Subdivision, number 520, was presented on March 28, 1955 to the municipality. This plan provided for homes to be constructed on Insley Road and extending Henley Road east of Insley to Second Line East (Stanfield Road). The Applewood Village Shopping Centre would open in October of the same year.

The population of South Peel was starting to explode with every new development and Applewood Acres certainly provided a kick-start to that growth. By the early 1950's it was evident that Peel's transition from a rural to an urban community was taking place.

Suburban growth in Peel was a response to population pressure on Toronto. After the Second World War, southern Peel started transforming into a residential urban pattern that linked to Toronto by means of major arterial roads and highways. The population of Toronto Township in 1871 was 5,974 and in 1946, some 75 years later, it had grown to 13,328. In 1966 the population exceeded 93,600 people, an increase of 603 percent in just a 20-year span. The Township of Toronto achieved official town status in 1967 and, in a contest, was named the Town of Mississauga, beating out the name Sheridan. In 1974 it was incorporated as the City of Mississauga.

Herbert W. Jarand parked his 1940 Oldsmobile Hydromatic in front of his new home at 814 Duchess Drive. Below is Harcourt Crescent.

2 Recipe For Sold Signs

Reindeer, stagecoach rides, ice-cream, airplanes, helicopters, radio and newspaper advertisements were all items found in the bag of tools Harold Shipp employed to sell and promote Applewood Acres over the years.

He had a recipe for sprouting 'sold signs' and the proof was certainly in the pudding. One of his promotional campaigns resulted in the sale of 135 houses in a seven-day period, with some 50 homes being sold on the weekend alone. Harold Shipp was the consummate salesman. When he sat down with Howard Wilson of McKim Advertising Ltd. of Toronto, the pair developed a marketing plan to sell Applewood Acres such as had never been seen before.

The plan consisted of inserting full-page advertisements in the three Toronto daily newspapers on Saturday (May 10, 1952), and running one minute radio commercials all weekend on a Toronto radio station. In addition, they arranged advertising support from suppliers and sub-contractors which ran in the newspapers in conjunction with the Shipp ads. A helicopter towing a banner "Visit Applewood Acres" was flown high over Toronto May 9 and 10 for two hours each day.

This advertising produced publicity ranging from an article and pictures in one Toronto paper to a wire-service release across Canada and a mention on the CBC Radio Canada newscast. On site, customers were treated to free ice cream courtesy of Borden's, more than two truck-loads in all.

The entire campaign proved to be an outstanding success. It had been carefully thought out and, anticipating the response, they knew it would be impossible for the sales people in the model homes to try and explain all the features and details to the public. A giant tent was set up and inside the area was divided into booths along the lines of a trade-show. Various sub-contractors and suppliers erected their own displays.

The tent performed two functions. It assured a steady flow of traffic through the model homes and provided more direct and comprehensive information to the potential buyers. A pretty girl was placed in each model home to keep traffic flowing, answer general questions and hand out more than 20,000 brochures.

Some 16 men and women acted as sales staff, mingling with the crowd and making as many contacts as possible. If a sale was anticipated, the salesman directed the prospect to the office where Mr. Shipp finalized the deal. When the 500th home was sold to Mr.and Mrs. Jack Utting, William Pope, Applewood Acres' General Manager, presented the family with a bouquet of roses, and of course, the news media was on hand to snap the picture. First year purchasers were presented with flowers on the following Mother's Day, the actual anniversary of the start of sales in Applewood. Also, in keeping with that appreciative touch, the Shipps delivered plants at Christmas to those first buyers.

A sales pavilion was the first stop for customers.

Aided by excellent weather the results were outstanding by any measurement. With the help of the Ontario Provincial Police and commissionaires, both automobile traffic and foot traffic were kept in hand and cars parked in an orderly fashion. A public address system played music and gave instructions not only to the customers but to the sales staff as well. If a home was sold, an announcement would be made instructing the sales staff to 'mark off a house number' from their list.

To keep tabs on the progress of the building, an ingenious, wall-length master plan, which showed just what stage each house had reached at any given time, was erected.

On Friday, May 9, a total of 10 homes were sold grossing $151,000. Saturday, crowds increased and business swelled to $174,000 and by Monday, $750,000 had been reached.

It was Mother's Day. Prospective customers tour the model homes.

Home-builders in the United States predicted the Shipps might set a record for the entire continent. In December, the firm was rewarded by being named the only Canadian builder to win the award in a U.S. builders' merchandising contest for their highly successful spring campaign. Shipp beat out two large California home building firms. The award is made only to firms which have sales in excess of 100 homes per year.

Catchy names were given to each of the eight styles of houses. These names have stayed with area residents over the years and are often referred to in conversations, but few people know what the names of their homes stand for or the origins of the names.

The Victoria model was named after Harold Shipp's daughter Victoria. The Breezy Brae was named after the 33 acres (13.3ha) of lands purchased from Harry Whitehead, a 'Gentleman Farmer'. He had purchased his farm from Charles Watson who had given it the name Breezy Brae. The Watsons were a prominent family who owned much of the property on both sides of Middle Road (QEW) and all had given their farms various names. The Hargord model got its name from the combination of Harold and Gordon, thus the Hargord. The Shipp-Shape model received its name from the company name. Two homes, the Mid Century and the Mid Century Deluxe were so named because the building of Applewood Acres took place at the Mid Century, the 1950s. The name Wedgewood, however, was selected, as Harold Shipp would say many years later, "because it simply had a nice ring to it". No explanation was given about spelling Wedgewood with an 'e'.

The Candish name is a combination of letters, Can-di-sh. It was selected to pay tribute to the firm that provided the first funding for Applewood Acres, Canada Life, the 'di' a tribute to Ron Dymond, Zone Manager of Canada Life and the 'sh' for Canada Life's staff architect, Bill Sheets.

Several roads in Applewood are named after apples. However, some were named to pay tribute to people who owned land here prior to the subdivision being established. Guthrie, Hedge and Stewart were named after landowners of the day. The name Johnathan, however, is one which stands alone. Originally selected for the name of the apple, a spelling mistake was made and never corrected, thus, the name Johnathan remains. Years later, in an article in the Apple Press, a short story about the spelling of the word Johnathan quipped that possibly the Shipps had a liking for words with extra letters, thus their name "Shipp."

The name Russett came by its second last letter through an error made somewhere in the workings of the municipality. The original Plans of Subdivision clearly show the correct spelling, however, present day maps and road signs differ. Another name that comes under question is the spelling of MacIntosh Crescent. The apple is spelled McIntosh.

28

The Second Line East, which had been known as Bloomfield Road, was changed in the late 1950's. Ruth Stanfield had been in touch with Colonel Thomas L. Kennedy, M.P.P. for Peel and in a response dated August 19, 1958, Colonel Kennedy wrote *"Dear Ruth, I think you have something and the Stanfield name should be given some thought to your road. They have made a great contribution to the village of Dixie. Only for them we would never have had either skating rink or curling rink. I will see if I can do anything. With best wishes, Yours sincerely."*

Cody Lane was named by myself when I was the Ward 7 Councillor. City staff had concerns that the original name, Haines Road, would be difficult for emergency people trying to get to that portion of Haines Road in Applewood. It was closed off at The Queensway and not connected to that portion of Haines Road north of The Queensway. At the time I was advised that these lands were originally owned by Philip Cody and that it was originally the dividing point between what became the Haines property and the Cody lands. It was a natural to name it Cody Lane.

When Westacres was developed, the Bell Telephone and hydro supply to all the homes, except those along Melton Drive, was fed from power lines at the rear of the houses. This was accomplished through an agreement among Bell, Hydro and the developer that the main distribution cables would be buried. Applewood Acres was one of the very first subdivisions in which Bell and Hydro buried their main cables underground. These distribution lines can be seen at some intersections, little square boxes about 3 feet (1 metre) high and six square inches (38 square cm) wide.

Those who arrived to view model homes were presented with a brochure. Actually two different brochures were used, one which featured six homes in the the eastern development and later, a newer brochure added the Victoria and Wedgewood models.

The brochures were 40.6 cm by 50.8 cm (16X20 inches) high quality heavy paper stock, printed both sides and folded into four panels. The brochure showed a drawing of the road plan and included numbered lots. Actual photographs of the model homes were shown with floor plans and a description of each home was given.

The features and specifications of the brochure contained the following as 'Optional Features' (without metric conversions).

Green, Blue or Sandstone coloured bathroom fixtures, including 5 foot recessed bathtub, compact style lavatory, and 17 inch by 19 inch chrome leg wash-basin, with chrome towel bars, combination fittings and pop-up waste. This is included in the "Shipp-Shape" and "Mid-Century" styles. In the "Hargord," there are two complete bathrooms in colour, In "Mid-Century Deluxe", "Breezy-Brae" and "Candish" styles, the extra 2-piece washroom has white fixtures of the same design.

Lino-Tile colours in Kitchen, Bathroom, Washroom (if any) and Vestibule. 8 Pastel Oil Paint Colours on the walls and ceilings (except halls and stucco ceilings). Option of Washable Wallpaper of your choice on Bath or Washroom Walls.

The second brochure added supplier names such as Dominion Oilcloth and Acme Paint and Varnish Co. Ltd. The brochure outlined the standard specifications in all homes, unless otherwise indicated, they were, "your choice" of;

● *"Fleetlite" aluminum windows, completely weather stripped, and including storms and screens* ● *Ceramic tile in neutral gray colour on all interior window sills* ● *"Fleetlite" steel door-jamb and trim units, for modern neat design* ● *Birch slab doors in modern mahogany finish* ● *Modernfold doors in easy to clean "oyster white" colour on all clothes closets and cloak closets* ● *Steel kitchen cabinets-stainless steel sink bowl-arborite counter top in pearl gray- drawers on rollers- magnetic catches* ● *Zonolite plaster aggregate used exclusively for additional fire-proofing and insulating features* ● *Lot sizes mostly 60-foot frontage by 130 in depth, except where otherwise indicated on Block Plan* ● *Steel Beam Construction for lasting durability* ● *Attached garage with easy-to-operate "Roly" steel overhead doors 8 foot wide supplied by Mor-Sun Ltd. Of Waterloo, Ontario.* ● *Ceilings insulated with fibreglas batts* ●*Outside walls insulated with Insul-Board lath, 15 lb. Felt Paper and plaster parging* ●*Outside doors weather-stripped* ● *All electric light fixtures included* ● *Crushed stone in driveway* ● *Open fireplace with marble facing and quarry tile hearth in living-room.*● *"General Electric" Oil-Fired Furnace with "General Electric" "Air-Wall" heating system* ● *"McClary" Automatic Electric Water Heater in gleaming white enamel finish with 5 year warranty*● *Front lawn sodded to street line*● *Rear and side yards are Rough Graded* ● *Bath recess tiled 4 inches high in gleaming Black Arborite* ● *½ inch Oak flooring throughout, with Parquet design on Main Floor Hall (except in "Candish" and "Breezy-Brae" models)* • *Oak stair treads* • *Three coat paint job on all interior and exterior woodwork* • *Attractive exhaust fan in the kitchen (except in "Candish" and "Breezy-Brae" models)* • *Weeping tile, rainwater downspouts (except garage) and floor drain connected to storm sewer* • *Clock outlet in kitchen* • *Utility outlet over kitchen cupboard* • *New 'No-Fuze" Electrical Panel* • *Shrubbery in front of house* • *Door Chimes, with pushbuttons on both front and rear doors* • *Foundation wall parged with waterproofing, according to N.H.A. specifications* • *Built according to N.H.A. specifications and controlled sale prices-all mortgages bearing interest at 5 1/4 %*

In the second brochure supplier names were added in the standard features section, names such as Sterling Aluminum, Tru-Trim steel door jams, Skeco supplied steel kitchen cabinets and Zonolite plaster. Gypsum, Lime and Alabastine Ltd. with Rockwool batts and Nutone Exhaust Kitchen Fans were named as suppliers. The brochure also contained an artist's sketch of what the Applewood Village "One Stop" Shopping Centre would look like. In the second brochure the sketch varied a little from the one first used

The brochure read as follows:
Comprising nearly 10 acres of ground, this centre should offer residents of Applewood Acres and surrounding district, a complete shopping service within easy walking distance. At the present time, the shopping needs of Applewood Acres residents are served by shopping at nearby Port Credit, Islington, the Kingsway and New Toronto-each just a few minutes drive.

In this pleasant suburban community, the home owner enjoys all the advantages of life in the country-with every city convenience. All delivery services of the Toronto area such as bread, milk, grocery and departmental stores are provided daily. Hydro is supplied by Toronto Township Hydro Electric System at rates comparable to those in the Toronto Metropolitan area. There is a daily rural mail delivery. Your address would be R.R. 1, Port Credit, Ont. Plans have been formulated and presented to the township for necessary schools and other community services. Roads, water and storm sewage installations are provided and paid for by G.S. Shipp & Son Limited.

Located in Toronto Township and the County of Peel, Applewood Acres has no water shortage in the summer. Tax assessments are in line with those of other growing municipalities. Bus and train commuter service is

available to and from Toronto. Driving time to downtown Toronto (King and Yonge Streets) is 30 minutes; Malton, 20 minutes; Ford plant at Oakville, 10 minutes.

By the time the second brochure was brought out the post office recognized Applewood as a distinct postal district and residents could now use the address Applewood Acres, Port Credit, Ontario. The second brochure also made mention of the plan for a junior high school to be opened for September 1955 and located on the eastern side of Westacres Park.

Bricks and blocks used to build the homes in Applewood came mostly from Argo Block and Cooksville Brick, both local firms. The white bricks used in a number of models, however, were from Harbour Brick of Toronto and the mortar application used with 19 of the homes with the white brick is unique as it looks as if the brick-layer forgot to properly clean off the mortar. This application is called 'slop joint' or 'French mortar'. Some of the bricks were also purchased from Booth Brick of Toronto, Milton Brick and McFarren Brick of Streetsville. Harold Shipp points out that while the bricks have stood strong and sturdy in the homes for a half-century, the companies supplying the bricks are no longer around.

In total, G.S. Shipp and Son registered Plans of Subdivision for 754 homes to be built north of the QEW. However, Plan of Subdivision 463 was amended by Plan 466 as detailed in Chapter One. Subsequently the total was reduced by 21 homes. The final tally has 733 homes forming the original Applewood Acres subdivision.

Breaking this figure down, a total of 72 Hargord, 77 Candish, 200 Breezy Brae, 60 Mid Century, 134 Mid Century Deluxe, 36 Shipp-Shape, 73 Victoria and 73 Wedgewood models were finally built. There were eight special homes built. One was the Better Houses for Canadian Living and the other, a Home for All America, both sponsored by national magazines (see Chapter 10) as well as six homes which G.S. Shipp constructed at the end of the project. The six homes, which were not 'rank and file' in terms of the eight model homes built throughout the area, are located on the North Service Road between Stanfield Road and Tolman Road and the east side of Tolman Road to Russett Road. The Shipp sales office was actually at 1177 North Service Road, at the corner of Stanfield. These homes do not have similar design or floor plans nor do they all have

32

fireplaces, which was a standard for Shipp built homes in Applewood Acres.

A little oddity about some of the early homes is the house numbers had to be changed. As an example, Ernie and Mary Nock originally had 1356 Primate as their house number, but it was changed later to 2155. Other roads were also seeing number changes, as an example, numbers on Russet Road were in the 1100 series and changed to 2000 series. Throughout the book street addresses will be noted, and in some cases will be the original street addresses.

If you check the current Mississauga Street Guide you will note that most municipal addresses within the City are based on a grid system with buildings numbered according to their relationship to a grid line. As an example, east-west grid lines are arranged to fall on main streets such that Lakeshore Road is 1000, QEW is 2000, Dundas Street is 3000 etc. The Township engineers must have had a few disgruntled homeowners on their hands when they made these changes.

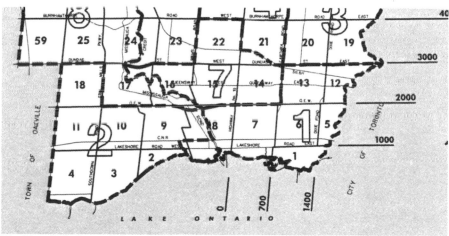

The City of Mississauga's house numbering grid

A great deal of time was spent doing an actual inventory of these homes and long time Applewood resident and friend, Al Cooper, and I, drove through Applewood recording the various models and numbers of each. This proved to be challenging as so many homes in Applewood Acres have been renovated, some to such an extent that nothing remained to provide a clue as to their original form. Knocking on doors eventually solved those problems.

Looking north on Second Line (Stanfield Road) as prospective customers park where the eastern portion of the shopping center now stands.

The following pages contain a description of the homes and floor plans, as printed in the original Applewood Acres sales brochures. Also shown is the listed selling price. When a number of homes went on the market for resale, Sheff Cassan, then with A.E. LePage Real Estate, prepared a listing of all homes sold in 1957. As an example of price increases, a Hargord at 942 Johnathan Drive sold in August 1957 for $21,700, an increase of $4,700 over the 1952 price of $17,000.

The HARGORD
May 8, 1952 priced at $17,000 with $7,000 down. The price increased September
25, 1953 to $18,315 with $8,315 down.

Photo by Dave Cook

*This is a beautiful home with a large living-dining room area (13'x23'6") for
entertaining. There are four bedrooms, two upstairs and two on the main floor.
One of the downstairs bedrooms would be ideal as a dining room or den. This
model has two complete bathrooms (both with coloured fixtures), one on each
floor; a bright, attractive kitchen provides a cheerful eating area.*

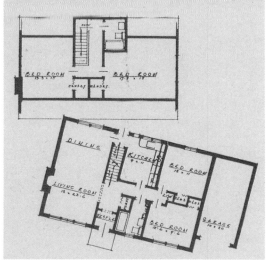

35

THE MID CENTURY DELUXE
May 8, 1952 priced at $15,400 with $5,400 down. Price increased September 25,1953 to $16,600 with $6,600 down

Photo courtesy of John Cassan Realty Limited

With the same basic plan as the Mid Century, this model has an extra two-piece washroom on the main floor as well as a complete bathroom upstairs with a dormer in front. There are separate dining and living rooms.

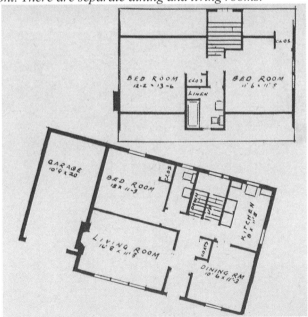

THE MID CENTURY
May 8, 1952 priced at $14,650 with $4,650 down. The price increased on
September 25, 1953 to $15,850 with $5,850 down

Photo by Dave Cook

*This attractive 6 room, story and a half model was designed to provide a free
flow downstairs with every room opening into the hall. There are separate dining
and living rooms. All three bedrooms, two on the second floor and one
downstairs, are convenient to the four piece bathroom on the main floor.*

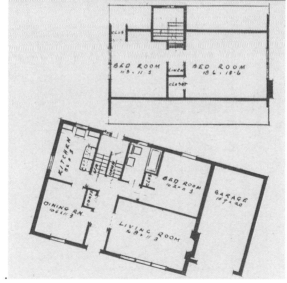

THE BREEZY BRAE

May 8, 1952 priced at $15,150 with $5,150 down. Price increased September 25, 1953 to $16,350 with $6,350 down.

Photo courtesy of John Cassan Realty Limited

Designed with four bedrooms for a large family, this model also offers the possibility of using the fourth bedroom on the main floor as a dining room or den. The large master bedroom and two smaller bedrooms are on the second floor. There is a large dining-living room area. As in 'The Candish', a two piece washroom for youngsters is located by the side door with a complete bathroom upstairs

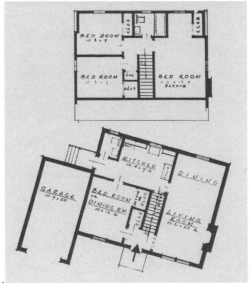

THE CANDISH

May 8, 1952 priced at $14,700 with $4,700 down. Price increased September 25, 1953 to $15,900 with $5,900 down

Photo courtesy of John Cassan Realty Limited

This home was designed with a large living-dining room area for the owner who likes to entertain. The other main floor room to the left of the entrance hall may be used alternately as a dining room or third bedroom. Two bedrooms are upstairs. The two-piece washroom is ideally located by the side door to allow children to wash after play without 'tracking up' the house. There is a complete bathroom upstairs; ample eating space in the kitchen.

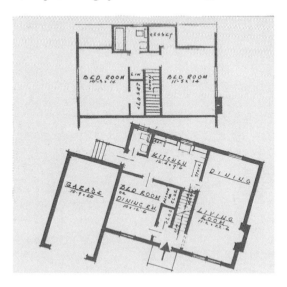

THE VICTORIA
September 25, 1953 price $17,330 with $7,330 down

Photo courtesy of John Cassan Realty Limited

In this home you will find all of the features as to size and convenience that you could hope to find in any 6 room bungalow selling at substantially more money than the price of this home. Large bright airy rooms with an abundance of storage space. A home that you will truly be glad to claim as your own.

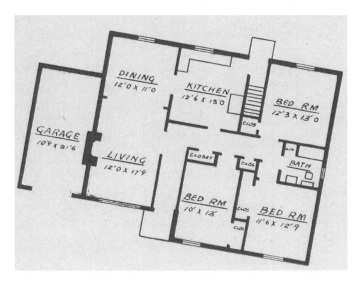

THE WEDGEWOOD
September 25, 1953 price $16,430 with $6,430 down

Photo by Dave Cook

We have a compact six-room bungalow that will serve all types of home owners equally well. The attractive living-dining room 'L' provides a sumptuous entertaining area. Three spacious bedrooms and a bright kitchen complete this fine home.

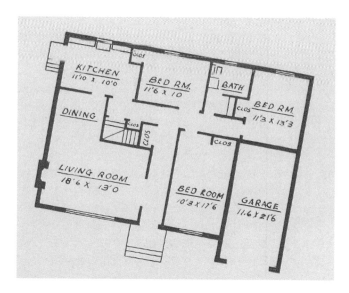

THE SHIPP-SHAPE

May 8,1952 priced at $14,500 with $6,000 down (a few 1951 models at reduced price $13,500 with $5,260 down) Price increased September 25, 1953 to $15,600 with $7,100 down.

Photo courtesy of John Cassan Realty Limited

Newlyweds or an older couple whose family has grown up and moved away will find this an appealing home. There are three spacious bedrooms, with the third bedroom ideally located for use as a dining room or den, if desired. This room would also make an excellent nursery, being adjacent to the kitchen. Again there is a large dining-living room combination.

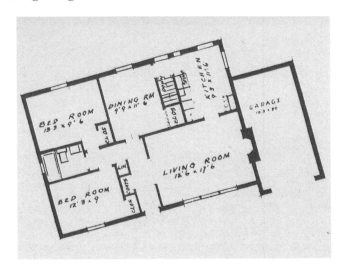

Six months after that historic April 1, 1953 meeting of Council, invitations were sent out for the official opening of Applewood Public School at 2180 Harvest Drive and on November 19, 1953 the ribbon was cut to mark the arrival of a school to serve the residents of Applewood Acres. The school was built by G.S. Shipp and Son and the architect was Hanks, Irwin and Pearson.

The administrator for the Board was H.J.A.(Jack) Brown, and according to Harold Shipp in an interview 50 years later, the Board agreed to pay G.S. Shipp 'cost plus 10 percent' of the raw land costs and 'half' of the cost of the road, sewers and water on which the school fronted. Jack realized that the shortest frontage would equal the least cost. According to Harold that was the formalization of all future school site acquisitions in Peel while Jack was administrator.

The guest speaker for the official opening was William Vanderburgh, Assistant Superintendent of Elementary Education who was introduced by Alan A. Martin, Public School Inspector. Representing the newly established Home and School Association was Orchard Heights resident Ken Crober. The area Trustee was Mr. J. Featherston.

The first school staff consisted of Principal Gordon Gracey and teaching staff Mr. David H. Brown, Mrs. R. Locking, Mrs. Norma Thomas, Mr. G.W. White, Mrs. Jean Green and Mrs. P. Poyner. The caretaker was Mr. K. Van Tuinen.

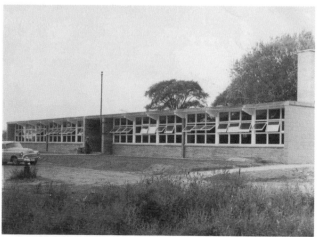

Westacres School almost ready to open: photo courtesy of Shipp Corporation.

In the school year 1954-1955 Westacres Public School opened. The original school went to Grade 8 and the Principal was Gord Finlayson and the Inspector was Allan A. Martin.

It was again Jack Brown who was responsible for the development of the school. In a written presentation prepared many years later for the school's 35th Anniversary, Mr. Brown wrote the following.

"Our Westacres Community was one of the better subdivisions that launched the post-war development of Toronto Township.

G.S. Shipp and his son Harold were responsible for the planning and development of this sub-division. Westacres was originally referred to as Applewood West. (I believe I am responsible for the renaming of the school to Westacres.)

The South Peel Board of Education purchased 7.51 acres of land for a site we originally conceived might serve both an elementary and a secondary school. The cost of the land was $35,500.00. The purchase was completed in January 1954.

The first school consisted of six classrooms and was approved for construction by the Department of Education on March 15, 1954. The estimated cost was $108,000.00. The architectural firm of Hanks, Irwin and Pearson was selected to design the school.(They had already designed the Applewood Public School in 1953.) Tatti Construction was the successful contractor and when the project was tendered the actual cost of construction came to $89,279.27. Fees, fencing and furniture totaled another $15,00.00 The total expense was approximately $106,000 for six rooms (about the cost of one room today).

The architect who designed the school and supervised its construction was Mr. Clark Pearson. He has recently retired but still lives in Mississauga. In 1955, a further six rooms were added at a cost of $67,300.00 and, in 1956, two more at $40,000.00. Since then, as you know, kindergarten rooms and general purpose rooms (library, gym) have been built.

The original school was staffed by an outstanding group of teachers. Mr. Finlayson, Doug Read, Rita Lambert, all went on to positions of added responsibility in the Peel system. (As a matter of fact, many of our former staff members over the years have now assumed very important roles in our educational system.)

The Westacres Community were very supportive of the educational system. (Nothing has changed here, folks.) One of the strong trustees who represented our area on the Board and served as Chairman for two years was Mr. Alan Bradley. (And one of his daughters is a present staff member at Westacres.) And we must mention the children and grandchildren of Mr. Chic Murray a former Mayor of Mississauga, who also live in and attended our school. What a neighbourhood!

(From left to right)Thomas Jackson, Deputy Reeve, Twp. Of Toronto, Reverend Lawrence A. Purdy, Applewood United Church, Leslie Hughes, Chairman, Board of Education, A.B. Lucas, B.A., B.Paed, President Ontario Education Association, and G.W. Finlayson, Principal Westacres Public School.

The park and school relationship that exists at Westacres was a pilot project later repeated in other communities. (I guess that it was successful here.)

The third school in Applewood Acres is located on Melton Drive, east of Stanfield where the Dixie Catholic Board built on 3.85 acres of land purchased from the Lloyd Leaver Estate.

The Dixie Catholic Board was constituted in November of 1953 due to the dedication and vision of Father Healy and Applewood Acres resident Ed LeMay. The Dixie Catholic Board undertook the building of its second school, St. Edmund, on Melton Drive, in 1959. The original purchase price was $7,500 per acre. Ed LeMay, who served as an elected member on the school board, is also noted in Chapter 11.

St. Edmund was designed by Servos and Cauley and constructed for $75,000.00 by Brampton Home Builders. By September 1961, St. Edmund housed 109 students in grades K, 3,4,5 & 6 while St. Patrick had the students in the remaining grades.

In 1962, the Dixie Catholic Board became part of the combined Roman Catholic Separate School Board. The first addition to St. Edmund School was in 1963. While St. Patrick was closed in 1967 and later served as the first Dufferin-Peel Board Office, St. Edmund continued to grow and change. Portable classrooms were added as numbers and classes increased.

Members of the community began seeking a permanent addition to the school. This addition, started in the summer of 1992, was ready for occupation by staff and students early in 1993.

The original plan for Applewood Acres called for the construction of a secondary school to be located east of Westacres Public School. However, those plans were eventually set aside and the students from Applewood Acres were to be enrolled at Gordon Graydon Secondary School located south of the Queen Elizabeth Highway.

Gordon Graydon Secondary School opened officially on Friday, November 16, 1956. The address was given by The Honourable John G. Diefenbaker M.P., who, seven months later, was elected Canada's 13th Prime Minister (June 21,1957-April 22,1963).

A note from the programme of the celebrated evening reads, "Mr. Louis Applebaum, noted Canadian composer, has written a "Graydon Overture".

The school opened with a staff of 24 under the administration of Principal W.J. (Wilf) Wood and Vice Principal J.E. Bailey. The student body grades were grades seven to11. The following year the grades were eight to 12. The third year grades 10 to 13. The new Junior High School, Allen A. Martin took grades seven through nine.

With the opening of any new facility there comes numerous administrative problems and challenges. Being a new school, there also came the need to develop a motto, crest, school colours and a school song, all of which would have to stand the test of time.

Miss Alice Turner and Mr. W.E. Ward, an ex-air force officer, composed Graydon's motto. Mr. Ward was familiar with the R.C.A.F. motto "Ad Astra Per Ardua." The idea of striving for success he felt should be enshrined in the school, hence the motto "Palma Per Ardua."

A competition was held to establish a crest for the school. Mr. Wood's idea, concerning the personal development of students, was taken from a passage in the New Testament. Luke 2:52 describes the ideal maturing process in these words: "Jesus increased in wisdom and stature, and in favour with God and Man." The prize in the crest competition was offered to the student who could embody this basic concept in a design. The winner was Silvio Perusini and Alex Fraser, the art teacher, transferred the student's design to masonite.

Mr. Wood chose the school's colours, Green and Gold, while the school song resulted from a competition won by Marilyn Stephenson.

Graydon's distinguishing landmark, The Rock, is among the school's most colourful legends, and actually arrived at the school as a result of coincidence, planning and showmanship, not to mention nerve.

In 1956, it was coincidence that the highway was being widened at the time a conference for principals was being held at Muskoka Sands Inn in Gravenhurst. Passing an area of extensive blasting, Mr. Ward noticed some impressive pink boulders. These gave him the idea for Graydon's Centennial project.

Mr. Ward then started the process to win approvals and transport the large rock to the school site. The Town of Mississauga and the Board of Education were also involved as the logistics of moving such a load

47

required a 25-ton flat-bed truck and crane on the ready to lift the rock over the wires and onto a concrete base. The base for the rock was actually the foundation of a re-located hydro sub station.

Once the logistics were taken care of the showmanship began. Michael Petrie, a student active in the Conservative Party, later a Tory campaign director, was Chairman of the May 4 Committee. He took the initiative to contact the Right Honourable John G. Diefenbaker who agreed to speak at the installation. The May 4 ceremony was planned as an outdoor spectacular complete with bands and flags befitting the presence of the Prime Minister.

Like most plans, these encountered a small hitch. About 90 days before the grand event an election was called. The Prime Minister phoned to say that he had to go to Prince Albert, but that he would send a videotape of his message for the installation.

The installation was a huge success: the weather was beautiful, 1,000 flags added colour, the band played and a capacity crowd watched Mr. Diefenbaker's video address. As at the opening of the school earlier, Mrs. Graydon cut the ribbon. Following this event, subsequent school newspapers were called "The Rock."

It's interesting to note that while many residents of Applewood Acres continue to return to their roots so to speak, and as it is not uncommon to hear of children purchasing their parents' homes or buying their own near their parent's homes, the list of students who have returned to Gordon Graydon to teach also grows with every passing year.

A quarter of a century after G.S. Shipp and Son Limited resolved the issue of schools with the Board of Education, the residents of Applewood Acres would become involved in the very emotional issue of school closings.

As John Walmark, who lived at 2098 Harvest Drive, said many years later, " It was indeed a shock as I had just moved into the community. My wife,Pam, and I had an 18-month old daughter and all of a sudden we were being faced with school closures."

John, who later was elected as the Education Trustee for Ward 7, had learned of the school board's plans when he attended the Annual General Meeting of the North Applewood Homeowners' Association (NAHA) meeting on Feb. 1, 1979. John, along with area residents Dave Chornomud, 844 Duchess Drive, Chairman of the Westacres Parent Teacher Association (PTA) and Mag Paulson, 1313 Melton Drive, who was a long-time executive member of the Homeowners' Association, immediately came forward to spearhead a committee to fight the school closings.

According to the Board of Education, enrolment at Westacres had dropped to 180 children in 1979 and lower to 156 in 1980.

At the next executive meeting of the NAHA, the then president Arnold Tremere, 2252 Haltrye Court, announced he would not seek re-election. John Walmark was elected the new president. The following is John's account of one of the biggest community actions ever organized in the City of Mississauga.

Initially the community was told that Westacres Public School would not be closed. The students from Applewood Public School on Harvest would be split between Sherway Drive Public School and Westacres Public School.

We tried our best to convince the Board of Education that all three schools should remain open given the resurgence in the area of young families like ourselves.

Our plight was much our own until the school board revised its plan for closure. Suddenly Applewood Acres, Westacres and Orchard Heights across the Queen Elizabeth Highway were targeted for closure.

This all happened within a six to nine month period. We had been having plenty of meetings with our community as well as Orchard Heights and Westacres. We never, however, had any success in getting the Sherway group to become involved with us. The community felt that the Board of Education was pitting communities against one another and to make matters worse, the only supportive area elected Trustee Mickey Reid had announced he would not be seeking re-election in 1978.

I was encouraged by the community to seek election as I was the most visible from the group and the most knowledgeable about the issue. It was felt the Board of Education needed a voice from this community and that voice was to be me.

We ran a very small campaign in 1978 and lost to a Sherway resident Bruce Robertson, by 54 votes. Our group continued to pressure the newly elected trustee and the Board not to close both our community schools.

It was then that we decided to run a high-profile campaign. What followed was to be a campaign unequalled in the community's history.

More than 500 lawn signs were placed throughout the area, one sign for every third home "Don't Close Both Our Schools" read the signs.

The community worked hard developing a game plan with delegations to the Board and of course the signs that blanketed the area. For more than two years our main push was to convince the Board not to close both the schools.

There was a great deal of animosity that grew between Applewood Acres and the Sherway community, and I feel that some of it remained many years later. It did not make sense to have half of the students cross Dixie Road to Sherway Drive when the flow was to the west with all other students. Indirectly we were suggesting it should be Sherway that should be closed and not Applewood Acres.

Many hours in meetings, delegations to the Board and of course the highly visible lawn signs, all brought the matter to the attention of television media. "Applewood Acres was once again in the national media."

The final big push was at a meeting at the School Board Central Office where more than 200 area residents gathered to show support for the community's position. The Board voted to close Sherway and Applewood Acres schools keeping Westacres open to the area residents.

The next year John Walmark was chosen by the Board of Education Trustees to fill a vacancy left when Mr. Robertson resigned. The following year, John was elected to office and remained Trustee until 1985. John continued to remain active in the community and served as President of the homeowners' association until 1991 when he moved to the Lorne Park area in southwest Mississauga.

The issue of school closings continued to dog the community for years to come, although certainly not to the extent that it did in 1978. The Board of

Education established a committee to review the Consolidation of School Accommodation Policy and in December of 1984, S.M. Campbell and M.B. Wilson, representing the Westacres Parent-Teacher Association, registered the concerns of the area residents with respect to any consideration of closure here. Under both signatures, they penned a letter drawing the Board's attention to the advantages with respect to small school enrollments.

"The major factor influencing the quality of education in the primary grades is without question the teacher. This consideration overrides all else. Low enrollment may necessitate split grades, thereby placing an extra burden on the teacher. At Westacres, we may be particularly fortunate with respect to the staff, but we are proud of the sound fundamentals learned by our children and their success on moving to middle school."

"The most important of these is increased staff/student/parent familiarity which we believe results in increased dialogue and the early identification of individual student needs. Security and confidence are fostered in the children by the scale of the facility and the increased familiarity. In addition to having kindergarten through grade 6, Westacres has three classes of mentally retarded students. We believe that this integration of students has been beneficial to both groups with respect to their understanding of the world they live in and the development of their character."

"We have concluded that Westacres provides our children with an excellent primary education and quality of school-life. We must, therefore, express to you these conclusions and request that this flexibility be inherent in any policy you develop."

J.L. Berges, Superintendent of Planning and Resources, Peel Board of Education, responded in early January 1985, thanking both for their written submission and assured the community that the Trustees would receive full attention as their work proceeds. Obviously, the concerns of the community prevailed as Westacres Public School continues to this day to provide the students of our community with an excellent educational facility.

4 In-Fill and Renovations

The expression 'in-fill' probably wasn't in the lexicon of the early Toronto Township Planners. But not too long after G.S. Shipp and Son packed up and moved on to construct new homes elsewhere, the 'in-fill' started.

On November 16, 1955, Edward Small and Son Construction registered a Plan of Subdivision and started to construct homes creating Watson Orchard Road and Sidney Drive. Mr. Small purchased these lands from Mel Watson who had an apple orchard, thus the name Watson Orchard. Sidney was named after Mel's son who was killed during WW11.

The Edward Small plan opened up a direct link to Dixie Road from Rambo and Melton Drives. Until then the residents had to come off Dixie Road at Primate and then travel to Courtland and north on Harvest Drive.

In January of 1956, A.B. Green built the homes on the west end of Melton Drive at Cawthra Road and also created Melton Court. This opened Melton Drive to Cawthra Road.

The third Plan in September of 1960, called for homes to be built extending Johnathan Drive easterly from Westfield. Lawsmith Holdings created the first curb and gutter road, complete with sidewalks. Prior to this, all roads were constructed as stone-chip and tar, which basically is what it sounds like. Stone chips are laid and tar is poured over it and when it hardens, you have a fairly sound road surface. In later years this gave way to oil based slurry-seal, which was laid by means of a spray-like application. When the slurry-seal dried, it gave the road an asphalt-like appearance. Today the roads are asphalted.

The Lawsmith Holdings plan also included a small number of homes on Baldwin Road as well as Stanfield Road. It wasn't until 1969 that Baldwin was completed when Edrich Construction registered a plan which also included Wyton Court.

Linby Street in Westacres was developed in March of 1965 connecting Duchess Drive and Harcourt Crescent. This plan was registered by Peter Augustinavicius of Alka Developments.

Melton Drive opened up to Stanfield Road when Stanfield Developments registered its plan in November 1966, which also included Kilgorie and Haltrye Courts. This completed the connection between Stanfield and Cawthra.

Edrich Construction returned with plans in 1972 and also in 1977 to construct homes east of Stanfield creating Promenade, Stir, Meander, Melton and some along Stanfield Road.

In February of 1977 Nicholas Rukavina, owner of Cape Developments, built along Melton east of Stanfield adjacent to the Hydro Right of Way.

In 1975 Mr. Italo Galassi of Corolla Investments Ltd. built the western wing of Harcourt Crescent. In 1995 F-F Construction developed a cul-de-sac on the western end of Duchess Drive.

PLANS OF SUBDIVISION (registered by groups other than the G.S. Shipp & Son Company)

Plan 532	Watson Orchard, Sidney Drive and parts of Kendall Road and Melton Drive. Nov. 16, 1955, Edward Small and Son Construction
Plan 537	Melton Crt., Jan. 7, 1956, A.B. Green
Plan 638	Johnathan Drive east of Westfield, parts of Baldwin and Stanfield, Sept. 28, 1960, Lawsmith Holdings
Plan 727	Linby Street, March 1965, Alka Developments, Mr. Peter Augustinavicius
Plan 772	Kilgore Ct., Haltrye Crt, Melton from 980 east to Stanfield, Nov. 24, 1966
Plan 845	Baldwin Rd. and Wyton Crt. Feb 10, 1969 Edrich Construction, Mr. Stanley Fujarczuk
Plan 936	Promenade, Melton, Stir, Meander and Stanfield, April 7, 1972, Edrich Construction

Plan M64	Harcourt Cres., Feb. 13, 1975 , Corolla Investments Ltd. Mr. Italo Galassi
Plan M183	Melton Drive, east of Stanfield, adjacent to the Hydro Right of Way. Feb. 14, 1977, Cape Developments, Mr. Nicholas Rukavina
Plan 215	Meander Crt., Oct. 7, 1977, Edrich Construction
Plan M 431	Ajyn Crt., and west end of Whitney Dr., Oct. 22,1981, VMA Construction Mr. Vittorio Vacca
Plan 43M-544	Hedge Road. June 14, 1984, Built by Gardi Homes, owner Noble Propane & Energy Ltd. Mr. Joe Stangl This property was the site of the mushroom houses where Leaver Mushroom Company stood since 1922.
Plan 43M-1170	West end of Duchess Dr., July 20, 1995 F-F Construction

In 1982 the Shipp Corporation was celebrating its 60th Anniversary and Harold Shipp had plans to build an anniversary project on the Leaver lands that were then being placed on the market for sale. He discussed the concept with me briefly as he obviously was looking for my support as ward Councillor. I was very enthusiastic about his idea, which was to construct homes that resembled the original eight models. They would be single-family dwellings on similar sized ' Applewood' lots. However, it was soon learned that the lower density and the cost to service the lots would not support the project financially and a higher density was required.

Numerous homes in Applewood Acres have since been extensively renovated. However, two homes have been totally replaced. The home of Norman and Ann McRoberts at 2041 Stewart Cres, which was destroyed by a fire after a lightning storm, was the first, while the other was a Shipp-Shape at 906 Ribston Road, which was demolished to make way for a much larger house.

When the fire destroyed the McRobert's home, Ann's father was visiting from California. He had a love for fine chocolates and had purchased a particular chocolate at the airport in California when he was leaving to come to Canada. After the fire, the firefighters would not allow anyone to go to the second floor of the house for obvious reasons, but one of the firefighters did go to the upstairs closet where the suitcase was located to retrieve the passport. Not only was the passport intact, but so was the chocolate! The McRoberts now have the wrapper of the chocolate framed, after it was eaten of course.

A third home, a Mid Century Deluxe at 1299 North Service Road, was demolished in early 2004. It was in such a poor state of repair the property owner, the Department of Highways, served notice to its tenants that the demolition was needed as it was going to be too expensive to bring the home up to municipal property and safety standards.

More than 30 percent of the original 733 Shipp-built homes have undergone visible renovations. An excellent example of a major renovation can be seen at 2077 Redan Drive. John and Barb Desjardins converted this Breezy Brae into a spacious gabled-Cape Cod style home. The architect was Randy Guthrie, who resided on Linby Street. Photo by Dave Cook

5 Churches

In December of 1954, the year following the Constitution of Applewood United Church as a congregation, G.S. Shipp and the Church teamed up to erect a large illuminated scene of the nativity.

Larger than life-size and beautifully coloured, it portrayed the traditional setting of the birth of the Christ-child, showing Mary, Joseph and the Babe lying in the manger. On one side the scene showed the shepherds in the fields with their flocks while the other showed the wise men journeying from afar.

The nativity scene, which could be seen from the Queen Elizabeth Highway, is probably the first major presentation of the congregation, which was established in a ceremony held Monday, December 7, 1953, and which served notice to the greater community that the Applewood United Church had arrived.

The history of Applewood United Church was first published in the 40th Anniversary booklet. The authors of the history, Lyle and Margaret McKay, prepared seven chapters providing an excellent historical outline of the church covering the background, origin and formation of the congregation to the construction of the building and the first few years in the new church.

This accounting will deal with highlights of that story, which was provided by the Applewood United Church. For the complete and detailed history, all supporting documents are in the United Church Archives, where they have been catalogued and placed in fireproof storage and are available for reference.

In April, 1952 the Toronto Home Missions Council sent Mrs. Mercer, a deaconess, to make a survey of the area. As a result of her efforts, the first meeting of about 20 families was held in Lakeview Central School on Meredith Ave. on May 4th with Dr. C.A. Myers and Rev. J.C. Torrance officiating.

After the second service on May 11th, a Women's Committee and a Men's Committee were formed. At this time every adult acted in some capacity. There were two teachers for every Sunday School class so the teachers could attend the full church service on alternate Sundays. H.W. Davies, a theological student, took over from Dr. Myers as the acting minister. By June, the Sunday School enrolment was 97 and at a picnic held at Miles Park, 45 adults and 60 children ate at one long picnic table.

The services would continue for one more year at Central School but following several meetings, it was agreed that the eventual location for the church would be north of the QEW.

During the summer of 1952 church student workers called on all the homes in North Applewood and Orchard Heights and reported 60 per cent were of United Church background.

In September, Mr. J. Story, who had completed his theological course but had not yet been ordained, became acting minister. Mr. Story later went into missionary work in India.

The service for constituting the Congregation of Applewood United Church was held Monday, December 8, 1953. Rev. A.J. Eagle, Chairman of Toronto West Presbytery, presided at this ceremony and was assisted by Mr. Kenneth Partridge, Rev. G.A. Payne, Bethesda Dixie United Church, Rev. A.C. Forrest, First United Church, Port Credit and Rev. J.C. Torrance, Toronto Home Missions Council.

The first meeting of the Committee of Stewards was held January 13, 1954. It was announced that the Toronto Home Missions Council would approve a $10,000 mortgage and a $2,500 grant for the purchase of a manse and a campaign committee had to be established immediately to raise additional funds. The funds were raised very quickly, thanks to the enthusiasm and generosity of the members and sizable donations from the Women's Association and Mr. G.S. Shipp. The original manse at 931 N. Service Rd. was purchased and Reverend Purdy and his wife, Lenore, took residence. Rev. Lawrence A. Purdy began his duties as the first minister of Applewood United Church on July 1st, 1954. However, the name of the church was not formalized until the annual meeting of the congregation on February 13, 1956. It was decided that three names for the church be placed on a ballot to be mailed to members of the congregation to determine the name of the church. The results of the vote were 143 for the name Applewood United Church, 81 votes for St. Paul's United Church, Applewood and 10 votes for Grace United Church, Applewood.

The first anniversary service was held December 5, 1954 and it was on that day that the Sunday School began at 9:30 a.m. and two church services were inaugurated, one at 10:30 a.m. and one at 11:45 a.m. The youngest children attended Sunday School in the portable, while the older children attended in the classrooms of nearby Applewood Public School, which was rented to accommodate the larger number which could not find room in the church.

In the days of the portable, which was used from 1953 to 1957, the church office was the dining room in the home of Mrs. W. Blacklock who continued as secretary at the new building until Mrs. Death took over in 1959.

The first step toward the building of a church edifice occurred on December 6, 1954 when the Board passed a resolution establishing three committees, one for Finance, one for Architecture and one for Development. This resolution was approved at the annual meeting of the congregation on January 17, 1955.

With the acceptance of the committee recommendation that Mr. James A. Murray be hired as architect, a Canvass Committee was formed in March, 1955 and on the 23rd of that month, a Loyalty Dinner was held in the auditorium at Thomas L. Kennedy Secondary School. 370 members and friends of the congregation attended. Sacrificial giving was the theme of the dinner. More than $126,000 was pledged and Building Fund envelopes were made available for Easter Sunday for contributions covering the next 150 weeks.

The land on which the church stands consisted of six lots which were purchased by the congregation from the Toronto Home Missions Council for $1,250 each, the price they had originally paid G.S. Shipp and Son.

One of the conditions of approval of the first mortgage was that it be guaranteed by 40 members of the congregation with individual liability limited to $200,000.

Parking was limited on the church site and later, in 1960, Applewood Church obtained parking rights in Applewood Village Shopping Centre at a rental price of $1 per year. In return, a portion of the church property was released to permit changing the road configuration.

On October 27, 1955 tenders were let. Olmstead and Parker Construction Company made the lowest bid. As the bid appeared too great for the money available, meetings were held with the architect so that specifications could be altered to permit economies. Finally, a reduced bid of $203,163 was accepted and construction began in December. During this period it was noticed that the old Guthrie Barn was about to be torn down and its wonderful stone foundation would have been discarded. It was decided that some of the stones would be used in the new edifice. It was reported in the Port Credit Weekly that by doing so, the dignity and stability of the old farm building, the interests and enthusiasms of the developers, G.S. Shipp and Sons, and the dreams and visions of the young congregation would come together in some measure to add to the quality of the church.

Meanwhile, a sod-turning ceremony had been held on September 25th. Total pledges had reached $135,000 and a second canvass was organized.

On Sunday, April 15, 1956 the Presentation and Laying of the Foundation Stone ceremony was held. As the church construction progressed, many excellent photographs were taken by Mr. J. Chittenden and a colour motion picture was made by Mr. E. Hyde with accompanying sound track by Mr. Purdy.

Finally the building was completed and Sunday March 17, 1957 was a day of great joy for all the people of Applewood United Church who had worked so faithfully to turn a dream into a reality. On that bright and sunny morning, A thankful congregation witnessed the opening service and symbolic service of dedication.

The service opened with the ceremony of Knocking at the Doors. Mr. C.N. Lucas, Recording Steward, opened the doors and welcomed the procession of clergy. The architect, Mr. James Murray, called upon the builder, Mr. Wm. Olmsted, to present the keys. In reply to a question by Dr. Vaughn, President of Hamilton Conference, Mr. D.W. Foley, Chairman of the Architectural Committee, proclaimed the name to be Applewood United Church.

Reverend Purdy conducts the first service in the portable. Photo courtesy of Applewood United Church

On June 9, 1955, the Applewood United Church site was selected as the location for Peel's first ever free X-Ray Clinic for the mass tuberculosis survey sponsored by the Peel County TB and Health Association and Ontario's Department of Health X-Ray unit.

In 2003 St. Lukes United and Bethesda United churches closed. Many members of the two congregations joined Applewood United Church.

In November 2003, an 86-page book was published to celebrate the golden jubilee of the church. Agnes Paterson was the coordinator for the publication.

In 1978 the Igreja du S. Salvador Do Mundo church opened on Melton Drive, east of Stanfield Road. This church serves the Catholic congregation from the area as well as hosting a religious festival and parade which annually attracts people from across the city.

6 Shopping Centre

The official opening of the Applewood Village Shopping Centre in October, 1955, was almost a celestial affair.

According to the news reports of the day, two giant searchlights beaming out the opening of the Dominion Store and the Bank of Nova Scotia threw the Malton Airport (now Lester B. Pearson) control tower into a tizzy.

Pilots of four aircraft saw the lights shining on low-lying clouds and thought they were over the airport, while instruments indicated they were still four miles distant.

"What's going on?" radioed one worried pilot to the tower. "Who's showing those lights?"

A traffic control officer checked and found permission had been granted by the Department of Transport for the searchlight and the tower notified. However, an airport employee failed to report the permit to the tower controllers.

The opening proved to be a grand affair with Dominion Stores holding a Carnival Contest in which a 1956 Buick automobile was the grand prize. More than 100 other prizes were given away ranging from a Frigidaire automatic washing machine to children's bicycles. And typical of Harold Shipp's entrepreneurial ingenuity, four tiny reindeer were penned in the large open area in what are now the garden beds in the indented section of the shopping centre.

HANKS & IRWIN, ARCHITECTS

Artist's sketch of Applewood Village Shopping Centre; courtesy of Shipp Corporation

Four tiny reindeer were penned in the indented garden area for the official opening; photo courtesy of Shipp Corporation.

While the shopping complex was always part of the plan for Applewood Acres, it wasn't until January 1955 that Toronto Township gave its approval and passed a resolution asking the Ontario Government's Minister of Planning and Development to give it draft approval. Had the approval for the shopping centre been approved at the time of the first plan of subdivision for Applewood Acres, the Applewood Village Shopping Centre would have been one of the first in the Province of Ontario. The first shopping centre in Ontario was Toronto's Sunnybrook Plaza, built in 1952. It consisted of 17 one and two-storey retailers.

Soon after Dixie Plaza opened becoming Canada's largest shopping centre. Just 10 months later, Gordon S. Shipp issued an open letter to the community inviting everyone to visit the new 11-acre shopping centre, which boasted enough space to park more than 1,500 automobiles. The shopping centre was built on lands originally owned and farmed by James Guthrie. G.S. Shipp and Son paid $4,000 for the 27 acre farm.

"Commencing with the opening of the Bank of Nova Scotia on Monday, October 17, 1955, you are invited to enjoy the facilities," wrote Mr. Shipp.

Mr. Shipp's letter listed the merchants and professionals now open for business. They were: (from west to east) Dominion Store, Bank of Nova Scotia, Darcelle Bakery & Delicatessen, Maher Shoe Store, Don Sproul Men's Shop, Glory Ann Children's Wear, Glory Ann Ladies Specialty Shop, Murray's High Grade Shoes, Shore's Specialty Shop, Chreston's Applewood Restaurant /Apple Villa Banquet Hall, Trans Canada Jewellers, Patrician Beauty Salon, McCormick's Barber Shop, Brodie's Shoe Repair and Luggage, Martin's Gift Shoppe, Mainprize Drug Store, Paramount Cleaners and Laundry, Kingsway Television Service, Jack Fraser's Men's and Boy's Wear, and Yott's Hardware.

At the eastern end of the shopping centre, was Haggart's B.A. Service Centre while at the western end stood Applewood Sunoco Station. The B.A. Service Centre was later owned and operated by Clare Wilson who lived on Henley Road.

While memories fade, there remained a tangible reminder which always brought a smile to many of the children who grew up here. For some time after Glory Ann Children's Wear had closed, and new merchants moved in, the entrance to the original store remained untouched. A door for the adults, and a tiny little door for the children.

Professional suites on the second floor in the centre of the shopping complex were occupied by Dr. P.J. Comrie, D.D.S., who had been practising out of his Applewood home, at the corner of Dixie Road and Primate Road. Dr. F.P. Giardine, Obstetrician and Gynecologist, and Dr. L.A. Eckert, Surgeon also had offices on the second floor. The executive offices of G.S. Shipp and Son Limited occupied the east block of the second floor space.

While promotions became the norm at every shopping centre or mall in the country, it's interesting to note that one of the first promotions organized for Applewood was in June 1956 when a three-day new car showing was sponsored by eight area automobile dealerships. It's ironic that one of the longest lasting promotions held at Applewood is also automobile oriented. Every Wednesday evening from May to September since 1989, California's Restaurant has promoted 'Cruise Nights', which brings together owners of a variety of types and models of automobiles for a walk-around display. Vehicles of the 1950's are again in abundance. This promotion was originally developed in 1986 by Janet Dixon, her daughter Addrene and Janet's sister, Jean McQuaid. The trio worked with the plaza merchants developing car shows, originally with an old movie theme.

One of the most unusual plaza promotions, however, had to be on April 27, 1957, when the Oshawa Racing Pigeon Club held its season opening event. More than 300 pigeons were released at Applewood and home arrival times were telephoned back to the site so that a winner could be declared. The biggest in terms of drawing people had to be the Western BBQ, as told in the next chapter.

In December 1959 the merchants and the Dixie Lions Club got together to bring Santa in for the month. Santa was housed in a beautiful five-room colonial cottage erected on the parking lot. Tickets were sold for a raffle with the cottage as the grand prize.

Expansion of the plaza was approved in 1960 and construction started in September. The little parkette at the bottom of Stanfield Road was eliminated. This expansion included the addition of a Miracle Mart, which was built at the most southeasterly part of the shopping centre. In later years Miracle Mart became Dominion Save-a-Centre. The expansion created seven new stores, including a bank and on the upper level, a bowling alley. Many residents of Henley Road were joined by one or two of the merchants, such as the Dominion Store, in opposing the expansion. The main battle seemed to be over the closing of Stanfield Road and the lack of notification about the expansion. However, in the end, approval was granted.

On August 5, 2003, Paul A. Mitcham, P.Eng., MBA, The City of Mississauga's Commissioner of Community Services, presented a report to the chairman and members of Mississauga's Heritage Advisory Committee recommending that Dominion Save-a-Centre be added to the City's Heritage Inventory on the basis of its architectural and contextual significance.

Mr. Mitcham's report focused on the stylistic aspects of the supermarket building saying that it is a traditional 1950's 'contempo' design something totally new for Mississauga in its day. And, new for the Toronto area as a whole, was the concept of 'bedroom communities', of which Applewood remains a prime example.

The 'contempo' design was popular for about 20 years, from 1945-1965 (John Blumenson, Ontario Architecture). The supermarket is one storey, built of brick, with stylistically exposed metal crossbeams visible within the glassed front facade, which is fashioned in the form of one large front gable.

There is liberal use of metal flashing around the edge of the roof overhang, and the roof itself is shingled. The interior of the building retains a styled terrazzo floor, thought to be original. The terrazzo floor is one aspect that adds to the 50's contempo flavour of the structure. Once used extensively throughout that era, this method of flooring is rarely seen today. The ceiling is slanted according to the gentle slope of the roof line, giving the interior a very pleasant and airy environment. From the exterior, the impression at a distance is that of an oversized bungalow house, which was in keeping with the surrounding residential subdivision's styles at the time of construction.

As a whole, the supermarket, in the context of both the rest of the Applewood Village Shopping Centre and the surrounding subdivision residential area, has a unique character of the emerging suburban landscape that, in its heyday, was a futuristic concept, and is today seen as an early example of the style of the development that has shaped Mississauga over the last 50 years.

Mr. Mitcham went on to write that the context of the structure within the larger Applewood Village Shopping Centre was the forerunner to a style of development that has come to typify Mississauga.

While not part of the Applewood story, a mention must be made of what almost became a reality just across the highway from Applewood Acres. An application for an apartment project and shopping centre on lands located on the south-west sector of Dixie Road and the Queen Elizabeth Way had been made to the Toronto Township by Benjamin Pass who was representing a Montreal syndicate. Meanwhile, consideration was being given to a hospital site on the east side of Dixie Road, north of the Queen Elizabeth Way, where the Sherway Community now stands.

Between 600 and 900 apartments were being planned on 28 acres of lands formerly owned by Charles Hemstead. East of this site, on the other side of Dixie Road, G.A. Rome of Islington was planning to develop 350 housing units and a shopping centre fronting onto the South Service Road with rows of apartments as part of the plan.

The Orchard Heights Community came alive the second weekend of September 1952 when more than 8,000 people came out to inspect six model homes, one of which was fully furnished. The builders, Daniel Saracini and his brother Allan, employed Doug Romaine, one of Canada's top comedians, to greet the prospective customers that weekend. The Saracini brothers built 60 homes in a 12-week period and priced them

at $17,700 to $19,000. Later, in partnership with G.A. Rome, the firm of Rome-Saracini Ltd. built and developed Dixie Plaza. The Saracini brothers were sons of J.V. Saracini, a builder who started his trade in 1910.

Serge Ovsianikov worked for close to four decades at Applewood Village. He was a friend not only to the merchants but to all the shoppers as well. Photo courtesy of the Ovsianikov family.

No story of the Applewood Village Shopping Centre would be complete without mentioning Serge Ovsianikov. From the opening of the Shopping Centre until his retirement in 1991, Serge was not only the maintenance man, but a friend to all shoppers and merchants. Everyone knew and liked Serge and would often stop and exchange greetings. Serge could often be seen chatting with old friends at the Shopping Centre long after his retirement. In 1970 Serge purchased a home at 925 North Service Road from Mr. Brodie, who owned and operated Brodie's Shoe Repair in the Shopping Centre. Serge and his wife Roza raised three children. His wife died in 1981 and Serge passed away on June 18, 2000 in his 76th year.

7 The BBQ

An old-fashioned western barbecue which attracted an estimated 7,000 people who consumed more than 2,000 pounds of prime beef was quite possibly the most successful promotional/charity event ever staged at the Applewood Village Shopping Centre, so successful in fact it was repeated the following year.

The actual site for the BBQ was on the parkette, which was located at the eastern end of the shopping centre. At that time, the shopping centre ended at the Second Line (Stanfield Road) which continued straight south to the North Service Road while MacIntosh Crescent veered off south-easterly. A little parkette was in the middle.

Meat from five steers, 150 pounds of flour, 30 pounds of salt, 15 pounds of pepper, 10,000 hamburger rolls, 16 cords of firewood, four barbeque pits, two firemen, six chefs, four helpers and 18 hours of preparation time made the Old-Fashioned Western Barbecue a resounding success.

The Port Credit Weekly along with all of the major Toronto media carried stories of the event. The Weekly's edition of Thursday, September 12, 1957 wrote the following on the day of the event.

"Barbecue five steers and add 10,000 rolls and you're all set for a luscious "Steer Burger" at the Applewood Benefit Festival, sponsored by the Merchants of Applewood Village Shopping Centre, tonight, Thursday, beginning at 8:30 p.m.

Dozens of community organizations and individuals are co-operating in staging the old-fashioned western event in the interests of the South Peel Association for Retarded Children.

And just to make sure that it's done right, the merchants of Applewood, after an exhaustive month's search came up with Elton A. Chisholm, an acclaimed expert in the art of western style barbecuing. He will supervise six butchers and two firemen in the preparation of 10,000 " Steer Burgers."

If you were at the C.N.E. you might have seen some of the 'burgers' —two of the steers, for tonight's repast, were special C.N.E. show steers.

The western-style "steer burgers" will be sold at 25 cents each by service clubs and associations on behalf of the Retarded Children. There will be no charge to view the proceedings, including the five barbecue pits, each three and a half feet wide by three and a half feet deep and 14 feet long. Also there will be two orchestras- one for general dancing and another for country dancing- fireworks, movies and western hats. Even the Boy Scouts and Cubs will benefit by selling special packs containing a towel to wash face and hands on the spot without the necessity of soap and water.

In all, everything adds up to good food, good company, a highly enjoyable time, a most unusual event and a big boost for a worthy cause. Everybody is welcome. Remember it all starts at 8:30 p.m., tonight, Thursday."

Bob Yott owned a hardware store at the eastern end of Applewood Shopping Centre. It was one of those old-fashioned hardware stores where just about one of everything could be found. Snow can be seen in the little parkette between the shopping centre and MacIntosh Crescent where the BBQ took place. Photo courtesy of the Shipp Corporation.

Preparation for the barbecuing started well in advance. The cords of hardwood were lit at midnight. Each pit was started one-half hour apart. Between six to seven hours later, the glowing charcoal from the hardwood was covered over by sand. The meat, in chunks of 15 to 25 pounds and boned out, were rubbed with salt and pepper, covered with cheese-cloth, then overlaid with a paste of flour and water, and finally encased in clean burlap. They were then cooked for about 12 hours. Mr. Chisholm, executive secretary of the Western Stock Growers' Association at Calgary, who was imported to supervise the preparations, said the one big problem with these old-fashioned ovens is that once the meat is placed in the pits, there is no control over it. The meat can come out not done well enough or over done. "That's the trouble with these old fashioned ovens, there are no timers on them," he quipped.

8 Parks, and Swimming

The Westacres Pool serves as a monument to the spirit of those who made it an Applewood Acres institution, namely the members of The Lions Club of Dixie- Mississauga and to the untiring efforts of area resident and Lions Club member Don McLean.

Don, who passed away in April 1997 at the age of 76, was one of the original Applewood Acres residents. He was instrumental in spearheading the drive to fulfill the hopes of the community in having the pool designed and constructed.

Don was born in Punnichy, Saskatchewan. Here he received his early education. Following university, Don enlisted in the Royal Canadian Air Force where he worked in Transport Command.

He met his future wife while posted in North Bay, Ontario and in 1949 married and settled in Vancouver, British Columbia. Marie was a nurse, having graduated from nursing school in 1942. Their first two children, William and Lawrence were born in Vancouver, while daughter Sue and son Don were born in Applewood Acres shortly after the McLeans moved here in June 1953.

By this time Don had left the service and was well established in a career with Air Canada. He started as a pilot and rose to the position of Captain.

It was in Applewood where Don became active with the Dixie Lions and, as Chairman of the Club's fund raising committee, Don and the Club were looking for a community project to sponsor and quickly came up with the idea of having a public pool in Westacres Park.

Don approached Robert Speck, the Reeve of Toronto Township, now The City of Mississauga. The Lions Club plan was outlined to Reeve Speck. The Club was to donate $15,000 if the Township could match that amount. Speck did not think much of the plan since the total budget of the Parks and Recreation was $15,000.

But Don and the members were not to be deterred. They continued to negotiate with the Township and, in 1960, managed to convince the Council that the pool was a good idea.

Westacres Pool was to become the first municipally owned sporting facility other than ball diamonds and soccer fields. Don, as Chairman of the Committee, started the Club's efforts to raise funds in the community. A large thermometer was erected at the Applewood Village Shopping Centre. It was divided into increments of $10,000 and the theme was "Get The Boy In The Pool." The thermometer had a sketch of a little boy as the marker.

Not too long afterward bad news struck. Cost projections amounted to almost twice the original amount. The planners estimated the costs to exceed $50,000. Don and his fellow members met with the planners and designers and came up with a few cost-saving measures.

After the site was chosen, the pool went to tender. More bad news followed. The quotes started at $90,000, which was the equivalent of six homes in Applewood Acres.

But Don and his fellow members were again not to be shaken. They persuaded the Township that the pool was worth $90,000 to the community and on April 11, 1963 it opened. It was built by D.A. Sinclair Limited, a local company from nearby Cooksville. The Lions Club had raised $25,000 toward the construction of the pool. The Township came through to complete the financing.

According to Jerry Love, Director of Recreation, who acted as master of ceremonics for the official opening, dignitaries from the Township, the Dixie Lions Club, along with many other notables, were on hand.

A cheque was formally presented to the Township by Don McLean and then the ribbon was cut. But it was the Deputy Reeve of Toronto Township, Applewood's own Chic Murray who made the biggest headlines that evening.

Mr. Murray was unceremoniously thrown into the pool, clothes and all. Fred Gunther, Lions Club historian, recalls it was all in fun and the Deputy Reeve felt so as well.

71

Bill McLean speaks at ceremony dedicating the pool as the Don McLean Westacres Pool while the McLean family looks on: Photo by Sophie Cook

As the Applewood Acres community started to celebrate its 50th anniversary in the summer of 2001, the Applewood Acres Homeowners Association joined with the Lions Club of Dixie Mississauga and The City of Mississauga in recognizing the truly monumental efforts of area resident Don McLean, who, during his many years in the community was never in the public eye, but certainly had the public's best interest in his heart.

The naming of the pool comes just 10 years after the City of Mississauga announced it was considering closing the pool forever. However, Parks and Recreation recommended that eight local pools should be kept open in 1992 and Council agreed.

It became an issue of 'use it or lose it.' During this period I sat as President of the Homeowners' Association, and I was outraged that Councillor Nando Iannicca, who succeeded me when I retired as Councillor, failed to inform our group of the City's plan to close the pool.

The City announced that it would hear comments in September, after the season closed. The report stated that attendance at Westacres Pool had increased by 17 per cent in 1991.

The report also stated that the cost of operating the pool had increased 100 per cent from 1986 to 1991. It was estimated at the time that it would cost $270,000 over the next 10 years.

Fearing the pool would be lost to the Community the Homeowners' Association decided to encourage interested area residents to form a committee to determine what action could be taken to save the pool from closure. Additionally, the Homeowners' Association decided to organize a BBQ and Free Swim in June to help create an awareness and encourage its use. This event became an annual fixture.

The first meeting was held at the home of Denise Ormonroyd at 1092 Melton Drive. At that meeting Cliff Barry, an Applewood resident who was an Olympic swimming coach (see Chapter 14), took up the challenge and set plans in motion to help save the pool. The group met a handful of times but the important meeting was when they sat down face-to face with Mayor Hazel McCallion to outline their concerns.

During this period, the City had set new Ward boundaries and Applewood Acres fell into the new Ward One alignment which was held by veteran Councillor Harold Kennedy. Councillor Kennedy worked diligently on the matter and by the spring of 1994 he advised the pool had been given a reprieve and would stay open indefinitely.

Following the decision, Mississauga City Council approved $70,000 annually for normal operation of the pool. A further $29,000 was approved to replace the slide, and for chemical handling facilities and drain repairs.

For 1996, the City set aside $46,000 for both interior and exterior renovations and further earmarked $300,000 for a total renovation in 1998.

The City promised to keep the pool open for the next 10 years if continued high use was evident. The Applewood Acres Homeowners' Association immediately instituted the Annual BBQ and Free Swim, held at Westacres Park, to promote usage of the pool.

Applewood is blessed with park space and green-open space for residents to enjoy. In total, Applewood Acres has more than 14 acres (5.7 hectares) all located within the boundaries of the community. Fred Halliday Memorial Park has 4.48 acres (1.81 hectares), while Alan Bradley Park has .35 acres (.14 hectares). Applewood North Park has 1.9 acres (.76 hectares) and Westacres Park, the largest, has 7.36 acres (2.97 hectares).

Fred Halliday Memorial Park, at Stir Crescent, is one of two parks named after an area resident. The following is a story prepared by The Halliday Family.

Although the Historiography is not dated, Frederick James Halliday lived in Applewood Acres. between 13 August 1953 and 30 August 1984.

Fred was born in Harlston, Norfolk, England on 25 July 1911. He and his brother Jack were twins and Fred, the youngest, weighed in at 2.5 lbs at birth. The family eventually moved to Ipswich where Fred started his long career with electric motors at E. R. and F. Turner. It was also at this time that he joined the Territorial Army (England's Reserve Forces).

Fred married Mary Daphne Jolly on 12 August 1939, and on 3 September 1939 WW2 was declared. During the war Fred served with the Royal Electrical and Mechanical Engineers (REME) of the British Army in Italy and Austria. Following the war Fred made arrangements for his wife and son, Tony, to join him in Austria. However, he was "demobilized" before the move and returned to Ipswich.

In 1948 the Halliday family, which had now grown to four with the birth of their daughter, Jane, moved to Sutton Coldfield just outside Birmingham. During this time Fred worked for an Australian Company, still selling electric motors.

In 1951 the Halliday family grew to five with the birth of Sally. In 1952 the British government introduced heavy import duties on Australian goods and Fred's company could no longer compete with British firms. All of a sudden, finding himself without a job, he wrote to an acquaintance with Bedard Girard Ltd. in Montreal to inquire if the previous offer of employment was still valid. Fred was offered and accepted a job as manager of Bull Motors Canada, selling electric motors made by E. R. and F. Turner in Ipswich.

Fred arrived in Canada on 11 November 1952 while his family remained in England. What a Remembrance Day this was as Fred found himself responsible for Bull Motors in all of Canada. But, he had no office, no staff, no customers, but electric motors starting to arrive. Hard work and

74

long days soon solved these problems. Fred found office and warehouse space on Kipling Avenue and so naturally looked in the west end for housing so he could have his family join him in Canada. Mary and the children arrived in Montreal via Trans Canada Airlines North Star on 17 July 1953, one of the hottest days of the year. The family stayed in temporary lodgings waiting for their Shipp-built home at 1324 Wealthy Place to be completed.

The scheduled date for completion was 31 July 1953 but the house was not available for occupancy until 13 August 1953. By today's standards two weeks is not bad. Thus commenced Fred's long association with Applewood Acres.

Mary Halliday remembers that in 1953 the electrical power in her home was DC but was changed to AC shortly after moving in. Also, Mary remembers Dixie Road as being unpaved in 1953. Fred loved his garden at 1324 Wealthy Place. A big lot that originally contained 13 apple trees provided many hours of pleasure and many days of work to get it into shape.

In 1959, 1960 and 1961 Fred's garden was judged to be the best in Applewood Acres. In 1976 Fred added a small greenhouse extension to

the side of the house. This addition allowed Fred to grow his flowers from seed. After several transplants and repottings he moved them to his garden.

It is in the community that Fred demonstrated his kindness, compassion and dedication. He will long be remembered for his continuous support in a variety of volunteer services. In particular Fred was an active supporter of youth activities. He spent many days working on the baseball diamond that was where the Sears Store now sits at Dixie Mall.

His support included fundraising, an activity that he did not like but knew was necessary. If those he approached could not help he still enjoyed meeting new people and just chatting with them. He also provided transportation for players when required many times driving some to Lancaster Depew even though none of them were his children.

75

Fred loved to entertain and often hosted barbecues and other social events at his home. In June 1955 Fred joined the Dixie Kiwanis and started his many years of activities with this service club. Fred was the mainstay in the support of the Lakeshore Psychiatric Hospital. bingo games and parties were Fred's specialty. Fred also was a familiar sight driving senior citizens, visiting the sick and aiding in local fundraising efforts. The Kiwanis Club used to hold an annual White Elephant Sale. It was during this event that the true salesman in Fred came out. Fortunately, when all items are donated free of charge, the sale of that item for any amount produces a profit. Fred would rather sell the item for $0.25 than have to put it back in the trailer at the end of the day.

Fred was President of the Dixie Kiwanis in 1962/1963. This memorable year taught the other Kiwanians the meaning of the term, "Are you with me?" Fred's non-confrontational relaxed enticing approach provided the help he was seeking. Then, when the job was done, Fred often thanked his helpers with the term "Bless you." Many times people who did not know Fred would think that he was from some religious order with this phrase. Whether it was at his home or in the community Fred would tackle almost any job so long as he had a "Mate." This "Mate" did not have to be qualified or trained to do the job, he/she just had to be there.

Fred retired after 50 years with Bull Motors on 15 June 1979. Now Fred had more time to putter in his garden and walk his Saint Bernard dog "Buffy." Work with the Kiwanis continued with Peat Moss sales in the Spring and collecting, preparing and delivering presents to the needy at Christmas. Fred died peacefully while enjoying a sunny afternoon in his lawn chair on 30 August 1984.

On 19 October 1985 Mayor Hazel McCallion, Ward 7 Councillor Dave Cook, Mississauga (Dixie) Kiwanis, family and friends gathered at Applewood South Park. Fred was instrumental in building this baseball park and it is very appropriate that it was named "Fred Halliday Memorial Park" in his honour.

The second park, actually a parkette, to bear the name of an area resident is located on Melton Court, just east of Cawthra, on the north side.

In 1998 Hydro Mississauga requested the City of Mississauga to have a park named in honour of Alan E. Bradley who had recently retired as

Commissioner of Hydro. Mr. Bradley was first elected to the Hydro Mississauga Electric Commission in 1970 and re-elected in the 1971 and 1972 elections.

Coincidental, with the formation of the City of Mississauga in 1974, Hydro Mississauga took on a new name and established a new commission. Four other members, Dr. Doug Sherbaniuk, newly-elected Mayor of Mississauga, Dr, Martin Dobkin, Brampton Mayor Jim Archdckin, along with fellow Applewood Acres resident Chic Murray, attended the inaugural meeting and it was at this meeting that Mr. Bradley was unanimously appointed its Chairman. He held the elected position of Chairman from 1971 to 1994 and was voted to the position of Vice Chairman from 1994 to 1997.

In view of his long-term service, commitment and contributions to Hydro Mississauga, the utility industry and the residents of Mississauga, the request to name a park in his honour went before City Council for endorsement and was subsequently approved. Hydro Mississauga announced the naming at a retirement dinner in March of 1998.

Born in Winnipeg, Manitoba, on August 23, 1913, Mr. Bradley went through public and secondary schooling and then graduated from the University of Manitoba in 1935 with an Electrical Engineering degree. He attended McGill University in Montreal graduating in 1936 with a Mechanical Engineering degree.

From 1936 through 1939 he was employed with Manitoba Bridge and Iron Works and also San Antonio Gold Mines. Following his marriage to Kay

Ray in 1939 the Bradleys moved to Quebec where he worked for Defense Industries Ltd, then later he joined Standard Brands Ltd.

By 1947 the Bradleys found themselves living in Long Island, N.Y. where Mr. Bradley had been transferred by Standard Brands. Moving to Toronto in 1954, Mr. Bradley established the eastern division of Canadian Lift Slab Construction Co.

In 1956 Mr. Bradley was elected Education Trustee to the South Peel Board of Education. He was subsequently elected each year and in 1963 was elected by his peers as Chairman. In 1964 and 1965 he was elected Chairman of the Board of Education of the Township of Toronto. The Bradleys had four daughters, Joanne (married to Doug Williams), Sue (married to Gord Turner), Margot (married to Jeff Remahl), and Betty (married to Barry Rudachyk). Margot became a teacher and taught at Westacres Public School. The Bradleys lived at 2163 Harcourt Crescent.

9 Citizens of The Year and Volunteers

Applewood Acres has the distinction of having two residents honoured with Mississauga's Citizen of The Year Award, a third being named the Young Citizen of The Year and three others being honoured by the Province of Ontario with volunteer awards.

Margaret Leslie, who lived at 2074 Breezy Brae with her husband Art and children, Judy and Sharon, was selected Citizen of The Year, April 29, 1980, the year the award was first established. The Citizen of The Year award was named the Gordon S. Shipp Memorial Award.

The annual award event is organized by the Mississauga Real Estate Board and The Mississauga News. All recipients of the Gordon S. Shipp Memorial Award have their photos on display at City Hall.

Below is an article originally published in the community newsletter, The Apple Press, in the fall of 1994. It was written by Doug Read of 2119 Russett Road and reprinted here with Mr. Read's permission.

"Marg Leslie, one of Applewood's senior citizens, died in May. I use the word 'senior' not to describe her age (she was only 79) but her accomplishments. She was a leader in her field. She would have scolded me for referring to her this way. She never thought of herself as a leader. When particular honours came her way, as they did frequently, she was always taken by surprise, believing that others deserved them more.

I first met Marg Leslie in 1954 when I joined the staff of Westacres School. The school had just opened; she was the president of the Parent, Teacher Association. The community was new and, wanting the best for it children, lent support to dozens of projects which raised a lot of money for the school and began the tradition of the Westacres Fair.

Marg and Gord Finlayson, the school principal, guided Westacres through those formative years with a skill, in my somewhat biased view, still unmatched.

At the time I did not know Marg was also a volunteer with the Canadian Red Cross. She had joined the society in 1946 and had worked at Sunnybrook Hospital. When she and her family bought a house in

79

Applewood in 1954, she transferred to the newly formed Peel Chapter of the Red Cross.

Long-time residents of Applewood will remember 1954 as the year of Hurricane Hazel, when the storm flooded their basements and shattered their windows. Others, like the residents of the Pleasant Valley Trailer Park, will remember seeing their homes swept away.

Marg Leslie was one of the first nurses to reach the area. It was not her first experience with emergencies on a large scale. In 1949 the S.S. Noronic had caught fire in Toronto harbour and burned out of control. The Red Cross was on hand to treat crewmembers and fire fighters injured in the blaze. Marg was part of the team.

Arthur Leslie was kind enough to let me borrow the family scrapbook to help prepare this article. To read it is to remember how often in its short history our local Red Cross has been called upon to give emergency help: the gas line explosion in Malton (1968) that destroyed the Four Corners; the crash of Air Canada flight 189 at Toronto International Airport (1978); the Texaco tank fire in Clarkson the same year; the C.P.R. derailment (1979); the fire at Queensway Extendicare (1980). By then under Marg's direction, the first blood donor clinics in Mississauga had been well established.

Without question, her biggest challenge was the C.P.R. derailment in 1979 and the subsequent evacuation-called the greatest peacetime evacuation in history. An editorial in The Mississauga News of the day reads: "Who was really in charge of the evacuation? The Mayor, the police chief or a grandmother? For countless local residents Margaret Leslie was by far the most important official during the entire crisis. She was Mississauga's Red Cross Emergency Chairman, a position which left her with the responsibility for guiding the lives of 240,000 homeless people."

Recognizing her efforts she was awarded the Gordon S. Shipp Award as Mississauga's Citizen of The Year. Her portrait hangs in City Hall. In 1987 she was awarded the medal of the Order of the Red Cross, the society's highest award.

In 1993 the Government of Canada awarded her the Commemorative Medal for the 125th anniversary of Confederation. The citation from the Governor-General reads in part, "The award is made to those persons who, like you, have made a significant contribution to Canada, to their community and to their fellow Canadians."

A final tribute came in 1993 when the Canadian Red Cross created an award to recognize each year the most outstanding Junior Red Cross Volunteer. Appropriately, it was named the Marg Leslie Award.

Art and Margaret Leslie lived at 2074 Breezy Brae Drive raising their daughters Judy and Sharon. Marg was named Mississauga's first Citizen of The Year on April 29, 1980 at a gala affair held at the Royal York Hotel in Toronto. The Honourable Pauline McGibbon, Ontario's Lieutenant Governor, made the presentation.

•**Bradley Butt**, born in Canada's Centennial Year 1967, arrived on the Applewood scene with parents Terry and Kathy Butt in 1969. In July 1970 Brad's sister Sharyn was born. Brad attended Westacres Public School, then Alan A. Martin and Gordon Graydon Secondary Schools. He attended University of Toronto-Erindale College where he studied Political Science and French Language.

His interest in politics came early in life as a result of being involved with his father's political career. Terry served on Port Credit Council in 1971-

81

1973 and later held a seat on The City of Mississauga Council in 1976-78, representing the Applewood Acres area.

"I became interested in politics when my dad was running for Council in 1977. It was a little later when I really got hooked. That was when Bud Gregory was running for MPP in Mississauga East," said Brad.

Brad was active in minor hockey, soccer and also in Cubs and Beavers. When he started high school, he quickly became involved in student activities. Brad served as President of the Student Council at Gordon Graydon. During the summers Brad held a job with the City as a swimming instructor and also as a life guard and in the 1980s he was coordinator for the popular Citi Swim.

He has been active on numerous committees, including the Library Board, Arts Council and Applewood United Church. He has sat on almost all committees of the church. One of his crowning moments came in 1986 as one of the founders and first Chairman of the Mayor's Youth Advisory Committee. He was also honoured by being named the 1986 Young Citizen of the Year.

Brad resigned the Chairmanship of the committee in 1988 when he decided to run for Council. In 1990 Brad won the Provincial Conservative nomination for Mississauga East. He again ran for office in 1994 when Councillor Harold Kennedy retired. Brad had moved into Ward One by this time.

Brad also established himself in the community with the airing of a Cable Television interview program, which has run almost every year since 1991.

It is almost a certainty that if a book is ever done on the Second 50 Years of Applewood Acres, Brad Butt will fill many paragraphs. The residents of Applewood Acres will most certainly be rewarded by his energies and enthusiasm in the future just as we have in the past.

•In the year 2000 The Provincial Government gave **Leonard Barrett** its Volunteer Service Award. In addition to that award he also received the Volunteer of The Year Award presented by the Mississauga Senior Citizen Centre. In the same year Leonard was nominated by the Ontario Senior Games, District 20, Mississauga Senior Games for five years of service.

Leonard moved into Applewood Acres in 1957 and it didn't take long for him to become involved with the Kiwanis Baseball and then with the area minor hockey groups. He became President of the Mississauga Reps, sat on the Board of Directors of the Toronto Township Hockey League and then eventually moved up the ladder to take an executive post with the Metro Toronto Hockey League (MTHL).

Leonard, who worked in the private sector in auditing and also a stock brokerage firm, began his employment with the Provincial Government in 1962, first with Treasury and later with the Transportation Ministry. He retired in 1988 but retirement only meant a slight change in his hectic schedule. He continued to work as a volunteer in the community.

In all, Leonard spent 22 years as Treasurer of the MTHL. He also chaired the Overseas Travel Committee. For 15 years he enjoyed the perks of taking part in the overseas trips with the organization.

His involvement with the Mississauga Senior Citizens Centre came after his retirement from his government job. He enrolled in a class to brush up on the French language. However, it didn't last too long as the class suffered low attendance. As a result, Leonard ended up taking men's exercise classes as his wife Marion was in a women's class. It was then that he became involved at the Centre.

He served as Vice Chairman for five years with the Senior Games, before moving on to other Centre activities.

•**Jim and Bertha Betts** moved into Applewood in June 1953 settling at 2194 Rambo Road. The Betts family came to the area as already established volunteers as Jim had been very active in community volunteering in Etobicoke. They immediately became involved in the community here and over the years have been dedicated to several causes. In 1972 Bertha was the founder of the Mississauga Chapter of Meals on Wheels, while Jim was involved in planning for the Distress Line of Peel. On Wednesday, December 10, 2003, both Jim and Bertha were recognized by the Province of Ontario and were presented with the 2003 Ontario Volunteer Service Awards.

•Johnathan Drive resident John Somerset was kind enough to write the story of **Jim Murray** and also he contributed the lead story of Mayor Chic Murray in our chapter on area politicians. John is probably the best writer for this particular task as he is Chic Murray's son-in-law.

Jim Murray's first contact with the law occurred at the cusp of his teenage years. Too young to face charges, as the Township of Toronto police officers decided, Jimmy Murray surely needed only to face a lesson regarding what is decidedly inappropriate behavior.

In the late 50s, Applewood Acres and surrounding areas were in the final stages of development with building sites and equipment evident everywhere you cared to look. All of this was tempting, perhaps too tempting, for young boys – especially the yellow earth moving tractors, sitting idle, some with keys in the ignition. Jimmy and his pals would explore these interesting sites after the work crews had gone for the day. They would sit upon the earth moving equipment while pressing pedals and pulling levers, pretending to operate the machines. One afternoon the inevitable happened. The boys started up one of the machines. Jimmy could barely reach the pedals as his machine sprang to life, lurching forward toward the road. He was horrified as it moved toward some parked cars, coming to a crashing, jarring and terrifying stop.

This is the same Jim Murray who would later be named Mississauga's Citizen of the Year in April of 1996. More ironic, this is the same Jim Murray who would serve on the Police Services Board as a commissioner, Vice-Chair and Acting Chair for six years. Yes, they gave him a badge.

James John Murray was born in London, Ontario, on September 24th, 1946. He arrived in Applewood Acres as a young boy of eight, when his family moved into their brand new Shipp-built home on Duchess Drive in 1954. Known to his family as James, he is the youngest of four and, by necessity, a decidedly spirited youngster. He and his group of friends threw their energies into the Applewood Rover/Scouts program, where Jim rose to the highest levels. After high school, he, and many from the same group of friends, would find similar satisfaction in the Kinsmen organization. In 1967 Jim joined the Kinsmen Club of Mississauga, which met upstairs in the Applewood Plaza. In Jim, Kinsmen fostered a strong purpose in serving the community while stimulating rewarding personal growth. He progressively chaired many committees before becoming Kinsmen president. After receiving several awards for contributions beyond the home-club level, Jim was awarded the Kinsmen's highest honour, a Life Membership. At 33, he was the youngest member to be so recognized for his outstanding contributions.

Jim is very good at the games of chance and just as good in pursuing a life that especially suits him. Jim would be the first to tell you that school was not the highlight of his life. Nevertheless, he never let this detract from his making a series of very smart moves early in his career. One of the smartest steps he took was in marrying Janis, his high school sweetheart. Another would be in hiring Wendy Thompson, his long-time, devoted secretary. Janis and Wendy are the team behind Jim's business, community and personal lives. They provide the fine organizational stability that allows Jim the freedom to lead an exceptionally busy life.

Fred Price, owner of a small local real estate firm, saw something special in Jim and in 1968 hired this young man in search of a career. From that time, Jim took his seat at the real estate table and decided to make something meaningful out of the opportunity. Four years later, and encouraged by Fred Price, Jim set out on his own to form a partnership known as Newton and Murray Real Estate, specializing in industrial, commercial and investment sales. This was to be Jim's area of expertise for all of his working life. In the period starting from 1975, when he bought out his partner, Jim was involved in ownership changes at Parsons Taylor and then Guaranty Trust, before joining J.J. Barnicke in 1983.

On the shelves and walls of Jim's Mississauga office, there is ample, tangible evidence of a man devoted to many business and community causes and the rewards for dedicated work. While these are too numerous to mention here, there are a few in which he takes special pride. He serves on the Board of Governors of the Credit Valley Hospital. There are numerous references to the Mayor's Gala, an annual charity event that Jim chaired in 1994 and in which he continues to play a pivotal role. There is an especially fine plaque for the Gordon S. Shipp Award for Mississauga's Citizen of the Year in 1996. In a more prominent place in Jim's office, there is a gorgeous family portrait of Jim, Janis and their three boys, Tim 29, Jason 26 and Frazer, 23. There is also a composite of the family cottage on the Severn River, the family escape hatch. Make no mistake

about it, Jim is, and always has been, a family man. He has supported his boys in their many activities through the years.

Jim has been with J.J. Barnicke for twenty years now and is currently a Senior Vice-President. He has served on the Police Services Board for the Regional Municipality of Peel since 1997 and is now Vice Chair. As he dresses for work each morning, Jim places his gold Police Services Board lapel pin on his jacket. It is similar in appearance to the badge he carries in his wallet.

Understandably, Jim takes particular pride in this. The old expression, that you can take the boy out of Applewood Acres, in this instance, but you cannot take Applewood Acres out of the boy, is quite apt in Jim's case. What he came to value in his younger years continues to serve him well. He remains, at heart, an Applewood Acres boy, as well as a citizen of the first order.

10 Unique Homes

Applewood Acres was selected to host two very special and unique housing projects. One was the *Better Houses for Canadian Living* and the other, a *Home for All America*, both sponsored by national magazines.

In February of 1953 the Canadian Home Journal magazine announced a series of annual architectural competitions to find new designs for *Better Houses for Canadian Living*.

All members of the Royal Architectural Institute of Canada were invited to compete, cash awards were offered, and in the contest period, hundreds of designs were received from across Canada.

Home '53', located at the south-east corner of Redan and Ribston, was designed by contest winners, Guy Desbarats and Fred Lebensold of Montreal. Their entry was declared outstanding, incorporating many modern imaginative ideas, while still remaining practical and completely livable.

Canadian Home Journal, feeling that this design should be brought before the Canadian public as soon as possible, decided to have Home '53' built for public inspection and approval. The problem of arranging for a reputable builder to erect 'Home 53' was solved in the easiest possible fashion. Mr. Jack Kent Cooke, publisher of Canadian Home Journal, had long recognized the ability and proven success of G.S.Shipp and his development, Applewood Acres, as easily being the most outstanding endeavour in Canadian building of the day.

Mr. Shipp shared the enthusiasm for 'Home 53' and plans were quickly put into effect, and the result of this new partnership is now evident.

Modern as tomorrow, yet as comfortable as a pair of old shoes, according to a feature story in the Toronto Telegram on September 15,1954, as how the home located at 849 Duchess was described.

The *Home for All America* was designed by Robert A Little and Associates, a leading U.S. architectural firm from Cleveland, Ohio. The home is a one-storey, three-bedroom home which represents a blend of ideas collected by Better Homes and Gardens Magazine from a panel of 12 families who explained just what they would like in a new home.

Added to this were some of Mr. Shipp's own ideas and these were enhanced by the interior decorating touches of the T. Eaton Company Ltd.

Intent on creating a home geared to young Canadians, the Duchess Avenue home came to reality after a visit by G.S. Shipp to the National Home Show in Chicago where a similar model was displayed. Mr. Shipp won the contract to build the first one in Canada.

The G.S. Shipp and Son Limited brochure said at the time that their decision to build the Better Homes and Gardens much-talked-about *Home for All America* was not one which was taken lightly.

" It was the result of many weeks of careful consideration and close study of plans and specifications."

The brochure stated that the reaction of those who visited the home would help decide whether or not to incorporate ideas from this controversial home in the designs offered in future residential developments undertaken by the company.

The house, 59 ft. X 24.5 ft. (17.9 m X 7.46 m) is of frame and stone construction with a two-car garage, covered patio 20 X 22 ft. (6 X 6.7 m) complete with a barbecue.

The press preview of the home was held Tuesday, September 14, 1954. The home opened to the public on September 17, 1954 under the sponsorship of the Progress Club, which was raising funds for the mentally challenged. Viewers donated to the Club during the three-week viewing period.

Attracting major interest was the activities room, a blend of informal living room and recreation room. It had access directly outdoors as well as to the children's rooms and a bathroom. The bathroom was situated in such a way as to back onto the bathroom in the master bedroom thereby saving additional piping.

The open plan featured the living room, dining room and kitchen combination, and wall space was saved throughout by the use of sliding doors. Only four doors were of the conventional hinge design.

Summer air conditioning went on automatically just as the furnace came on in the winter, and a remote control bedside switch provided auxiliary control of the lighting throughout the entire house.

There was an accent on colour in the interior decorating. A careful blend of colours added spaciousness to the open areas yet tied everything together. Eaton's also provided furnishings boasting that they were flexible enough to suite the varied activities of a growing family.

There stands a number of homes along Dixie Road, North Service Road, Cawthra Road and at The Queensway and Stanfield Road which pre-date Applewood Acres. Some are smaller homes which housed employees of the orchard owners of the area, while others were houses built and occupied by relatives of some of the major landowners.

As an example, Ken Watson, a relative of the Watson Apple Orchard family, who owned property along the QEW and Dixie Road area, lived in a house which is still quietly tucked almost out of sight, snuggled up to the east bank of the Dixie Road overpass at 1345 North Service Road.

Ken's daughter, Nora, married Carl Stewart, who could well be this area's first elected politician as he sat on Township Council before the Shipps came along. Carl and Nora built the home at 835 North Service Road.

The house at 915 North Service Road was built by William Henry Hedge in 1928 and is certainly noticeable as you travel along the North Service Road. Construction on the house was a family affair. William Henry Hedge cut all the stones, while his relatives did the carpentry work. The fine carpentry inside the home is oak paneling and gumwood cabinetry in the kitchen.

Fred Hedge lived in the house until the 1980s. He fell off the roof while working on it. He never recovered sufficiently to return to the house, and resided at Chelsea Park Nursing Home until his death in January of 1995.

The Hedge House is one of several homes built and still majestically surviving as a reminder of when the Applewood area was a thriving agricultural community.

On the west side of Dixie Road just as it turns to rise over the QEW stands a large home built around 1913 by Hector Death. The house, at 2116 Dixie Road, a two storey, 10-room home, once sat in splendor with a large veranda overlooking a 15 acre orchard. Once inside the house, it is abundantly evident that much skill and care were taken in its construction. Much of the construction was done using oak wood throughout.

Just to its south, about where the Dixie overpass stands, was another beautiful home. While no longer there, it was on a 42-acre spread owned by Hector Death's brother, Walter.

Hector Death sold off part of his property to Shipp and part of it to the Ontario government to establish the overpass. When Hector's wife died, his son Ivan and wife Dorothy moved in to live with Hector. Ivan and Dorothy had two sons, Bob, who went to Thomas L. Kennedy Secondary School and Marshall who went to Gordon Graydon Secondary School. The Deaths sold the house in the 60s.

Thomas Stanfield arrived in Canada in the 1840s and purchased 100 acres south of Dundas Road and established his home on the west side of The Second Line East near Middlegate Road.

However, Applewood Acres cannot lay claim to Thomas Stanfield's home. The Stanfield's house was located just where the Fruehauf Truck Company was once located, now the site of modern warehousing   and   is just north of the northern boundary of Applewood Acres.

But, on the south-west corner of Stanfield Road and The Queensway, at 2250 Stanfield, is the original home of Lloyd and Ruth Stanfield. This home has a unique story in that it was originally constructed on property near the Thomas Stanfield home above Middlegate Road. Just prior to the establishment of Applewood Acres. Lloyd had his home moved to its present location. It had to be totally re-bricked.

The home of Garnett Phillip Goddard and his wife Elma Sarah was built around 1913 on the south-east corner of The Queensway and Stanfield Road (2265 Stanfield Road).

The home took an inordinate amount of time to finish. The walls are solid concrete to the top of the first storey. Garnett had little money when he first purchased the 20-acre site and his chosen method of construction was to pour concrete a little by little. Each day, the walls would rise one more foot. The veranda was finally built 12 years later.

The house had three bedrooms and a bathroom upstairs. There was a pantry, a sunroom and kitchen and living room. His son Jack, who was born in the house in 1919, and his wife Marg remained in the community and now live at 1253 Melton Drive.

One year after Garnett purchased the property, he sold off a portion to the Provincial Government for the hydro-electric transmission corridor. He made enough on the sale to pay for his purchase. On June 6, 1989, roughly 75 years later, this house was placed on the City's Heritage Inventory list.

Further east, at 2240 Dixie Road, on the south-west corner of The Queensway and Dixie Road, is a beautiful home constructed of stone. Originally this house was a small stone cottage but after it was purchased in the late 1920's by William and Lydia Clarke, who moved from Toronto to settle in the country, an architect was hired and the house greatly expanded from what it originally was. The house was completed in 1929. The original walls of the house are more than a foot thick and the interior is adorned with gumwood throughout. Bob Watson, one of the last remaining members of the Watson family, says that he recalls that the Clark house was originally owned by a family known as Wood who were part of the Wood Gundy investment family.

The Clarke's sons, Norman and Victor, built the detached garage before World War ll. Upon close inspection it is not hard to see the outstanding craftsmanship. They would spend hours shaping the stones, in many cases working an entire evening on just one stone. The garage was completed in the early 1940's, just before Norman enlisted for service.

It was in 1942 that Norman married Dorothy and at that time he was posted to service. Dorothy moved into the home to keep Lydia company as she was then a widow. Following the war both Norman and Dorothy remained in the house. Dorothy lives there to this day.

On August 5, 2003, the Commissioner of Community Services of the City of Mississauga, Paul A. Mitcham, P.Eng.,MBA, presented a report to the Chairman and Members of Mississauga's Heritage Advisory Committee, recommending that the Clarke house be added to the City's Heritage Inventory on the basis of its contextual and architectural significance.

One cannot drive north on Stanfield Road without noticing the four large red brick homes which once housed the Leaver families and staff along with the large white office building just north of the hydro corridor.

The white building, at 2170 Stanfield Road, once a garage, eventually became the office for Leaverleigh Farms and continues to this day to function as an office building, albeit not for its original occupants. On June 6, 1989, this building was placed on the City of Mississauga's Heritage Inventory list. According to the list, the style of the building is listed as being a one and one-half storey residential structure with plaster and lath, vertical wood siding on the east façade first storey. The roof is a hip roof with asphalt shingles and gabled and flat roof wall dormers. There are 15 pane windows with some hinged at top muntins, and concrete sills. There are wood brackets over the cornice of gabled wall dormers. There are commercial plate glass windows on the upper storey.

At 2196 Stanfield, on the west side, stands the house originally constructed for Leo and Marie Kline. Leo was brought into Leaverleigh Farms in a senior position. Leo and his family lived there for a short while until Leo died of a heart attack at an early age. The house then became the home to Lloyd Leaver's in-laws, George and Amy Clarkson, who were dairy farmers located on the south side of Dundas Street, just west of what is now Highway 27. They lived in what was then known as Summerville.

According to John Clarkson, whose father was Amy Clarkson's first cousin, George Clarkson lost his farm as a result of a legal judgment against him after one of his cows wondered onto Dundas Street causing a tragic accident. John is now living in Duncan, British Columbia where he moved after retiring from political office. He was once the Mayor of the Town of Caledon and sat on Peel Regional Council as a colleague of mine.

In an interview many years later, Diane Richards, Lloyd's daughter, would recall that her grandfather, George Clarkson, raised budgie birds in the garage until his allergies ended his hobby.

The house, like many of the homes of the period, was trimmed in rich woods with hardwood flooring. This house had a fieldstone fireplace.

Across the road, on the east side, stand three more Leavers homes. The first, at 2169 Stanfield Road, was the home of the family patriarch, George Leaver and his wife.

Not too far north, at 2183 Stanfield, is the 'staff' house where the more senior members of the business would be housed. Two people, who would have been very popular with its occupants, were the cooks, Mrs. Ethel Bagshaw and Mrs. Jessie Grice.

Probably the most interesting of all the Leaver buildings still standing is the home of Lloyd and Amy Leaver at 2199 Stanfield Road. Prior to 1947 this home stood immediately north of the office on the west side of the road. The home has a centre hall plan with four bedrooms, a living room, dining room and kitchen. Oak is used throughout the house.

In around December of 1947 or 1948 it was decided to move the home to its present location on the east side of Stanfield Road and build a new home on the old foundation to accommodate a new senior employee who was coming from the United States. All the details and logistics were worked out on how to move such a massive home, bricks and all, and the move started.

After the house had been severed from its foundation and jacked up, large timbers fashioned as rails and logs acting as rollers were used to literally slide the house across Stanfield Road in a northeasterly direction. Once there, the house had to be turned about 180 degrees to have the house face west instead of east. It was a mammoth undertaking in that day and age.

The house was literally rolled across the street on logs. Below in the middle of Stanfield Road.

photos courtesy of Diane Richards

Just as the house was in the middle of Stanfield Road, at midnight, the telephone rang to advise Lloyd Leaver that the new employee had changed his mind and that he would not be joining the firm.

Diane Richards would later say that she felt that her father really should have just built a new home in the first place and she could never figure out why it became necessary to move such a large home.

In doing so they had to destroy all of the trees in the front yard including her most favourite trees, a Blue Spruce, Scotch Pine and a Mulberry bush.

According to hand-written notes provided by Stewart Petrie, of the Stewart family, the house at 871 North Service Road is the Graham homestead (Con.1, S.D.S., Lot 9). A log cabin was originally constructed by Thomas Graham shortly after he purchased the lands in 1838. When the Graham's decided to build a larger house they would call it Lakeview House. They built Lakeview House extremely close to the log cabin. Thomas Graham's son started to build the house but before it could be completed he died leaving his son, R.H. Graham, to finish the work. As an interesting side note to the story, Mr.Graham was 'laid out' in the log cabin and since the log cabin was so close to the new house, the coffin had to be stood vertically in order to get through the door.

According to newspaper accounts of the day, R.H. Graham was born here and educated in Brampton public and high schools and also at the "Toronto Normal". As an adult he taught for 10 years at the first school in what is now New Toronto.

In 1887 he was elected alderman for St. Stephen's Ward and served Toronto Council for 20 years. During this period he became a member of the first Board of Control, and was also Chairman of the Board of Health and also the Library Board. R.H. Graham was a member of the Eaton Memorial Church for 25 years and also was the recipient of the Masonic Jewel from the Grand Lodge of Canada presented on the completion of 50 years as a member of St. George's Lodge.

For a period, the property and house was rented to a family named Donnelly and then in 1908-1909 the Lakeview House was purchased by John Stewart. Later, about 1918, the property was divided between Harvey Stewart and his brother John.

The community of Lakeview actually was named after the house. It seems that Harvey Stewart suggested the name at a public meeting held at the old Lake Shore School during the time when the residents of that area were trying to find a name for their community. The name Lakeview was voted on and accepted.

The homestead was redesigned and modernized in 1936. Originally the house was a two-storey wood fame structure. A brick veneer was placed over the wood frame, a sunroom was added and the upper floor was redesigned with three windows replacing the single window. The original front porch, which ran across the entire front of the house, was replaced by two bay windows, each with shingled tops and a smaller porch with a roof and Georgian style pillars on each side of the front door. The 2,500 square foot (232 sq. metre) house has five bedrooms and a bathroom upstairs, a very large country kitchen, living room, dining room and a pantry. Originally there was a staircase leading off the back of the kitchen to the bedrooms. The foundation was of stone, approximately two feet (.6m) thick. To this day the original floor beams are being supported by 'two by six' beams. The original beams were trees cut from the surrounding area and trimmed flat on the top.

Dr. Thomson had to engage tradesmen to shore up the floor of the living and dining rooms when he purchased the house in 1953. The floor in both rooms had actually sunk and warped nine inches (22cm). Dr. Thomson made minor changes inside the house. His office occupied the entire east side of the home for 20 years. He created a small washroom and a lab by adding one wall between the pantry and the dining room. The dining room was the waiting room. His patients would then enter his office through the connecting hall. On the right was the washroom, while the lab was located on the left side.

The grounds surrounding the house reveal hints of years past. Water was once delivered by a well. Its cement top can still be seen in the back yard of the property next door. Also against the west basement foundation there are tops of a cement structure which once was two cisterns. Five very large maple trees stand tall providing natural air conditioning for the house. On June 19, 1999, the house was placed on the City's Heritage Inventory list.

The City of Mississauga has about 600 heritage properties on its Heritage Inventory list and only about 90 of those are actually designated as a

Heritage property. A property is added to the Heritage Inventory (listed) when it is deemed to have cultural, historical, architectural, archaeological, or natural significance and value. A listing does not have any legal status, and is not subject to a formal review or permit application fee. The listing is made for the purpose of flagging the property in the City's internal records, so as to assure that any development on or near that property will be sensitive to heritage concerns. It also allows the property to be studied in the future, in greater detail, should it be deemed worthy of upgrading to Heritage Designation under the Ontario Heritage Act. Designation of a property is a far more involved process and has legal status, through a designation By-Law. The property is then formally protected under the provisions of the Act.

John Stewart, who purchased the property from R.H. Graham in 1909, is seen tending to his beehives at what is now 871 North Service Road. The home was 'modernized' in 1936.

It has been written that the call to public office is the highest calling a person can have and Applewood Acres has been blessed with several people who have answered that calling. The first 'urban' politician to hold office in rural Toronto Township may well have been Charles (Chic) Murray. John Somerset, who lives at 1001 Johnathan Drive, is Chic Murray's son-in-law and tells the story.

By John Somerset

Chic Murray's long political career began with an impromptu session at Wally Beaupre's home on Duchess Drive. Wally had the neighbourhood guys in to show off his newly built recreational room. Finishing the 'rec' room was a task that all homeowners in the new subdivision faced, sooner or later. Among the keen admirers were Chic, Al Bradley, Ken Rowe and the proud carpenter. They discussed the finer points of constructing a comfortable room from a bare space in the basement.

The discussion soon turned to politics in Toronto Township, in particular how it was that the long-established families, mostly in the rural population, controlled local government. Those in newly formed subdivisions, such as Applewood Acres, had little or no voice. As he had some free time on his hands, and as he had not yet started his own rec room project, Chic was centered out as a prospective council member for the emerging suburban population.

Five neighbours each donated ten dollars toward publicity costs for the 1957 Ward Three Council race. While Chic was soundly defeated, he was determined to run a winning campaign the following year. With a newly gained admiration for the political process, and continuing support from his neighbourhood volunteers, Chic set out to win a seat on Council. He visited and courted the very people whom he saw as influential in the course of local government. Chic pitched his case and, like the fine salesman he was, gained their respect and, more importantly, their votes. This included T.L. Kennedy, himself. Robert, Chic's second son, remembers accompanying his father to visit Tom Kennedy on several occasions. Even as a young child, Robert could sense the closeness between the two men.

The election was a landslide. In 1958 Chic took his seat as Councillor for Ward 3 in the Township of Toronto. Thus began a municipal political career spanning eighteen years (1958-1976), including the office of Mayor of the Town of Mississauga (1972-1973).

Chic and Jo moved into their new home at 839 Duchess Drive in June 1954. They had previously lived in Etobicoke for a short time, but the Shipp house there would not work for the young Murray clan, as it had but one small bathroom located inconveniently on the first floor-hardly sufficient for a growing family of four children and a dog. Chad was the oldest at 13, followed by Susan, 11, Robert, 10, and James, just seven years old. The Applewood Acres house was larger, had more bedrooms and two ample bathrooms on separate floors. Additionally there was a near-by school for the children adjacent to a park and for the Irish setter, Clancy, to run through Applewood Acres. The Township of Toronto held great promise for the active, young family.

In the autumn all of the Murray children were enrolled at Westacres Public School. Their father initiated and chaired the first June Fair to raise funds for the new school. Chic was becoming a participating member of the community.

Born in Toronto on February 9, 1914, Chic was the younger of two boys and girls. Before he could start school, Chic's family moved to Buffalo, New York, where his father had purchased a light manufacturing company. He attended Bennett High School, where he excelled at sports, track and field in particular. After graduation, Chic's first job was as an *office boy at Ralston-Purina Company at $15 a week, a respectable salary during the depression.*

In 1937 Chic returned to Toronto on his own to accept a job selling for a book binding company. The following year, he would marry his high school sweetheart, Josephine Keith. Chic and his brother-in-law, Art Graham, started a construction company and built small houses in the Chestnut Hills area of Islington. As World War II grew darker, building supplies became increasingly scarce; the company did not survive these severe difficulties. With their new baby boy, Chic and Jo moved to London, Ontario, in 1941, where Chic worked as a $0.40/hr mill worker for Quality Steel Company before being promoted to a more suitable sales position in 1944. He was successful in sales, and in 1950, Chic accepted an offer to become National Sales Manager of Erie Iron Works in St. Thomas, Ontario. The position required that Chic and Jo move their family of four children to the Toronto area in 1953 and Applewood Acres the following year. The post-war years were full of promise for the Murrays. The Township of Toronto would be good for the young family and lead to fulfilling adventures, especially for Chic.

Chic had not long been on council when he and Reeve Robert Speck recognized a special bond between them. They seemed to complement one another's strengths and had the same vision for the future. After two years, Speck supported Chic in a bid for the position of Deputy Rreeve of the Township. In 1960 Chic defeated Caye Killaby to become Deputy Reeve of the Township of Toronto, a position he held from 1960 through 1967. When the township, along with the Towns of Port Credit and Streetsville, merged to become the Town of Mississauga in 1968, Bob Speck was elected Mayor, and Chic its Reeve.

Mayor Speck was forced to rely more and more on his Reeve for support, as he began to experience severe heart problems. When this resulted in one of Canada's first heart transplant operations, Chic was named Acting Mayor for the period of 1971-197; then, upon the death of Robert Speck, the popular councilor was unanimously acclaimed mayor to serve out the term through 1973. Mississauga was to achieve city status in 1974; Chic was eager to see his and Speck's wish become a reality. It was not to be.

Dr, Martin Dobkin ran against Chic on an anti-development platform. He claimed that the town officials were too cozy with the developers and that Chic was part and parcel of it all. With his unsupported allegations,

Dobkin became the first Mayor of the City of Mississauga in January 1974. Chic was devastated and admittedly depressed at the totally unexpected outcome. Nevertheless, he was not about to walk away, he believed he had more to give. He later ran for councilor of Ward Three, narrowly defeating Frank Bean by a mere 50 votes. He retired two years later with an enviable eighteen-year record of service to his city, 1958-1976. Chic finally felt free to pursue his various business interests and spend more time with Jo at their cottage and villa in Barbados. Jo died in February of 1979.

On January 21st, 1984, the City named the arena at Burnhamthorpe Community Centre, Chic Murray Arena in recognition of a long and dedicated service to his city. Chic died in July of the same year, a contented and proud man.

•**Terence (Terry) Butt** and his wife Kathryn moved into Applewood Acres and settled on Guthrie Lane in 1969. Their son Bradley was just two years of age. Brad's sister, Sharyn, was born in 1970. Terry soon found himself active in the community and was elected to the Port Credit Town Council in 1971. While he lived in the Township of Toronto, he owned a real estate business in Port Credit and was eligible to hold office there. He sat on Port Credit Council until amalgamation brought Port Credit into the new City of Mississauga.

Years later Terry was encouraged to run for the vacant seat on Mississauga Council when Councillor Ron Searle, who lived in Orchard Heights, announced he was going to run for the office of Mayor. Terry was elected in 1976 and served as a City and Peel Regional Councillor until 1978.

Terry was born in Thunder Bay, Ontario, April 19, 1945. He became a Real Estate agent after successfully completing his Provincial examinations in 1965 and became an agent in his father's business R.W. Butt Limited, Realtor, in Port Credit. He worked with his father until 1971. He had qualified as a broker in 1969. By 1972 he incorporated his own business, Butt Realty Corporation, with head offices in Mississauga and branch offices in downtown Toronto and Oshawa, Ontario. At its peak, Butt Realty employed 28 agents and, as president and owner of Butt Realty Corporation, he successfully built a company from its incorporation in 1972 to total sales of more than one billion dollars. In 1990, due to the recession, he closed his brokerage and transferred his license to Hurontario Realty Inc. In 1992 he joined Realty Corporation of Canada I.C.I. Limited, as manager of the Industrial, Commercial and Investment Division.

In September 1998 he transferred his broker's license to Coldwell Banker Sturino Realty. Terry successfully negotiated the sale of more than $84,000,000.00 of I.C.I. real estate. In 1999, 2001 and 2003 he was awarded the Coldwell Banker "Canadian Sterling Society" designation. For the first quarter of 2000, he was recognized as the "Number One" agent in Canada in gross commission income. For the year 2000 he was awarded the Coldwell Banker Canada "President's Circle" award. He was also inducted into the Coldwell Banker International "Diamond Society" in 2001 for his production achieved the previous year. His I.C.I. sales for the first nine months of 2003 totalled more than $9,000,000.00 and he was subsequently recognized as one of the "Top 50" agents in Canada in gross commission income for the first quarter.

His dedication to the community has spanned 35 years and he has served on numerous committees and organizations. He is a founding member of the Port Credit Businessman's Association, founding member and original fundraising chairman and executive board member of Distress Line Mississauga and original fundraising chairman of the Salvation Army Red Shield Appeal Mississauga. He served as chairman and member of the executive committee of the Applewood United Church and also as chairman of fundraising, Peel United Way Campaign.

•As author of this book, I find myself in the position of writing about my own political career. I grew up in Applewood. I moved here with my parents in 1957 and lived at 2218 Rambo Road until my father passed away in 1974. I attended Applewood Public School and then later Gordon Graydon Secondary School. In 1966 I became employed as a newscaster for CHIC Radio in Brampton, and later in Toronto at CHIN Radio. In 1974 I joined the Mississauga News as a reporter and for many years covered local politics. I married in 1974 and moved to Toronto. In 1978 my wife Sophie and I purchased a house at 860 Hedge Drive. It didn't take long for me to become involved in the North Applewood Homeowners' Association as its secretary and it wasn't long after that I was encouraged to seek office as Councillor. I was elected in 1980 and re-elected for two more terms, retiring at the end of 1988.

•**Carl Stewart** lived at 835 North Service Road and could be considered the first Applewood resident to hold public office. He was one of the Stewart clan, a cousin to the Stewart Family who farmed the land here. In the Foreword it was noted that the Stewarts purchased their lands from the Graham Family in 1909 and later, around 1928, William Henry Hedge purchased from the Stewarts.

Carl sat as a member of Toronto Township Council for two terms. He was elected in 1952 and again in 1953. He was one of the owners of the lands purchased by G.S. Shipp and Son that became Westacres in December of 1953. Carl lived in what was originally built as a 'cottage' to the west of the Stewart farmhouse at 871 North Service Road. After Carl's second term of office no one from Applewood sat on Council until Chic Murray won a landslide election in 1958.

Summary of terms of office to Township of Toronto, Town of Port Credit, Town of Mississauga and City of Mississauga Council by Applewood Acres residents.

Carl Stewart- one year terms
1952 and 1953, Councillor, Township of Toronto

Charles 'Chic' Murray-
1958, 1959, Councillor, Township of Toronto
1960-61, 1962-63, 1964-65, 1966-67, Deputy Reeve, Township of Toronto
1968-70 ,Reeve, Town of Mississauga
1971-73, Reeve, Town of Mississauga (April 10,1972 appointed Mayor)
1976 ,Ward 3 Councillor, City of Mississauga

Terry Butt
1971-73, Councillor, Town of Port Credit
1977-78, Councillor, City of Mississauga

Dave Cook
1980-88, (three terms) Councillor, City of Mississauga

•Schooling in this area has always been a major concern and, oddly, the voter turnouts for the election of trustees has never been what one would call brisk. However, one trustee captured the minds and hearts of his electorate and established the foundation of schooling in this area for the Catholic voters. **Ed LeMay** was instrumental in the development of what is now the Dufferin-Peel Catholic District School Board. When Ed and his wife, Val moved to Applewood Acres in 1953 and settled at 2140 (originally 1331) Primate Road, they found there were no Catholic schools for children to attend. Ed immediately started to encourage other parents to join him in the development of a Catholic school system in Toronto Township.

The group, under his leadership, raised enough money to establish a tiny school board known as the Dixie Catholic Board and a subsequent school, St. Patrick, on Dixie Road, near Dundas St.

Ed LeMay served as trustee from 1953 to 1959 and then as its chairman from 1960 to 1962. With the amalgamation of four small boards in South Peel, he became the first chairman of the combined Roman Catholic Separate School Board and held that position until 1967. When the Mississauga Board was established in 1968, he was its representative on the interim separate school organizational committee, and then became chairman one year later of the new Dufferin-Peel Roman Catholic Separate School Board. He held that position until 1972.

He was appointed the board's assistant business administrator and then its business superintendent until his retirement in 1988.

Ed LeMay was a former Royal Canadian Air Force Pilot, who served with 426 Squadron in World War II.

A long-time resident of Applewood Acres, Ed was 77 when he passed away on June 19, 2000 at the Trillium Hospital. He leaves his wife Valrea and four children, Judy, Terry, Sharon and Mary, and 10 grandchildren.

• The South Peel Board of Education became the Board of Education of The Township of Toronto in 1964. For a period Applewood Acres also boasted that another of its residents sat as a school board chairman. **A.E. Bradley,** who is profiled in Chapter Eight, sat first as education trustee for the South Peel Board of Education, then as its vice chairman and then chairman. He was elected in 1960 and subsequently each year until 1967.

John Archer, who lived at 1167 Russett Road, was the first trustee to be elected to the public board when he won the 1957 election. The following year **W.F. (Fraser) Hughes** of 2138 Russett Road was elected.

Al Warrick of 2136 Harvest Drive was elected to represent Ward Three in 1966 while Mr. Bradley was representing Ward Seven. Al Warrick was elected again in 1968 and then for a two-year term, 1969-70.

Councillor Dave Cook, left, celebrates on election night with education trustee John Walmark

John Walmark, the last area person to sit on the school board, was profiled in Chapter Three.

105

12 A Footbridge and the QEW

On October 16, 1956, The Globe and Mail newspaper reported that a bailey bridge, spanning the Queen Elizabeth Highway at Applewood Acres, would be sought from the highways department.

"Toronto Township Council decided today that the new Gordon Graydon Memorial High School on the south side of the four-lane highway has made the oft-proposed bridge a necessity.

Police Chief Garnet McGill told councillors he had talked last week with department officials and that they were "receptive" to the idea.

Students and other pedestrians, to cross the highway from Applewood Acres, must now walk either more than a mile to the Dixie Rd. lights or take their chances with four lanes of traffic."

It was the concern for a safe crossing of the Queen Elizabeth Highway that produced what may be described as Gordon Graydon Secondary School's first student involvement in political issues. Mary Jane Miller, the first President of the Student Council, contacted the area M.P.P., requesting that a bridge be built from Ogden Avenue over the highway. A number of accidents resulted in delegations from the school going to Queen's Park. Graydon's first political venture was a success. The students received more than they asked for. They petitioned for a bailey bridge; the government gave them a permanent one.

Mary Jane Miller only lived in Applewood Acres for five years but her contribution to the community has had a lasting affect. Mary Jane, who went on to become a Professor of Dramatic Literature at Brock University, now lives in St. Catharines with her husband, Jack. Mary Jane contributed the following story about the bridge over the highway.

By Mary Jane Miller (Miller who married a Miller)

It began with a high school made up of students drawn from two rival schools – Port Credit and Thomas L. Kennedy – as the war baby boom rolled through. It also began with a bad piece of suburban planning which put the newer part of Applewood Acres on one side of the Queen Elizabeth and Gordon Graydon Memorial Secondary School on the other.

Applewood Acres north had nowhere to expand in the 50s, surrounded as it was by industries and the railroad. It was not likely that a high school would ever be built on that side of the highway.

Students for GGMSS, therefore, had to be bussed up and over the highway. Although the high school actually included grades seven and eight when the junior high school was built next door, the number of students to be bussed would rise again and the new Cawthra overpass, when it was built to the East, would make no difference. But the real problem was that the QEW was inadequately fenced with ordinary farm fencing and wooden posts. Students quickly learned to cut holes in the wire then dash across the four lane highway – inconceivable now, of course, and dangerous even then since the highway had 33,000 cars a day passing that point (I can still remember the numbers). But what finally brought the issue to a head was the fact that a young child was killed wandering out on to the highway through a large hole in the fence. The phrase we used in our arguments was "legal murder" and it did not overstate the case.

Meanwhile, a few of the grade 11 students from the two schools had been interviewed and I was selected to be the president of the student council of the brand new school. Our cohort became the senior grade for three years as grades 12 and then 13 were added on. That continuity proved to be useful in our campaign. I had just turned 15. Teachers at Graydon and the student council were looking for a project to pull the school together more substantially than the football games we always lost (there were no grade 12 or 13 boys at first). I don't know who first suggested we look into trying to get a bridge over the highway – probably Walter Ward who was advisor to the school council. Ignorant of what such a project might entail, including the economics and politics, the council thought that a campaign to get a bridge would be great for "school spirit." The fact that it is the only pedestrian bridge across the QEW for its entire length suggests the odds against such an idea succeeding – but the bridge is there.

It took almost two years from the spring of 1957 through the winter of 1958. First it became a research project. How many cars per day? What would happen when the highway turned into a six-lane highway? How many accidents caused by pedestrians crossing the highway? The answer was ten with one fatality. What would be the cost of a chain link fence running from Cawthra to Dixie Road? $50,000 in 1950s dollars was the estimate. What about a "Bailey Bridge" such as the two over the

Lakeshore from the CNE to the waterfront which were used only two weeks in the year? One was said to be surplus. Would army engineers build it as an exercise? Buses cost $2,500 a month. To their great credit the various companies took us seriously and gave us answers, on the phone or by letter.

500 students (the whole school) had signed a petition requesting the bridge but to succeed we knew we had to build support in the community. I was spokesperson and made speeches to Toronto Township Council, the Board of Education, the Rotary, the IODE, the Kinsmen, Home and School groups and whomever else would listen. One by one the organizations swung behind us. In fact Toronto Township had already asked for either a bridge or an underpass with no success, but Reeve Mrs. Fix then realized, shrewdly, that a group of high school students might have more luck. We met with Colonel Thomas L Kennedy, a very kindly man as well as MPP for Peel and ex premier, who had a lot of influence with the Conservative government. He arranged for us to meet with Jim Allen, the transportation minister, who was the person who could make it happen. When, after many months of work we finally went to Queen's Park to see Mr. Allen, the rest of the delegation, which included adults from the South Peel Board of Education, and Mrs. Mary Fix, Reeve and Robert Speck, Deputy Reeve of the township, stood aside and insisted that the students make the case.

Since we had assumed that they would do the talking – it was the 50s after all - I, at least, had not been apprehensive beforehand. Suddenly it was too late to worry. The fact that the Minister knew my grandfather broke the ice and we made our now familiar case.

It was not all hard work, speeches and praise. The school petition notwithstanding, there were other obstacles, because both the local community and the students were not unanimously behind the idea. Many students preferred a warm school bus to a cold, half to three quarter mile walk to school and said so vocally to me one night on the school bus. Merchants in the north side shopping centre feared that easier access to the larger shopping plaza on the south side would draw away their business. People still walked to the stores in the 50s. Families had only one car but the bridge would mean that mothers with toddlers in strollers and kids on bicycles could now reach the other side. Their fears, which were inevitably conveyed to their children, created an ugly scene or two at school. Although we had done some research on what would now be

108

called demographics, as students we didn't think about changing shopping habits or anticipate box stores. Yet the fact that the bridge was designed with ramps has meant foot traffic of all kinds can flow north as well as south. It is good to see that the north side shopping centre still flourishes.

One of the most decisive factors in our success was the long since defunct Toronto Telegram. In an era when few people thought of radio or newspapers or television as "the media," sophisticated media manipulation was in its infancy. Nevertheless, looking back as a scholar who does research on and writes about television, I can see that what happened was a media dream, captured in the scrapbook my mother made at the time. As teenaged students on the warpath we made good copy. I learned in those months that what is reported is not necessarily what was said – as in, the student council did not really threaten to go on strike- but it made a good headline.

They took pictures of students climbing the fence so that they could stay longer for after school activities. Barbara King, Barbara Rice, the "secretary" and "comptroller" of the student council and I had our pictures in the paper in June. The next November the deputation of Bob Norcross, the next school president, Linda Simpkins, Freda Roberts and I (otherwise known as "the Bridge committee") were photographed on our way to the Toronto Township council, clutching our binders and looking very young. The paper interviewed me several times because The Telegram, which had a regional insert, loved the idea that a 15-16 year old " young miss could speak out for such a project, presumably because young women who did such things were anomalies in those days. Yet I do not remember thinking about the experience in terms of gender at the time. Certainly the message from the teachers and, particularly from my parents, was "of course, you can do this." Nowadays, their faith would be seen as 'empowering,' which it was. Also, at the time, quite scary.

In the end it took the efforts of many people to make it happen. The papers said that Bob and I would open the bridge formally and published artist's sketches of it. However, construction was inevitably delayed. We were in university and the bridge simply opened without us. But it would not be there if the little high school that could, the community leaders who were persuaded to help, and the politicians, had not made it happen. Long before my 30 plus years as a university professor of Canadian television and dramatic literature (the struggle for the bridge certainly was 'drama' at times) who helped shape Brock University over the years, I learned that *if you really work at something, stick your neck out and put pressure on the people in power, sometimes you can make a difference. Every time my husband and I drive into Toronto from St. Catharines on the QE there is the bridge, still standing after more than 40 years, to remind me that you can win a few.*

Many years later, H.J.A. Brown, Business Administrator and Secretary-Treasurer of The South Peel Board of Education, wrote a newsletter which was circulated at the 35[th]Anniversary of the Westacres Public School and, in it, made reference to Mary Jane Miller and her campaign to have the footbridge established.

A pupil, Mary Jane Miller, began a campaign to get a footbridge across the QEW. She was very effective and finally convinced councillors and trustees of the necessity. A Township of Toronto Engineer, Ernie Bodner, designed the pedestrian over-pass and we proceeded to build it. However, no one would come forward with the money to pay for it. I had an idea. I'd get the Board of Education to pay for it and charge it to the bus transportation budget. I received a nasty slap on my wrist from the Ontario Department of Municipal Affairs for charging it to transportation. But, by then the bridge was in use (and has been used since then! Thanks Mary Jane).

Late in 1958, members of council were considering a report on the costs, being estimated at $57,728. Reeve Mary Fix had asked the township engineer, W.J. Anderson, if putting in traffic lights might be a better idea. Chief McGill's horrified expression puzzled the Reeve and she asked what the problem was, veteran councillor Roy McMillan, quipped "it is easy to see why the Reeve doesn't drive".

The Queen Elizabeth Highway (QEW) forms the southern boundary of Applewood and is the reason we are here today. The highway made it possible for development to move west out of Toronto. Imagine what structure our city might have taken had it not been for the development of the Queen Elizabeth Highway. The city might well have developed like ripples when a pebble is dropped into a pool of water, from the center outward. Would it have been Cooksville as the financial district or 'hub'? Or possibly Port Credit as a natural trade and commerce center due to it being a port on the Great Lakes? Whatever shape or form our city might have taken, it is doubtful in my mind that it would have blossomed into Canada's sixth largest city with the so called downtown core still in its

110

planning stages some 30 years after being formally declared a full-fledged city.

And for trivia buffs, the highway is the only Ontario Provincial highway that is not assigned a route number and was not named after England's Queen Elizabeth 1, who reigned in the 16th century, but rather the highway was named for Queen Elizabeth, wife of King George V1.

The highway's namesake, known in modern times as 'The Queen Mother', was born August 4, 1900 and became the longest-living British Royal in memory. She passed away on March 30, 2002.

Barely three years after King George V1 and Queen Elizabeth became King and Queen, and three months before the outbreak of the Second World War, the months of May and June 1939 were electrifying for Canadians from coast to coast. Newspapers across the nation carried story after story. The Royal visit to Canada was the first ever by a reigning monarch to North America. Then, on June 7, 1939, the Royal couple opened what became one of the longest multi-lane divided highways in the British Empire. In fact it was North America's first "Super Highway."

Construction on the QEW started in 1931 and by the time it was completed and opened in 1939, the seeds for the creation of Applewood Acres were just a decade away from becoming a reality. It was the existence of this highway that made it possible for G.S. Shipp and Son to build Applewood Acres. I think many people might even say that was it not for the highway opening and the Shipps' foresight, Mississauga, as we know it today, may not have developed as quickly as it has. As a sideline to the story, every house in Applewood was built with an attached garage, simply because of the necessity of vehicular access to the area and its proximity to Toronto. When Gordon and Harold Shipp began negotiating the funding to build Applewood Acres, a very wise banker insisted that garages be included in the design.

According to the Ministry of Transportation Ontario, the need for the QEW arose after the Toronto-Hamilton Highway (built in November 1917), and later known as Highway 2, became overloaded and a new route had to be considered. The Dundas (Hwy.5) was also at its capacity. As a result, planning began for the Middle Road, which became the Queen Elizabeth Highway.

At this point it should be noted that the Queen Elizabeth Highway did not follow along the original alignment of the Middle Road. The best example of the Middle Road can be seen at the eastern limit of Sherway Drive. The bridge that spans the Etobicoke Creek is in fact the historic Middle Road Bridge. It was also nicknamed 'White Bridge'. This particular bridge stands out above all others as it was the first of its kind ever built in Canada, and only the second of its kind ever built in North America. The bridge was designed in 1909 by Frank Barber and C.W. Young. It's a concrete truss or tied arch bridge and was celebrated for its light weight and strength. The bridge was tested on opening day when 40 cattle were herded across its span. On October 14, 1986, I had the pleasure of co-officiating the ceremony with Etobicoke Mayor, Dennis Flynn, that designated this bridge as a heritage structure. This bridge became the only structure in Ontario to be designated and renovated jointly by two municipalities. Applewood Acres resident and artist, Leonard Crump, who lives on Courtland Crescent, presented me with one of his outstanding drawings of this bridge that he did in 1978, prior to the restoration.

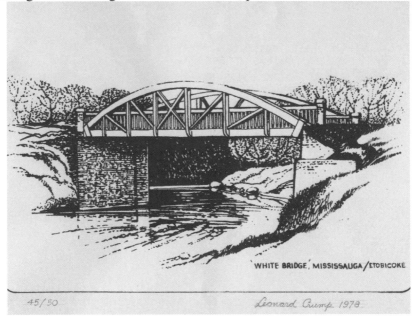

WHITE BRIDGE, MISSISSAUGA/ETOBICOKE

45/50   Leonard Crump 1978

The QEW was designed as a four-lane divided highway having a median strip which would vary from three feet to 10 feet in width with the remaining less traveled sections as undivided roadway. It wasn't until 1940 that a 4-mile (6.4 km) section from the Humber River to then Highway 27 (now the 427 Highway) was opened.

Originally Dixie Road, like many other roads, crossed the QEW as a level crossing. There was a need to eliminate these level crossings as it had been reported, in 1952, that almost a half-million motorists crossing the highway in Oakville ignored the traffic light during the study period. Traffic lights were installed at Dixie Road at the QEW on August 1, 1951 and operated until the bridge opened in October 1953.

Canada's first-ever cloverleaf interchange, at Highway 10 (Hurontario Street), however, was constructed much earlier having been completed in 1937. Obviously the 1952 study showed the need to eliminate at-grade crossings and develop more overpasses such as the one at Hurontario Street.

Construction drawings for the Dixie Road bridge over the QEW were completed in April of 1952 and the bridge was about to become a reality. At this section the QEW was a four-lane, undivided highway. According to Bob Watson, who lived not far from the crossing, this general area of the QEW was responsible for numerous deaths before the Department of Highways constructed the Dixie Road overpass.

In fact, according to reports in the Toronto media, there were 128 accidents at this crossing between 1948 and 1951. Seven people lost their lives in auto accidents there. It wasn't until October 1955 that the Department of Highways obtained approvals to close 13 level crossings which intersected the QEW between Highways 10 and 27 and build the north and south service roads. In 1948 there were no deaths but 24 accidents. In 1949, four people were killed and 25 accidents happened. In 1950, two people were killed and the accident rate rose to 42, while in 1951, three people were killed in one of the 37 accidents that took place that year.

The QEW became a divided highway a little further west, about where the footbridge is now located. The North Service Road re-entered the QEW at about the mid-point of where the Applewood Shopping Centre now stands. With the building of the western parcels of land creating what is now known as Westacres, the service road entrance to the QEW was incorporated into the Cawthra overpass. The overpass was built in the summer of 1957 and re-constructed to its present configuration in 1977.

In December, 1976, plans for the proposed Cawthra Road overpass show a pedestrian underpass further east at Ogden Avenue. This was partially in response to the concerns raised by the students lobbying for the footbridge and also because the Hurontario-Q.E.W overpass had a pedestrian underpass. The Ministry later decided not to built the Ogden Avenue pedestrian underpass. In fact, 26 years after the Cawthra Road overpass was completed, the Ministry announced they were taking a second look at the Hurontario Street pedestrian underpass and might be closing it completely and re-designing the entire overpass at Hurontario. The QEW highway would continue to develop and, in 1971, it was widened to six lanes along the Applewood frontage. In 1983 the sound wall was erected and, just as Applewood Acres approached its Jubilee, the Department of Transportation refurbished the footbridge.

Standing at the foot of Annapolis Road looking west, one might wonder why a fire hydrant would be stuck in the middle of the cluster of rather mature trees on the north side of the service road. It all has to do with the original road alignment. If you stand at the fire hydrant and turn back looking to the east, you can almost see where the original frontages of the homes ended and where the municipal road allowance started. The triangular section of green lawns seems to make it all fit. Later, when the service road was continued west, there was a traffic island and flashing light just past Annapolis Road to caution drivers that the road took a very sharp turn. All that was done away with when the road was changed to make the curve what it is today.

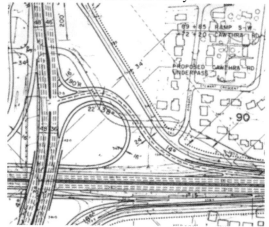

Later, in the 1980's, as Councillor, I negotiated the transfer of surplus lands, created with the re-alignment of the road, to the owners of the homes there. In fact, parts of the actual asphalt road surface are still there covered by top soil.

Cawthra Overpass drawings showing the new service road alignment. Notice the original service road alignment at the foot of Annapolis Road.

114

In 1954 the homes on Melton Drive in Westacres were still being landscaped The QEW is at the right side of this photo and the Dixie Road overpass, top of photo,is clearly shown.This photo shows the exact location on the North Service Road where it re-entered the QEW, about the mid point of where the shopping center (not yet built) now stands. You can see Charles Watson's home at the foot of Second Line East (aka Bloomfield Road for a short while before being named Stanfield Road by T.L. Kennedy, MPP). Leaver Mushroom operations on both sides of Second Line and the little park between Stanfield and MacIntosh is clearly shown with a barn .The off-set of Dixie Road north of QEW to Dixie Road south of QEW is clearly illustrated by the alignment of the Dixie overpass and you can see where the North Service Road ends just west of Annapolis. Photo from the personal collection of friend Elmer Gittings. Below, the North Service Road is being built. Notice the QEW in the upper right. Photo courtesy of Shipp Corporation

13 Notable People

Over the years, Applewood Acres certainly has not been at a loss having some very interesting and notable people in our midst. Such was **Colonel Harland Sanders**, who was one of the world's most recognizable people.

Col. Harland Sanders owned a home at 1337 Melton Drive and would occupy it for about four months of every year from the mid 1960's until his death in 1980.

In the early 1960's the Colonel would often visit the Applewood home of Edward Gogoff, President of Kentucky Fried Chicken of Canada.

One day in 1964 while walking through Applewood, the Colonel made up his mind to move into the area. Coincidentally, there was a home for sale immediately beside the Gogoff's. Since he was the roving ambassador for KFC and literally hated staying in hotels, this presented Col. Sanders with an opportunity to have a home he could enjoy while in Canada. He decided to purchase the home and retained Toronto lawyer Terry Donnelly to handle the transaction.

In an interview years later, the Colonel quipped that he loved the area and the home he had here was like a 'doll house' compared to the one he and his wife Claudia shared back in the United States.

In 1998, Edward Gogoff, who acted as the Colonel's 'right hand man', carried out one of the final wishes of the late Col. and presented the Mississauga-Queensway Hospital with a cheque for one million dollars for its Family Care Centre. The donation was the largest single donation in the hospital's history. According to Mr. Gogoff, the Colonel considered Mississauga his adopted Canadian hometown and he wanted to do something significant for the community.

The Family Care Centre brings together a wide range of services including mammography, an unscheduled primary care service and specialized children's programs including pediatrics, diabetes and asthma education. The centre has a special focus on education, promotion of personal and family health, wellness and prevention of illness. This concept met with the Colonel's wishes to support families and children.

Harland Sanders was born in Kentucky on September 9, 1890. He actively began franchising his chicken business at the age of 65 and today, even long after his death, the quick-service restaurant pioneer is recognized as a symbol of entrepreneurial spirit.

When the Colonel was six, his father died, his mother was forced to go to work, and young Harland had to take care of his three-year old brother and baby sister. This meant doing much of the cooking. By age seven, he was a master of a score of regional dishes.

At age 10, he got his first job working on a nearby farm for $2 a month. When he was 12, his mother remarried and he left his home near Henryville, Indiana, for a job on a farm in Greenwood, Indiana. He held a series of jobs over the next few years, first as a 15 year-old streetcar conductor in New Alban, Ind., and then as a 16 year-old private, soldiering for six months in Cuba.

After that he was a railroad fireman, studied law by correspondence, practiced in justice of the peace courts, sold insurance, operated an Ohio River steamboat ferry, sold tires and operated service stations. When he was 40, the Colonel began cooking for hungry travelers who stopped at his service station in Corbin, KY. He didn't have a restaurant then, but served his customers on his own dining table in the living quarters of his service station.

Eventually he expanded, moving across the street to a motel and a restaurant that seated 142 people. Over the next nine years, he perfected his secret blend of 11 herbs and spices.

His fame grew: Kentucky Governor Ruby Laffoon made him a Kentucky Colonel in 1935 in recognition of his contributions to the State's cuisine. In 1939, his establishment was listed in Duncan Hines "Adventures of Good Eating."

Disaster struck in the early 1950s when a new interstate highway by-passed Corbin, Ky., and seeing an end to his business he auctioned off his entire operation. After paying bills, he was reduced to living on his $105 Social Security.

In 1952 the Colonel started a chicken franchising business. He traveled across the country by car from restaurant to restaurant, cooking batches of chicken for restaurant owners and their employees. If the reaction was favourable, he entered into a handshake agreement that stipulated a payment to him of five cents for each chicken sold. In 1964 the Colonel sold his operation, which had grown to more than 600 franchised outlets in the U.S. and Canada. He did, however, remain as the firm's public spokesman.

Until he was fatally stricken with leukemia in 1980 at age 90, the Colonel traveled 250,000 miles a year visiting the KFC empire he founded. It all began with a 65-year old gentleman who used his Social Insurance to start a business.

"Good afternoon, I have come 'a-callin' on Miss Colleen." Words that Colleen Ryan, a child who lived next door to Colonel Sanders, will never forget for the rest of her life. The world-famous Colonel Sanders coming to her door asking her to come out to play.

The Colonel just loved to throw snowballs and with regularity would call upon young Colleen to be his snowball packer. Colleen's mother Connie, tells the story of what it was like to be living next door to one of the world's most recognizable people.

"Our Ryan family, Ken, my husband, myself and our three children, Kevin, Colleen and Tricia, lived on Melton Drive. One cold Saturday in late November of 1966, it had snowed overnight. Ken and I decided to go out to the front of the house and plan on where to put out our Christmas lights.

While Ken had gone back into the house to get his gloves, I stood on the driveway facing the house. I didn't hear anyone walk up the drive behind me. Suddenly I heard a man's voice say "Hello ma'm." Turning, I was so very surprised to see Colonel Harland Sanders. He smiled and said "I come 'a-callin' on Miss Colleen to come walking with me."

The Colonel enjoyed the snow and, while they were "a-walkin," Colleen would make snowballs for him and he loved to throw them. They had fun.

Ken and I had not been aware that Harland was our neighbour. There was an elderly gentleman we knew who also lived in our immediate area. He had white hair, moustache and a grey beard. Our son Kevin and the other children called this man 'Mississauga Fats'.

We assumed Colleen, age six at the time, thought of him as Col. Sanders. Miss Colleen became very well acquainted with Col. Harland and his wife Claudia. She was invited to their home frequently and enjoyed lunch with them often at their house.

On another visit to our home, Harland asked Miss Tricia, age two and a half, to go a-walkin with him and Miss Colleen. She was delighted. When the threesome were approximately five houses away, Tricia rushed back home. She had a confused expression on her little face. Ken asked her why she didn't go for the walk. Her reply was, " I don't really know if I like that Santa Claus. "

In the summer of 1969, I responded to a knock on the front door. To my surprise there stood a man with white hair, moustache, goatee and wearing glasses. His facial and head features were identical to Col. Harland, but he was taller and had a different voice.

He spoke and said, "Hello ma'm, I am Colonel Jim. Uncle Harland suggested I ask Miss Colleen if she would walk with me and show me the way to the local grocery store at the nearby plaza." Colleen had just returned home from Brownies, and still in her uniform, they walked to the Applewood Village Shopping Centre. No doubt shoppers imagined they were seeing things. While there shopping Colonel Jim told Miss Colleen she could choose anything in the store she would like for herself. She chose a Fudgecicle.

Colleen and other neighbourhood children loved to call at the Sanders' home at Hallowe'en as Harland gave each child a quarter (a fortune to the children). Colonel Harland Sanders was a very caring and loving man. In my opinion, despite his fame and fortune, he was a very humble and considerate man."

Connie Ryan

Colonel Harland Sanders and Colleen Ryan. Photo courtesy of the Ryan family

Photo above right is Colonel Sanders with his wife Claudia. (at left) Colonel Sanders with Tricia Ryan. *Note the rare photos without his trademark white plantation-style suite. Photos courtesy of the Ryan Family

120

•Persistence pays off and a glowing testimony to that old adage can be seen in the story of **Dr. H. David Archibald**, who, on November 17, 1988 was appointed a Member of the Order of Canada and his investiture was held on April 12, 1989. This is Canada's highest honour for lifetime achievement.

One of the original residents of Applewood Acres, David and his wife Ruth moved into Applewood in 1954 settling at 867 Johnathan Drive. During the next 29 years the family would grow with the addition of their children, Lynda, Janet, Gordon and Susan. Eventually they would move to 868 Melton Drive, and then, when David retired, to a condominium not far from Applewood Acres.

David was born on a farm on July 22, 1919, two miles from Truro, Nova Scotia, and he can count among his early ancestors, Sir Adams G. Archibald, a Father of Confederation, Sir Edward Mortimer Archibald, British Consul in New York and Thomas Dickson Archibald, member of the Dominion of Canada Senate. Certainly an impressive lineage and no doubt they would be proud of the accomplishments of their descendant, who is a recipient of so many lifetime awards. David received his Order of Canada in 1985, two years before his brother Gordon, who was also recognized by the same Governor General, Madame Sauve. Gordon was appointed June 29, 1987 and his investiture was October 28, 1987 as an Officer and Companion.

David had three sisters, Florence, Edith and Helen, who all became school teachers, and three brothers, Frank, Gordon and George. Frank became a United Church Minister, George went into the grocery store business and Gordon became President and Chairman of the Board of Maritime Telephone and Telegraph.

Among his educational accomplishments, David received a Bachelor degree in Social Science in 1946 from the University of Western Ontario, a M.S.W. in 1948 from the University of Toronto and an Honorary Doctorate of Science in 1971 from Acadia University.

While serving in the Air Force during WW2, David became interested in the study of alcoholism after having observed some men who were drinking in a way that was very different from the average person. His interest became more focused as he researched Alcoholics Anonymous (AA) and later studied under a scholarship at the School for Alcohol

121

Studies at Yale University. As a social work lecturer at the University of Toronto he often spoke about the need for research into the use of alcohol. He became known for his outspokenness concerning the subject and that led to his being hired in 1949 as the Director of Research for the Liquor Control Board of Ontario.

That same year he was commissioned by Ontario's Premier Leslie Frost to study the problem of alcoholism in Ontario. His conclusions were that an organization independent of liquor interests should be established. That same year the Ontario Government passed legislation establishing the Alcohol Research Foundation (ARF) and he was appointed as the founding Executive Director and first CEO, a position he held until 1976 when he became Executive Vice-Chairman. He retired in 1981, but would continue to work as a consultant until 1983.

Premier Frost met with David to discuss the establishment of the ARF and also just how the organization would be operated. It was to be at arms-length from the political world but founding legislation would require the ARF to report to the Provincial Cabinet. During his more than two and a half decades as CEO of the ARF, David has been credited with operating the organization as it was originally intended.

Having also been involved with the World Health Organization (WHO) as a consultant, he would travel extensively and participate with many other national and international organizations in Canada, United States, Europe, South East Asia and Latin America. In 1976 he was sent by the WHO to Thailand to advise on development programs providing basic health care for the "Hill Tribe Villages" found in the north jungle region. From 1981 to 1989 he served as President of the International Council on Alcoholism and Addictions. In 1983 he was appointed as a one-person Royal Commission on the Use and Misuse of Illicit Drugs and Alcohol in Bermuda. In 1988 he became the Chairman of the Canadian Centre on Substance Abuse and, in 1991, he drafted the National Drugs Strategy, the forerunner of the National Drugs Commission.

•**Mildred (Belford) Belleghem** was raised on a farm, located on Cawthra Road just north of The Queensway. She became a resident of Westacres in her later years when she moved into the Melton Court home of son-in-law and daughter Fred and Janet Dixon at 2292 Melton Court.

Mildred was a schoolteacher in South Peel for 42 years. She married Jack Belleghem in 1931.

As a child Mildred attended the two-room Cooksville Public School, the same school that Mildred's parents attended when they grew up in the area. Mildred went on to attend high school in Streetsville and then Etobicoke Collegiate. She became a teacher in the 1940s.

Mildred had what might well have been one of the keenest interests in local history for her time. She devoted endless hours writing and her efforts produced two paperback books. She wrote "And The Mill Stone Still Turns" and "From Creag Kenagh to Port Credit-A Belford Story."

In 1969 she was asked to write for the Streetsville Review Newspaper. While she didn't feel comfortable writing a column, she agreed to write in the form of a letter to her daughter Ruth, who with her son-in-law had just transferred to Vancouver. She would write her a letter each week, which was published in a column titled 'A Letter From Home'.

Both Mildred and her husband Jack were involved in community activities. Jack was one of the founders of the Toronto Township Hockey League (TTHL) and served as its President in 1949 and 1950.

He also was a member of the Recreation Committee for the municipality, he coached softball and was on the Township of Toronto's Centennial Committee in 1950. Jack passed away at age 53 in 1984.

Mildred was a volunteer at the Mississauga Hospital where she organized many events including Daffodil Teas in Westacres. She was also involved in the Cooksville School's 100th Anniversary. She was a member of the United Empire Loyalists-Lord Simcoe Branch, Halton and Hamilton Genealogy Societies, the Mississauga Historical Society and she was a lifetime member of St. John's The Baptist Anglican Church.

When the Cawthra Arena expansion was underway, the community advisory committee, which was established to consult with the City and architects of the project and which included the Applewood Acres Homeowners' Association, reviewed and selected names for rooms to honour Mississauga's deserving citizens. Mildred Belleghem's name was unanimously supported and the facility's Community Office was named in her honour when the building officially opened January 23, 2000.

A plaque outside the office door reads:

MILDRED (BELFORD) BELLEGHEM,
1908-1997- A devoted historian, dedicated teacher and lifelong resident of the Ward 1 community, Mildred's passion for teaching and the love of history has touched the lives of so many residents. The memory of her outstanding achievements and commitment to recording Mississauga's history will always be remembered.

Mildred's entire collection of newspaper articles, scrapbook and paperback books are in the Mississauga Library System and can be read in the Canadiana Reading Room.

●An Old Fashioned English Gentleman, always impeccably dressed, was **Bill Pattison**, who purchased his Westfield Drive house in 1954.

Bill moved to Canada and immediately found a job with Simpson Stores in Toronto and at the same time sent for his future wife Jeannie to join him in his new adopted land. They married at the historic Trinity Church in Toronto.

He would rise through the ranks to management at Simpson's but as he said, he first had to spend almost 10 years in the Customer Service Department listening to people's complaints. His career at Simpson's lasted 29 years.

The Pattison's purchased a home at 2041 Westfield Drive after having visited a Shipp display at the Canadian National Exhibition.

While Bill never boasted about his past, his friends soon discovered Bill was at one time Valet and Secretary to Lord Beaverbrook (William Maxwell Aitken). Bill's stay with Lord Beaverbrook lasted from 1936 until he joined the RAF in 1940. He would write many years later in an unpublished personal memoir, "Of Lords And Ladies", that in all the years of service to England's aristocracy, his years with Lord Beaverbrook were the highlight of his life.

Lord Beaverbrook, the son of a Presbyterian minister, was born in Maple, Ontario, in 1879. He became a stockbroker and by 1910 had made a fortune from Canadian cement mills.

He moved to Britain and eventually became the Conservative member for Ashton-under-Lyne. In the House of Commons Mr. Aitken became private secretary to the Colonial Secretary, Andrew Bonar Law.

Mr. Aitken authored several books including "Canada at Flanders" (1917). In 1918 David Lloyd George granted Mr. Aitken the title Lord Beaverbrook and appointed him as Minister of Information in the wartime coalition government.

During the war Lord Beaverbrook acquired a controlling interest in the Daily Express and turned it into the most widely read newspapers in the world.

He founded the Sunday Express (1921) and in 1929 purchased the Evening Standard. In the Second World War, Winston Churchill recruited Lord Beaverbrook into his Cabinet where he served as Minister for Aircraft Production (1940-41), Minister of Supply (1941-42), Minister of War Production (1942) and Lord Privy Seal (1943-45). Lord Beaverbrook died in 1964.

A little known fact about Bill Pattison was that while he served as valet and secretary, he would pen Lord Beaverbrook's letters and they would be written without ever being changed.

Page after page of Bill's personal memoirs provide a fascinating first hand look at his time in service of Lords, Countesses and Earls. His meetings with Lawrence of Arabia and with King George V and Queen Mary, are described with great respect and a kind touch of humour.

Bill's career started on the heels of the great depression. His first job was actually as a paper boy, but the economies of the time forced him into full time employment. As a youth as he worked as a "Marker Boy", marking rivet holes for the Blyth Shipbuilding and The Docks Company. However, Bill was out of work when the depression arrived.

A friend, who had earlier become employed in the household of a wealthy family, urged him to follow his example.

Bill contacted an agency in Newcastle and was hired by Major and Lady Clementine Waring. His job was to serve their food on trays when called for. One of the highlights of time with the Warings was when Lawrence of Arabia visited for a weekend. "I was surprised to find him a very small and unimpressive person, despite all that was known about him," he would write in his memoirs.

Later Bill would succumb to the harsh treatment of the housekeeper and decided to leave his employment with the Warings. He quickly became employed as Third Footman for the Earl and Countess of Shaftesbury. The Shaftesburys were close friends of King George V and Queen Mary and had actually rented a house in Windsor to be close to the King and Queen.

One day King George V and Queen Mary arrived for tea and Bill was to greet them at the door. "They both looked shorter than I had expected, however, they both, without a doubt, were very important and distinguished personages. Indeed Regal must be the word," said Bill.

Later Bill would be employed by Lord Monsell but hard times forced a lay-off. He then became employed for a short time with Brigadier Richard Howard-Vyse. However, this position would also not last long and Bill decided to enter the private sector.

"I saw an ad for a company named Airways. I learned very soon it was an American firm recruiting vacuum cleaner door-to-door sales people. I decided to stay on and give it a try," said Bill. However, after one month and one sale, he again was seeking other employment.

It didn't take him long to be hired as Second Footman to Sir Bolton and Lady Eyres Monsell. Sir Bolton was a Member of Parliament representing Evesham. He stayed with Sir Bolton and Lady Eyres for five years.

It was in the summer of 1936 he had applied for the position with Lord Beaverbrook. He wrote that Lady Eyres was very gracious about his resignation and wished him well.

Bill would leave Lord Beaverbrook to join the RAF where he found himself at Middle Wallop in Hampshire where he was in Signals in the Operation Room. He was posted to the Gambia in British West Africa where he stayed 18 months.

Back in civilian life, Lord Beaverbrook had promised Bill a position at the Daily Express but a union closed-shop prevented that. He remained in the private sector and eventually obtained a position with Marquis of Linithgow, who was Chairman of the Midland Bank. It was the Marquis who had been the Viceroy of India and the man who kept putting Ghandi in jail.

It was during this time that Bill met his future wife Jeannie. She was an expert needlewoman and looked after the Marchioneses' clothes.

Following the death of his wife Bill established a memorial at Applewood United Church in his wife's name. The memorial fund is for future candidates for the Ministry. Bill died December 6th ,1989, at the age 77.

•**Peter and Lillian Langer** purchased their house at 2193 Rambo Road in 1953 and, for the next five years, Peter would not only be kept busy with a young family and a new home, but with the fast growing suburbs of Toronto as a salesman with Farlinger Real Estate.

Born in Vienna, Austria in 1916, Peter went to England for his university education and then immediately into the War with the British Army. Normally university-educated recruits would immediately be placed into officer training, However, Peter was not born in England and therefore was only permitted to enter the service as a private.

But Peter would rise through the ranks and before the war ended he became a Field Major assigned to co-ordinate the local industry. It was during this time that he met Lillian, who was a dancer with one of the groups which provided entertainment for the troops through the Entertainments National Service Association (ENSA), set up during the war to provide entertainment for the troops at the front. Many legends built their careers in mess halls, barracks and off the back of military vehicles.

Lillian, who was born in England, trained as a dancer and eventually she joined the Blue Bell Girls in Paris, a highly successful and world renowned dance group. When the Germans invaded Paris, Lillian quickly returned to England and then went into service.

In 1946 the Langer's arrived in Canada and within seven years found themselves in Applewood Acres raising a son Peter and a daughter Ann. Soon Peter Senior became a partner in the real estate firm and very quickly Farlinger and Langer Real Estate began developing housing. They

127

started and developed Bayview Village and in 1958 the family moved from Applewood Acres into a home in the Village.

Peter, however, was sought after by A.E. LePage Real Estate owner Brian McGee and eventually became Vice President of the firm. Soon the firm was involved in the original land assembly for the Erin Mills community. At the same time, both were also assembling lands for the Meadowvale community. They formed Markborough Properties primarily to develop the lands for Meadowvale. Peter became the Executive Vice President, then President and then Chairman of the Board. He retired in 1985.

Soon after his retirement he began doing some independent consulting and actually ended up going back to Markborough for a brief period. He finally retired in 1995 at age 80.

During his business career Peter would serve as President of the Toronto Real Estate Board (1962), Director of the Canadian Real Estate Board and President of the Urban Development Institute. He also served as a Director and Special Advisor to the Metro Toronto Housing Authority and was also the founding Director of the Ontario Housing Corporation.

•A colour photograph of a smiling 18 year-old **Karyn Walmark**, accompanied by a story about the young Applewood Acres student's amazing academic achievement, graced the front page of the August 17, 1996 edition of The Toronto Star. The story was carried nationally, from coast-to-coast. Karyn Walmark is probably the only Ontario student ever who can claim scoring 100 percent in her six top Ontario Academic Credits (OAC). The Ministry of Education of Ontario spokesman did say it really is a remarkable achievement. Based on existing data, annually less than one percent of students who took OAC courses obtained 100 percent in at least one OAC. Her top marks determined her final graduating average from Cawthra Park Secondary School. She achieved perfect marks in Calculus, Algebra and Geometry, English, Finite (which is a form of math), Chemistry and Biology.

John Walmark, who contributed the article in Chapter Three on the battle to keep the schools open, and also once served as the elected Education Trustee for Ward 7, moved to Applewood in 1976. John and Pam Walmark's older daughter, Jennifer, was just one year of age at the time. Karyn was born January 2, 1978, just missing being a New Year's baby.

128

During her formative years Karyn attended Westacres and Kenollie Public Schools in the "Mode 3" program, which was established for bright children. In 1991 Karyn showed great promise in creative writing by entering and winning the Mississauga Library Writing Contest. She wrote a short story called Mississauga Murder Mayhem and Macabre Meet. Five years later she was awarded the John Fraser Scholarship for creative writing.

All during her youth Karyn was also an accomplished dancer having studied ballet, tap, jazz and ballroom dancing at the Van Buskirk Studios of Dance, located on Dixie Road at The Queensway. She started dancing when she was three and by the time she was in her teens she had competed in more than 40 competitions, averaging a top three finish each year.

Now, at age 26, Karyn teaches English and Guidance at Mentor College in Mississauga and continues her involvement in dance. She also teaches ballroom, tap and jazz at Van Buskirk as well as ballroom dancing at C.K. Dance Studio, also located in Mississauga.

Name a sport and you most certainly will find someone in Applewood who participates. And a number reached national or international levels. From figure skating, hockey, football, tennis, track and field, auto racing, watersports, equestrian, lacrosse, field hockey, badminton, baseball, rifle shooting and golf to the Ironman Triathlon, Applewood residents have made their mark.

•Courtland Crescent residents **Louise Brown** and her son **David**, are two excellent examples of people who rose to excellence in the sport of tennis. Both hold the honour of being inducted into the Mississauga Sports Hall of Fame. Louise was inducted in its very first year in 1974 while David was inducted in 1993. They hold the distinction of being the first mother/son combination inducted into the Hall of Fame.

The Mississauga Sports Hall of Fame has a permanent display at City Hall. Excerpts of the storyboards on display are reprinted here and certainly tell the story of Applewood Acres' First Family of Tennis.

For a long time Applewood's Louise Brown stood tall as one of the best and most competitive female tennis players in Canada, ranked among the nation's top 10 players in four decades for a total of 26 consecutive years (she was 15 times ranked in the top three) from 1946 to 1971, a feat that has yet to be matched. This fact was recognized on September 28, 1991 when Louise Brown was one of six inaugural inductees into the Hall of Fame of Canadian Tennis.

A self-taught and self-coached player throughout her career, Louise Brown first burst onto the competitive tennis scene in 1946, making her debut at the Toronto Lawn Tennis Club and showing enough promise to earn a place among the top 10 in national rankings. Her first real taste of success came at age 35, when, in 1957, she won the Canadian National Singles title. Then, teaming with Hilda Doleschell, she added the Doubles crown as well.

She won her second Canadian Open National Doubles title at age 40 when she teamed with Ann Barclay and in 1969 she won a gold medal at the first Canada Games. Years later, in 1990, she added a pair of National Senior Women's Singles and Doubles championship trophies.

A member of the original Canadian Federation Cup Women's Team in 1963, Louise was chosen playing captain two consecutive years, and then she was selected non-playing captain for three more years in 1966, 1967 and 1969. Her achievements and successes earned her an invitation three times to the All-England Championship at Wimbledon, one of the glamour stops on the grand-slam tournament circuit.

For many years Louise was women's representative to the Player's Association while her husband Ross was at one time the President of the Ontario Tennis Federation. Louise Brown passed away at age 81 in November 2003.

David Brown, left, with mother Louise and Canadian golfing great Al Balding, share a special moment. Photo courtesy of David Brown

David Brown was around five years of age when the family purchased their Courtland Crescent home in 1952. He grew up in a tennis atmosphere and it was only natural that he would have more than a passing interest in the sport.

David showed promise as a tennis player when he won his first tournament playing at Westacres. Six years later, he won the first of his Canadian Junior Championship titles in Doubles.

Where David really got hooked on competitive tennis was earlier at the Toronto Telegram Tournament, a popular event in the 1950's. He won the Regional Finals at Kew Gardens in Toronto and the seed was planted.

From Kew Gardens, David went on to loftier heights and to the University of Indiana where, exposed to top-notch coaching, his talents really started to blossom. It was at university that David met his future wife, Jody, also a tennis player.

In four years at the University of Indiana, David rose to become captain of the tennis team and earned the coveted "I" letter, the only Canadian ever to do so. He also reached the finals of the NCAA Men's Singles in Minnesota in 1969, once again, the only Canadian to claim that distinction. He was ranked both Indiana's top singles and doubles player.

David was chosen for the Canadian Davis Cup Team several times while at the University of Indiana. However, his commitment to the tennis program prevented him from playing for his country as often as he would have liked.

The memorable moment of his competitive tennis career came at a Davis Cup event in which he did manage to compete. It was in Bogota, the high-altitude capital of Columbia where visitors have to battle not only thin-air atmosphere, but the highly partisan crowds not above throwing coins at opposing players in an attempt to distract (and often completely destroy) their concentration. "You cannot imagine the feeling of standing there and having the Canadian National Anthem being played," he was quoted.

Internationally, David competed in the Canadian, United States, New Zealand and West German Open Tennis Championships. To date, he and his mother are the only mother/son combination to have competed in the U.S. Open (1967) and the only mother/son combination to represent Canada in Federation Cup and Davis Cup play respectively.

Nationally, David proved his mettle winning five consecutive Canadian Doubles Championships (1972-1976) with four different partners. He also has a Canadian age 35-plus doubles title.

David moved to the Clarkson area of Mississauga where he opened a business, David Brown Sport Enterprises. He also became tennis director at the Fitness Institute at Cliff Road and the North Service Road. David was inducted into the Hall of Fame in 1993.

•Harvest Drive resident **Fred Doty** was another athlete from Applewood Acres to leave his mark in sport and was inducted into the Mississauga Sports Hall of Fame in 1977. His story is also presented on a storyboard displayed at City Hall. Fred lived in Applewood from 1953 to 1957.

To the young generation, the name Fred Doty may not mean a whole lot, but those who go back a long way have no trouble remembering him. He was a football star who shone as bright on the horizon of the Canadian Football League (CFL) as the best of them during the post Second World War years.

Frederick Kenneth Doty shares a couple of Toronto Argo football records with some of the luminaries of the game that have stood the test of time very well over the years. In the days when players played for the joy of the game (and maybe pocket money and a case of beer here and there), Doty left his mark on the Argo record book by performing some big-league feats, such as intercepting three passes in one game and running back two intercepted passes for touchdown-two in one season. While playing for the Argos, he led the team in punt returns four years in a row from 1945-1948.

But what Doty remembers most vividly (and fondly, of course) are not so much the great punt returns or picked-off passes run for touchdowns, as the sweet taste of nectar out of the Grey Cup. Doty played football with the Toronto Argos of the Interprovincial Rugby Union (the name of the circuit before it became known as the Canadian Football League) from 1945-1949. During those years, the powerful Argos were the toast of the nation from coast to coast and won the Grey Cup three consecutive times 1945, 1946 and 1947.

Born in Toronto on October 25, 1924, Doty attended the University of Toronto and, in 1946, he actually played football for two teams, on the college level with the Varsity Blues and the Canadian league level with the Argos. Before turning his attention to professional football, Doty played basketball while stationed in Calgary with the Royal Canadian Air Force during the war years in 1943 and 1944. It was in Calgary where the love of the gridiron won out when he first played football at the junior level. An all-around talent (not a rare thing in those days), he played both defense and offense right through his Argo career, a feat he considers his most outstanding achievement.

Fred was inducted into the Mississauga Hall of Fame in 1977, the same year his son Cole (Canadian sprint champion who represented the country in various international competitions and starred for the Southern Methodist University track team in Dallas, Texas) was named Mississauga Amateur Male Athlete of the Year.

•In 1993, twenty years after **Dick Thornton** moved out of his Duchess Drive home in Westacres, the Canadian Football League (CFL) named him to the CFL All Time-All Star Team as one of the best 28 players in the history of the league. He was a Defensive Back, Quarterback, Running Back and Wide Receiver.

Dick, affectionately known as 'Tricky Dick', actually moved into Applewood in 1967 when he rented a basement apartment "just for a few days" from friend Bobby Leyden, who lived on the south-west corner of Breezy Brae Drive and Duchess Drive. That was the year the Winnipeg Blue Bomber standout star was traded to the Toronto Argonauts after jokingly making a comment on a Winnipeg radio station that the best thing about Winnipeg was the road out of town. That comment turned out to be the final straw in a tension-filled relationship in Winnipeg and management pulled the plug. Interestingly, the next season when the Blue Bombers came to CNE Stadium, Dick Thornton led the Argos to a 53-0 victory. The Argos had not been a stellar team prior to Dick Thornton's arrival.

"As a member of the Blue Bombers when we played in Toronto for the 1961, 62 and 65 Grey Cups, I became good friends with Bob Leyden, a television football statistician. When I got traded to the Argos, I asked him if I could stay with him for a few days. Well, I ended up living there for four years," said Dick Thornton in an interview many years later.

Bobby Leyden worked as a statistician for CTV from 1959 to 1989 and presently works for CTV's Sports Net and also does work on The Sports Network (TSN). Bobby's father owned Leydon Auto Radio on Roncesvalles Avenue in Toronto and Gordon Shipp actually purchased a number of fridges and stoves from him for Applewood houses. Bobby lived on the south-west corner of Breezy Brae and Duchess Drive from 1965 to 1972.

Dick married a Wardair stewardess in March 1970 and moved to an apartment on Dundas Street near Hwy 427. Bob Leyden called shortly afterward and told him that a house across the road from him was up for sale. The house, as it turned out, was the home of Chic Murray, then the Reeve of the Town of Mississauga.

"I purchased the house at 839 Duchess Drive in the spring of 1971 for $22,500", said Dick. "This was the first property I had ever owned. Often Bobby and I would laugh about how we were now neighbours, after having lived with him and his family for so long. You know, I only was to be there for a few days."

Things turned bad for Dick Thornton in 1973. On New Year's Day his wife flew out on a trip and never returned. She had run off with a pilot. Tragedy struck 12 days later when his father passed away and, in July, the Argos let him go following their first exhibition game.

"However, being in my 30's and single again and working downtown, suburbia wasn't my thing anymore. So, I sold my house toward the end of the year in 1973 for $76,000 and moved into the Sutton Place Apartments on Bay Street."

Life started to look up. He was immediately hired by The Toronto Sun as a columnist, covering his old team of course. But soon afterward the phone rang and John Bassett Jr., who had just started the World Football League (WFL) offered him a chance to play again. Unfortunately for Mr. Bassett and Canadian fans, a resolution in Parliament was about to be enacted preventing the WFL from playing in Canada. Fortunately, Memphis, Tennessee had just been denied a National Football League (NFL) franchise, so it didn't take long for the Toronto Northmen to become the Memphis Southmen. Dick was elected defensive captain and had an outstanding season, intercepting five passes, returning one for a touchdown and made 127 unassisted tackles leading the Southmen to a divisional title in 1974.

Dick Thornton (25) intercepts a Calgary pass intended for wide-receiver Jon Henderson (20). In the 1971 Grey Cup, Calgary defeated Toronto 14-11. Photo courtesy of Dick Thornton

While he was living in Applewood he managed to put his university education to good use. He authored a book titled "Get it While You're Hot, Cause Baby, You're Going to be Cold for a Long, Long Time". The problem is, it never got published. It was deemed to be too sexually vivid and a direct attack on the establishment.

During his career Dick played on the Grey Cup winning Blue Bombers in 1961 and 1962. He was with Winnipeg when they were finalists in 1965 and then with Toronto when they reached the finals in 1971.

He received All Star Recognition by the CFL in 1963, 1965 and 1971. Some of his records standing to this day include most interceptions returned for touchdown at eight, second most interceptions returned for touchdowns in one year at three and second most interceptions returned for touchdowns in one game at two. He holds the Grey Cup record for the third longest interception return at 54 yards. He has been placed on the 'short list' for the Toronto Argonaut Wall of Fame and one year was selected as an All Star on the Playboy Magazine football picks. Dick Thornton now lives in Manila, The Philippines, where he is working as an international merchandising specialist and contract consultant with Thai Pure Drinks Ltd., the bottler of Coca-Cola Products in Bangkok. He writes for Beverage World magazine and also writes a football column for the Bangkok Post, SE Asia's leading newspaper.

•Tolman Road resident **Geoff Fullerton** competed in the 1994 Ironman Canada Triathlon held in Penticton, B.C. and finished under the 15-hour mark to be classified as a finisher. There was a time when he couldn't swim between two docks at his cottage and he says he decided to do something about it and learn to swim.

Soon he joined a swim club which introduced him to triathlons. After completing his first triathlon, a conventional swim just short of one mile (1.5 km), a 40-mile (64km) bicycle race and a 10-mile (16 km) run, he was hooked. He said it was very addictive as when you finish a triathlon, you never want to do it again, but a few days later you get the urge.

Geoff said it was also very exciting to watch his weight drop and his heart rate drop as he got into better shape. His training meant swimming 90 minutes every second weekday and on other days he would run or cycle the 27 miles (44 km) to his work and home. On weekends he would cycle to Barrie, Ontario and back.

When the Fullerton family returned from Penticton, B.C., on Labour Day weekend in the fall of 1994, he had a newly acquired limp and a broad smile of satisfaction. Geoff Fullerton became an official Ironman Finisher.

Winning the title didn't come easy. The triathlon is an international event with competitors from 36 countries. The event lasted all day, starting at 7 a.m., when 1,350 entrants splashed into Okanagan Lake for the swim portion. They then cycled through hot and dry temperatures and mountainous terrain for their bicycle portion followed by their long distance run.

Geoff swam 2.4 miles (3.8 km), bicycled 112 miles (180 km) and then completed a long distance run of 26.2 miles (42km). His effort took 14.5 hours.

•It could be said that the first athletes who gained any degree of recognition and who hailed from Applewood Acres could well have been teenage brothers by the name of **Brian and Dick Runstedler.**

The Runstedler family moved into their brand new home at 2162 Harcourt Crescent in 1954 and by the time the first ever Westacres June Fair was completed, on June 11, 1955, the Runstedler family were setting the benchmarks for future competitions.

Brian, who was just about to turn 12 years of age, won several events at the first June Fair registering wins in the 80 yard hurdles, 80 yard dash, 100 yard dash, high jump and the broad jump. His older brother, Dick, was victorious in his age group in the dash, boys' senior discus (he tied with Nick Rampling, who in later life set marks of his own in automobile racing). Dick also won the sack race, 330 and 100-yard dash races, the boys' hurdles, senior relay, high jump, broad jump, and to top the day off, he was declared the Most Outstanding Boy in the day's competitions.

But it was his younger brother Brian who would continue through his school years to compete nationally across Canada and set numerous records. Brian actually broke an all-Canada record in track and field while running with a fractured foot. Brian's outstanding achievements, however, came after the family had moved from the area to the western Ontario town of Tilbury, near Windsor.

Brian competed for the Windsor Legion Olympic Club. He was the 1959 Western Ontario Intermediate Champion and also won the 1963 South Western High School Senior title. His many friends in Applewood Acres were delighted one day when he established a Canadian record in the 100-yard event winning the race held in a Toronto meet. Brian's picture was splashed all over the front page of the June 30, 1962 Toronto Globe and Mail newspaper. Sadly, Brian died, in May 2001 having succumbed to cancer.

•**Lloyd "Mickey" McDonald** moved into Applewood Acres in 1952 with his wife Elizabeth, or Betty as she was better known. Mickey rose to the highest levels of lacrosse just 10 years before he moved into his home on Melba Road. His speed and athletic ability earned him the opportunity to play lacrosse at the highest level in Canada when he won the Mann Cup in 1942. He was also Senior Eastern Champion in 1947.

 The Mann Cup was presented by the late Sir Donald Mann, builder of the Canadian Northern Railway, for the Senior Amateur Championship of Canada. It was originally a challenge cup and, in 1910, was first won by the Young Toronto's. It is a gold cup with a value of several thousands of dollars and is one of the most valuable trophies in sport. Mickey played lacrosse for the Mimico Mountaineers 1935 to 1951. The McDonalds moved from Toronto's Parkside area to try the suburban life and soon became a fixture on Melba Road. Mickey's ability and love for sport was quickly transferred to the neighbourhood and its children. The winter months turned into "Hockey Night at 1171 Melba" with numerous outdoor rinks in the backyards of his neighbours. On the street during the summer you would often find a game of road hockey, lacrosse, basketball, football or baseball.

Mickey was regarded as one of the best hockey coaches in the area. He, along with Gord Stanfield and neighbour Harry Russell, became one of the three founding fathers of the Metro Toronto Hockey League's Mississauga Reps, which has won numerous hockey championships. Mickey's hockey knowledge was recognized by Yale University, which utilized his services as an area scout.

After attending Mimico High School Mickey joined the Navy. He was stationed in Halifax and served on a Corvette during WW II. After the war Mickey joined Anaconda American Brass in New Toronto and served as its purchasing agent until his retirement.

During the summer months Mickey would be at his cottage in Haliburton but he was not far away from either his garden or the golf course. He was a member of the Brampton Golf and Country Club and, in 1990, he won his age category in the Royal Canadian Golf Association's Amateur Championship.

On September 20, 1997 the Ontario Lacrosse Hall of Fame and Museum held its Inaugural Induction Ceremonies in St. Catharines, Ontario. Lloyd "Mickey" McDonald was among those inducted as a member. Mr. McDonald passed away in 1999 at the age of 84.

•**Sharon Hrinco**, who moved into 2157 Harcourt Crescent in 1994, joins Mickey as a member of the Ontario Lacrosse Hall of Fame. Sharon was inducted into the Hall of Fame in the Builder Category. She has been involved in lacrosse since 1978. In 1984 Sharon was presented with the Al Austin Award for her outstanding contribution to the sport in Etobicoke and, 10 years later, she was presented with the Thomas 'Tip' Teather award for her outstanding contribution to the sport province-wide. She continues her involvement and is known for her positive 'make things happen' attitude. Her vision has had a profound effect on shaping the administration of the sport and taking it into the future.

•**James Laverty**, who lived at 1163 Greening Avenue, was not only active in the Applewood Baseball League but also was very active with the Applewood Hockey League and with figure skating at Dixie Arena, the forerunner of the Mississauga Figure Skating Club. His interest in figure skating came as a result of being at the Barton Street Arena in Hamilton where he played hockey in his youth. One day he met a figure skater by the name of Leona James and eventually they married.

James Laverty was an accomplished hockey player. He had played hockey at the Barton Street Arena and even attended the Detroit Red Wing Hockey Camp where he tried out for the Detroit Red Wings of the National Hockey League (NHL). However, the Government of Canada had other plans for him as he was drafted into the armed forces at the start of WW II.

The Laverty's resided in the Kingsway area and James had a thriving business in the elevator industry. Later, he was approached by the government and asked to become a government elevator inspector. Accepting the offer he sold his business. When he arrived in Applewood in 1952, television was in its infancy and he started a television repair service which blossomed in the area. Both James and his wife became very involved in community activities. Leona was a very talented singer (I

140

write about her in the chapter on Arts) and she became one of the founding members of the Applewood United Church choir.

James eventually realized that young hockey players need an activity during the summer to keep themselves fit for regular season play and he decided to start a hockey school at Dixie Arena. Eventually, he expanded the school into Chicago and also Detroit. While in Chicago and Detroit, he also had time to make contacts for baseball tournaments.

•Courtland Crescent resident **Warren T. Marshall** never played hockey but the sport became an important part of his life. He dedicated himself totally to the development of minor hockey in Mississauga.

Spending as many as five evenings each week in hockey arenas around the community, Warren Marshall rose to become the 20th President of the Mississauga Hockey League (MHL). On Saturday, April 21, 1973, at age 47, he suffered a fatal heart attack.

He was a very successful businessman in Mississauga, operating LCN Closers of Canada Ltd., located on Rangeview Road in south Mississauga.

Connected with the MHL in numerous roles for more than 12 years, from the time when there was just a handful of boys playing out of one arena, he lived to see a player enrolment of more than 6,500 boys.

He was an area rep for the Applewood Hockey Association for a number of years before being elected president of that group in the mid-1960's. In 1968 he was elected to the Board of Directors of the MHL. He was secretary for the MHL from 1968 to 1972 when he was named Vice President.

One of the two ice arenas located at the Cawthra Road complex south of the QEW has been named to honour Warren T. Marshall. The plaque at the entrance to the arena reads as follows, *" A dedicated man who gave freely of his time for others. The memory of his constant effort in the interests of minor hockey will live on in all who shared moments with him."*

• **Marcus Vujacic,** who lives at 2078 Tolman Road, could well become one of Canada's top men's golfers After all, he is already one of the top junior players and he is only just starting his golf career.

Marcus started playing golf at age 14 when his father bought him a membership at Rattlesnake Point Golf Club. The first two years he played on a regular basis and then decided to enter tournaments. Since then he has won the club championship twice, played six tournaments in his third year and 15 tournaments in his fourth season. He was on the winning squad playing for Team Canada in a junior tournament in 2001. In 2003 he was named to the McMaster University's Golf Team. His plans are to continue playing amateur golf while he pursues an education. He hopes to one day attend medical school.

•Living just around the corner from Marcus on Melba Road is young hockey player **Matt Foy**. Destined to become an NHL player, Matt graduated through the Ottawa 67's organization and in 2002 was selected by Minnesota in the NHL draft. In 2003 season Matt played 68 games with Ottawa scoring 61 goals and 71 assists for 132 points. He notched 11 goals and 20 assists in the playoffs.

•**Nick Rampling** lived at 819 Melton Drive and was one of 20 Westacres Public School students involved in a gymnastics demonstration, which was televised on the Dominion Network (CBLT) Toronto in 1957. As a student Nick was very competitive having excelled in sports at Westacres. Just nine years later Nick went on to enjoy a successful career in short-track stock car racing and was a fixture at tracks in southern Ontario including the famous Pinecrest and Canadian National Exhibition (CNE) speedways.

In 1966 the Rampling racing team ventured into the world's highest echelons of stock car racing competing in three races sanctioned by the National Association of Stock Car Auto Racing (NASCAR). He drove a 1965 Plymouth in races at Fulton, New York, Islip, N.Y. and at Daytona Beach, Florida. His attempt to qualify for the classic North American race, the 1966 Daytona 500, was cut short when problems sidelined him from the event during one of the Daytona 500 qualifying runs. The race was telecast on ABC's Wide World of Sports and won by Richard Petty at an average speed of 160.627 mph (258.497 kmh) and Petty won $28,150. Not bad for the time; after all, the 2003 event paid $1.4 million to win. Nick Rampling may not have made it past the qualifier race but he was sure in good company.

•The year IOC President Juan Antonio Samaranch brought the Olympics to his native Spain, in 1992, marked the first renewal of the Summer Games since the fall of communism in Eastern Europe and the reunification of Germany in 1990. A record 10,563 athletes from 172 nations gathered and this was the year that the IOC threw open the gates to professional athletes.

It was also the year Baldwin Road resident **William Hayes** represented Canada as a diver specializing on the 10-metre tower in the Barcelona Olympics. William was ranked 21st in the preliminary on the 10-metre tower.

Born in 1968, William attended Westacres Public School, Gordon Graydon Secondary School and then went on to the University of Michigan on a diving scholarship.

•Hockey great **Howie Meeker** once lived in Applewood Acres, albeit for a short period of time. As he recalls it was about 18 months. " I lived on Melton Drive, just two houses removed from Col. Harlan Sanders," said Meeker who had moved from Toronto to Applewood when his wife developed rheumatoid arthritis.

The name Meeker is synonymous with the National Hockey League and certainly conjures up different memories for many people, depending on the age. Older generations remember Howie as a solid hockey player with the Toronto Maple Leafs in the 1940's and 1950's. Younger generations may better recall his television colour commentary work on Hockey Night In Canada and other assorted broadcasts throughout the 1970s and 1980s. He also ran his own hockey school and had his own television show designed for helping players improve their skills.

Howie started his NHL career in 1947. In his first year he beat out such greats as Gordie Howe in winning the coveted Calder Memorial Trophy, presented to the top player in his rookie year. Meeker played outstanding hockey for the Leafs and was on their squad winning three consecutive Stanley Cups and then added a fourth one before he retired to become a coach and also a general manager.

Howie Meeker was also a parliamentarian as he sat for four years as a Conservative in Ottawa. He has been named to the Hockey Hall of Fame and now lives in British Columbia.

•Possibly the first active professional sporting celebrity to settle in Applewood Acres was **Jerry Doucette**. This standout 19 year-old Etobicoke Collegiate Institute athlete had just signed to play as a

quarterback in pro football with the Toronto Argonaught Football Club, when he purchased his home at 1374 Kendall Road. He played six seasons for the Argos, 1954 through 1959, and then one year each with Calgary and Montreal. At 6' (1.8m) and 190 pounds (86k) Jerry also found time to play basketball and excelled in that sport as well. He played guard for the Thompson Lumber Saints in the Toronto Township Basketball League. The team, coached by well-known sports builder in Mississauga, Jerry Love, went on to win the inaugural All Ontario Intermediate A Basketball Championships in 1958. Jerry was second highest scorer in the two championship games played against Brockville His high school career was dotted with winning championships. Having guided his school to many titles, he also played for the Balmy Beaches Toronto squad and took them to a championship as well.

In 1956 he led the club out of the woods to end the season with three consecutive victories. He had earlier been replaced in an experiment that failed miserably. The Argos suffered seven straight losses. Doucette engineered his team back to glory when he threw 112 times and completed 61 for 858 yards.

•**Dave Quantrill and Cederic Rackett** were born in India and were childhood friends attending Sherwood College there. Time and distance brought about their separation until one day Dave and Cedric met up again, this time living in Canada. Both were actively involved playing field hockey and both were founding members of the first Toronto Field Hockey Club in 1956. They received a great deal of support and assistance from Bobbi Rosenfeld, a sports writer with the Toronto Globe and Mail, who held the distinction of being named Canada's Female

Athlete of the First Half Century. The easiest way to describe Bobbie Rosenfeld is to say that she dominated every sport she tried from track and field, softball, basketball to lacrosse and hockey.

In the late 50's Cederic played internationally and was selected to be a member of the squad from the Toronto Field Hockey Club chosen to represent Canada in the Olympics, to be held in Rome in 1960. Unfortunately he was injured in 1959 during a series of international exhibition games and that brought a halt to his career. Both Dave and Cederic were also founding members of a second club, the Toronto Gymkhana. Later, the sport of Cricket was included in their efforts and they played at the site of what is now the Toronto Cricket Club.

Dave and Cederic were once again separated as family matters took priority but in 1963 Cederic was living at 2187 Sidney Drive and was out for a walk one day when he bumped into Dave, who had just moved into his home at 1308 Kendall Road.

Dave also had a love for a vastly different type of sport and was very much a part of the scene of Canadian motorsport. Just prior to the sport being developed into a nation-wide club structure in the late 1950's, Dave worked as general service manager for Ensign Motors, a major English automobile dealership in Toronto. He strapped on a helmet most weekends and could be seen racing Jaguar XK140's and Mercedes Gull-wing Coups at the Harewood Acres airport racing circuit 100 miles west of Toronto.

•**Danny Baxter** lived at 2049 McIntosh Crescent with his parents Robert and Henrietta and brother Bob, who in later years purchased a home just around the corner on Russell Road. The Baxters were among the first arrivals in 1952. When Danny graduated high school he became involved in motorsport with the Oakville Trafalgar Light Car Club. Most years he was involved in the administrative side but for 13 years he raced formula racing cars. His activity in the sport lasted for more than 40 years.

•Another Applewood resident highly involved in motorsport was **Al Cooper** of 2187 Harcourt Crescent. Al spent more than 20 years in the Antique and Classic Car Club of Canada, Mississauga Chapter, most of those years serving as its president or secretary.

•**Kevin O'Sullivan** arrived in Applewood in the late 1950s with his parents and brother Brian and settled on Johnathan Drive. Kevin went to

T.L. Kennedy Secondary School, later married and continued to live in Applewood. Kevin was a car racer and raced in the highly competitive Bulova Watch Formula Ford Series at Mosport. He graduated from the Jim Russell Racing School at Mont Tremblant, Quebec in 1971 and raced Formula Fords from 1972 through 1975. One season he competed against Gilles Villeneuve, who went on to become a World Championship Formula One Grand Prix racer for the factory Ferrari team.

•**Bill Lefeuvre** who lived at 2206 Rambo Road from 1952 until the mid-1960's became one of Canada's top Off-Road Racers (Baja desert style racing). He raced in a major North American series known as the B.F. Goodrich Off-Road Racing Series which sanctioned events across Ontario and Quebec. Bill started racing in 1960 competing in ice racing events held on frozen lakes. He raced during the winter season for the next five years winning championships in several classes. From 1962 through 1967 he competed on the asphalt in a formula car at Mosport and, in 1969, he started his Off-Road career which lasted until 2001 and produced several overall Canadian Championships. Bill married Joan Turk, who lived at 2303 Stanfield Road, at the north-east corner of Stanfield and The Queensway. Joan retired in 2004 after more than 40 years with The City of Mississauga, ending a most distinguished career as City Clerk.

•**John Lightfoot** of 784 Whitney is an accomplished competitor in the world of vintage motorcycle racing. He regularly competes at tracks such as Mosport, Shannonville and Cayuga Speedways in Ontario. His crowning achievment in the sport, though, came in 1985 when he took part in two races at the famous Daytona International Speedway in Florida, finishing fourth in one event riding a Honda and 13th in another on board a Harley Davidson Aermacchi. John moved into Applewood with his wife Chris Jackson and two children, Daniel and Jamie. He is an artist operating Lightfoot Art and Design Inc.

•**Mary-Jane Hall** was just an infant when her parents, George and Marguerite Peal, purchased their new home at 2063 Snow Crescent. The Halls were among those early Applewood "pioneers" who answered the advertisements in the major daily papers and moved to this new exciting development west of Toronto. In a way, Mary-Jane inherited those pioneer qualities as, later in life, she forged new roads for women in Canadian golfing.

Mary-Jane was the first woman in Canada to play against men. And, in 1981, she became the first woman head-pro in Canada. She followed that up with being the first woman in Canada to play against men in a Canadian professional golfing event and later, in 1987, she was instrumental in establishing the Canadian Professional Golf Association (CPGA) Women's Championship. The founding of the women's competitions originated basically because, as a teaching pro, Mary-Jane couldn't find any professional tournaments in which to play.

Her father introduced her to the game when she was 12 and she very quickly showed she had a higher than average skill level in the sport. She continued to enter, play and win, some very prestigious tournaments. One of the first major tournament wins for Mary-Jane came, when as a teenager, she won the Toronto and District Junior Championship. Her career was on path and she has never looked back. Her schooling, however, did not take a back-seat as a result of her golfing. She was educated at Applewood Public School, Gordon Graydon Secondary, Holy Name of Mary on Mississauga Road and then St. Mary's University in Halifax, Nova Scotia.

•Primate Road has been the home address for a couple of Canada's top-ranked badminton players over the years. In the 1960s **Ernie Nock,** who lived at 2155 Primate, was ranked in the top 10 in Canada while in the late 1960s and early 1970s, David Wowchuck, who lived at 2119 Primate, rose to become the National Age Group Champion.

Ernie W. Nock, his wife Mary Louise and son Ernie settled at Burnhamthorpe and Second Line area in the 1940s and established a small family-run chicken farm business. By 1952 they decided to moved into Applewood Acres. Young Ernie Nock, who was born in 1942, attended Dixie Public School, then the newly-opened Applewood Public. He entered Gordon Graydon Secondary School when it first opened becoming a Charter Member. It was at Graydon that Ernie started playing badminton and by 1961 realized he had a little more than a passive interest in the sport. He joined the Boulevard Club in Toronto and started playing competitively in 1961.

He played one year Junior, Singles and Mixed and played in Team Doubles. He was ranked in the top 10 in Canada playing with John Tomlinson in Team Doubles. His second year proved to be a little tougher. He continued to play with John and also, his wife Vicki played as well.

Badminton is surely a family love for the Nocks as daughter Melissa started to play when she was seven years of age. Melissa, also playing out of the Boulevard Club, rose to a third place national ranking in Singles and Doubles and ranked fifth in Mixed. In 1999 she won Gold at the Long Island, N.Y. Eastern U.S. under age 23 Competition in Singles and Doubles. She also took home a Silver medal in the Mixed category.

Ernie and daughter Melissa also share other sporting interests. Melissa excels in golf and equestrian riding (western pleasure) while father Ernie is a barrel racer. He was recently appointed to sit on the Ontario Racing Commission as he is an owner of two quarter horses.

Today Ernie and his family live in Oakville where he owns and operates E.J. Nock Realty, which he established in 1969.

•William and Elaine Wowchuck moved into their home at 2119 Primate in 1968. The Wowchuck's had two children, Brad, age eight and David, age six. **David Wowchuck** attended Applewood Public School, Allan A. Martin and then Gordon Graydon Secondary. He was an outstanding athlete and in Grade 13 was named Graydon's Athlete of the Year.

He joined the Boulevard Club and began playing badminton competitively to become the National Canadian Age Group Champion and along the way he collected three Singles, one Doubles and three Mixed Doubles Championships.

David attended the University of California Los Angeles (UCLA) and majored in Physiology and Bio Medical Science. He is now employed in the group insurance industry in Canada and is an executive vice-president of sales for a major firm.

He lives in Oakville today with his wife, Patti, and children Matt, age 10 and Brooke, age eight. David no longer plays competitive badminton but has continued to enjoy an active athletic career. At age 40, David is racing in marathons. He has competed twice in the Casino Niagara and once in the New York Marathon.

•While **Dixie Arena Gardens** is not in Applewood Acres, the arena played such an important part in the lives of so many here a little mention must be made. Dixie Arena Gardens actually opened November 22, 1949 for public skating and the first actual hockey game was played Monday December 5th. NHL player Ray Timgren of the Toronto Maple Leafs was on hand and signed autographs for all youngsters in attendance that night. The first hockey game was a Tadpole contest in which Dixie defeated Lakeview 3-1.

The official opening was held on December 16, 1949 and proved to be a gala affair with the area MPP, Col. Thomas L. Kennedy, Minister of Agriculture, and Ontario's Premier, Leslie Frost, among the invited guests. Col. Kennedy opened the evening ceremonies saying, "who knows, someday a second Barbara Ann Scott may begin her career on this very ice." Premier Frost added, "This is the most amazing community venture in Ontario."

Dixie Arena Gardens President Leslie H. Pallett added that the realization of the facility was a result of the efforts of many people who gave so unstintingly of their time, labour and talents.

"In February of this year a public meeting was held to discuss the erection of this arena. The citizens of Dixie decided that the incorporation of a company was the most advisable and efficient method of transforming idea into fact. The charter was granted on the first of March, permission was received to sell stock on April 22nd, the contracts were let (with the intentions of being completed by Novemeber 15) and, on November 22nd, there was skating in Dixie Arena Gardens," said Mr. Pallett.

The authorized share capital amounted to $200,000 with estimates of $135,000 for completion of the arena.

The 64-page souvenir program that night listed more than 255 names of people who purchased shares and contained more than 100 advertisements from local business operations. A read through this program provides an excellent insight into the activities of the community in the 1940s.

The seed to develop Dixie Arena Gardens was actually planted when a group, unofficially known as the Silver Seven, met at Nuttall's Supertest Garage, located on the north-west corner of Dixie and Dundas. Nuttall's was a popular gathering spot for the men in the area and soon the talk about the need for Dixie Arena Gardens became more than just a dream. The Silver Seven were: Leslie H. Pallett, President; James Sherman, Vice President; W. Howard Pallett, Secretary; Victor G. Stanfield, Treasurer and Directors Wilfred D. Goddard, Lindsay L. Death and James McCarthy.

Dixie Arena Gardens became the first indoor hockey arena in Toronto Township and for years not only provided a centre for all types of ice sports, but for many other activities. In August 1952, it played host to the largest flower show in North America when the International Gladiolus Show was held there.

The first major hockey teams calling Dixie Arena home ice were the Ontario Hockey League (OHA) Junior B Dixie Staffords, sponsored by the Stafford's Hot Chocolate Company, and the OHA Dixie Intermediates. The Stafford's played St. Michael's College on opening night beating the St. Mike's squad 6-1. In the second game played on opening night, the Dixie Intermediates defeated the Toronto Township All Stars 2-1. A few years later the Junior B team became known as the Dixie Beehives and was sponsored by the St. Lawrence Starch Co. Ltd. of Port Credit. The Beehives became an affiliate of the Chicago Black Hawks of the National Hockey League and, between 1954 and 1986, the Beehives won three Ontario Junior B division titles and three league championships.

Ron Rutledge, whose family farm was on the corner of what is now The Queensway and Cawthra Road, started working at Dixie Arena when he was 15. He attended Westacres Public School and a half year at Gordon Graydon Secondary. Ron worked at Dixie Arena for 28 years, much of that time as its operating manager. He has fond memories of his days involved with the thousands of kids who played hockey there, including the more than 30 players who passed through the Dixie Junior B team and later made their mark playing in the National Hockey League.

Dixie Arena Gardens closed its doors to the community as a hockey arena on May 31, 1986. For a short while it was used as a nightclub and later, razed by fire. A 155 unit town-home housing development, known as Applewood On The Park, now stands in its place. However, there is a plaque telling the story of a landmark that once defined Dixie Arena as not only a community recreational place but a Canadian hockey powerhouse.

Dixie Arena Gardens wasn't the only idea born around that little stove at Nuttall's Supertest by those early day entrepreneurs. At the same time the Arena was conceived, plans were also planted by the Silver Seven to establish the Dixie Curling Club, located to the east of the arena. The end result was that after 13 months of construction, and $175,000 in capital, more than 400 people had become playing members. Ten were given lifetime memberships. Vic Stanfield was President; Jim Johnson elected Vice President while John McLean was Secretary and Pat Patterson Treasurer. Members at Large were: Tom Jackson, Lou Goodfellow, John Pallett, Iver Murray and Duncan Campbell.

•It's not inconceivable to think that any one of the children splashing around in the Don McLean Westacres Pool may one day be an Olympic swimmer. And, living within ear-shot of the pool is **Clifford Barry**, a gentleman who could actually make that happen if the right swimmer came along.

Clifford moved into his home at 905 Hedge Drive in July 1990 with his wife Susan and daughter Carling. Clifford is a Canadian Swim Coach

Certified Level Three and working on Level Four. He is one of this country's leading swim coaches and has coached Gold winning swimmers at virtually every major games in the world including the Olympics, Pan Pacifics, World Championships, Commonwealth, Pan American, Students Games, World Cups, National and Provincial Championships.

Born in Montreal in 1946, Clifford graduated with a Bachelor of Arts from Sir George William University, Montreal, then completed two years at the University of Western Ontario (Physical Education) working toward a Masters Degree.

His coaching experience reads like the who's who of swimming. He was Head Coach at Gloucester Ottawa Swim Club in 1972-73, Head Coach in Guelph with the Marlins Aquatic Club in 1976 through 1979 and Head Coach of the Waterloo Swim Club from 1980 through 1986. He also taught aquatics at Wilfred Laurier University in 1985-86 and from 1986 through 1989 he was Head Coach for the Pointe Clare Swim Club in Montreal.

He moved to Applewood when he became Head Coach for the Etobicoke Swim Club, a position he held until 1997 when he was appointed Head Coach for the Etobicoke Olympian Masters Aquatic Club.

Clifford's career highlights include his being named as a Member of the Ontario Aquatics Hall of Fame. He was Canadian Swim Coach of the Year in 1982, 1984 and 1986. He coached on the 1984 and 1988 Canadian Olympic teams. Clifford was Head Men's Coach in the 1986 World Championships in Madrid, also in 1986 in Edinburgh, Scotland and was Head Coach on the 1982 World Championship team in Equador, in 1983 in Venezuela and 1991 in Cuba. He coached on the Pan Pacific Games in 1981, Tokyo, Japan in 1989 and 1993 in Kamloops. In 1986 and again in 1988, he was awarded the prestigious Longines-Wittnauer Coaching Excellence Award.

Clifford coached Victor Davis and Mike West in the 1984 Olympics in Los Angeles. Davis won Gold and Silver and established a world's record while West won Silver and Bronze. Victor Davis was tragically killed in 1989 when an automobile struck him. A Memorial Foundation was established in his name. Clifford is its founder and present Chairman.

The Victor Davis Memorial Fund was established to remember this champion's contribution to competitive swimming in Canada, and to encourage young Canadians toward excellence. Each year awards may be made from the Fund to promising, high performance Canadian amateur swimmers to assist them to continue their training, education, and pursuit of medals at the international level of competition.

Clifford has considerable experience as a competitor having competed on the Canadian Olympic Water Polo Team. He was its Captain in 1972, a member in 1976, Captain at the World Championships in Columbia in 1971 and Captain at the World Championships in Mexico in 1975. Clifford was a member of the 1967 Pan Am Games in Winnipeg and Captain of the 1969 Canada Games team in Quebec. He was named Canada's Most Outstanding Water Polo Player 1967-1972.

•For a short three seasons, from 1957 through 1960, little league baseball was big league in Applewood. Thanks to the **Kiwanis Club** of Port Credit, the many children who played in the Applewood Baseball Association got to play in a 600-seat stadium, complete with floodlights and all of the usual amenities found in more professional stadiums.

Many of the Kiwanis members lived in Applewood and included people such as Les Pilkington, who lived on Courtland Crescent with his wife Audrey, as well as Fred Halliday, whom I write about in chapter eight. The Pilkingtons were good friends of my mother and father and often Les would talk about the stadium when he visited my home on Rambo Road. He was one of the original Applewood Acres salesmen selling homes for G.S.Shipp and Son.

The stadium was located on the north-west corner of Dixie Plaza and, was in fact, the first of its type in Canada. A total of $10,000 was raised by selling $1 'planks' and the first person to step up to the plate to make a purchase on June 20, 1957 was the Honourable John Pallett, MP Peel. Many of the materials needed to build the stadium were donated by area firms and a list of the donors and plank purchasers was carried each week in the Port Credit Weekly. Vic Tedder who lived at 2080 Russett Road was the organizer for the earth fill that was needed to complete the job. Other happenings to make the stadium a reality were the work of the Kweens Club, which were actually wives of the Kiwanis members, who sold soft drinks at games at Westacres and Dixie fields. The chairman of the opening day ceremonies was Clare Wilson, who owned and operated the automobile service station at the foot of Stanfield Road. Opening day was Thursday, June 26, 1958 and more than 300 people attended. The voice of Toronto baseball, radio announcer Joe Crysdale, acted as Master of Ceremonies. The first ball was hit by 'Mr. Ontario', Col. Thomas L. Kennedy and, in what seemed like three short seasons, it all came to an end in 1960 when the plaza required the land for expansion.

•One of the very first world-class sportsmen living in Applewood Acres was **Dr. Lou Douglas** who lived at 2074 Stewart Crescent. In August 1955 he traveled to Bisley, England to participate in the Bisley Rifle Matches held annually at Bisley Camp, Brookwood, Surrey. More than 1,500 competitors from around the world took part. The winner is declared from scores achieved when 10 shots are fired in each of three distance events, 200 yards (182m), 500 yards (457m) and 600 yards (548m). Dr. Douglas scored 146 out of a possible 150 to win the championship. The competitions have been held at Bisley since 1870.

Dr. Douglas, who was the School Medical Officer for York County, also competed in the Colin Doyle Memorial Trophy Match where he placed third with a score of 48 out of 50 in the 900 yard (822m) event. He also competed in the Wimbledon Cup. In 1955, his rank in competitions was given as Captain and he competed as a freelance competitor. He did not belong to a national team in 1955, however, he did compete with Canadian Teams in 1961 and 1967 shooting in the Mackinnon matches.

•Teenager **Gail Heath** of 2081 Russett Road proved to be an accomplished equestrian as her career started to blossom in 1956 when she competed in the Royal Winter Fair. By the end of the season Gail had won more than 40 ribbons, bringing her career ribbon count to more than 70. Gail followed this with several major victories, including the Umphrey Challenge in Toronto, the Bloomfield Hills, Michigan jumping match where she represented Canada, the Master's event on Thanksgiving Day, the Olympic Horse Prep Trials and then starting off New Year's, 1958, at the Toronto Junior Horse Show where she tied for the championship. Later that year she shared the laurels with three other riders in winning the Junior Equestrian Championship of North America. At the 1958 Royal Winter Fair Gail impressed when she placed second in the Sage Trophy event which boasted the largest ever entry for a Canadian competition. She also placed first in the Junior Hunt Team. Gail had earlier competed in Illinois as a member of the Toronto and North York Pony Club team, bringing home a third place. In the absence of a structured North American Championship tour at the time, Gail Heath had to be considered one of the top Junior competitors in North America. Olympic great and Hall of Fame equestrian Jim Elder told me in an interview for this book, that he remembers Gail as an outstanding competitor.

•Sacrifice is the 'name of the game' in most highly competitive sports and Figure Skating is no exception. Applewood's **Donna Taylor** can tell you all about it as she looks back on her many national and international ice dance figure skating championships. Donna, who competed in the mid to late 1960's with partner Bruce Lennie of Etobicoke, recalls skating practices at Dixie Arena Gardens with the Credit Valley Skating Club, now known as the Mississauga Skating Club, and then renting ice time to continue after hours.

Photo courtesy Donna Taylor

"We would often rent ice time between 12:30 a.m. and 1:30 a.m. and many times would travel to Weston's Pine Point Arena at 5:30 a.m. for additional time," she would recall. The pair was coached by Bruce's sister, Mary Janc, who later in life became a National Coach Consultant with

Skate Canada and married Louis Stong, Skate Canada's Director of Skating Development.

Donna and her older sister Lynda grew up in Applewood, living at 910 Johnathan Drive. She was five years of age when the family moved into Applewood in 1955. She attended Westacres Public School, Allen A. Martin and then Gordon Graydon. When she graduated, she attended Teacher's College and today is a schoolteacher at Hillcrest Public School. In 1967 Donna and partner, Bruce, won the Junior Canadian Championship. The pair rose to the world stage in 1968 when they placed 13th in the World Figure Skating Championships in Geneva, Switzerland. The following year the pair clinched the Canadian Championship and then, with a solid victory in Oakland, California, won the North American title. They capped off the year placing 11th in the World Championships in Colorado Springs, Colorado. Unfortunately Ice Dance had not yet been established as an Olympic event, otherwise, Donna and Bruce would surely have competed.

•It is always difficult to write about one's self but I do have a little sporting history and I felt it should be shared here. My first involvement in the business side of motor sport came in 1961 when I was a member of the Oakville Trafalgar Light Car Club (OTLCC), which had just become one of three founding clubs providing the funding to establish Mosport Park in Bowmanville, Ontario. I was asked to be the Secretary of The Meet for the first ever car race to be held at Mosport. The event was scheduled to be held three weeks prior to the Player's 200, an international world-class race which was won by England's Stirling Moss.

The OTLCC race paved the way for my motor sport career, which over the next 40 years would bring me into close contact with all of the world greats of car racing. My involvement in car racing ranged from being a race-car owner, general manager of Mosport, play-by-play announcer, not only for Mosport, but for international events held at various circuits across the eastern seaboard of North America. I also had the pleasure of doing a voice-track for a film documentary on rallying.

My announcing at Mosport then led to a career in radio. One weekend the opportunity came to travel to Watkins Glen for an international race and in order to gain admission to the press box, which always has the best view and is free for the working media, I had to become a 'working media'. I contacted CHIC Radio in Brampton and offered to phone back live reports on the race- all they had to do was issue me press credentials. It must have been a successful move as I was hired as a news reporter upon my return.

My career in radio lasted a few years, some of which was spent at Toronto's CHIN Radio. It was there that I became good friends with my employer Johnny Lombardi, who would play a key role in helping me win my first election when I ran for municipal office in 1980. There is a very large Italian population in Ward 7, and Johnny Lombardi actually attended as my guest at a social evening at the local Celano Club and that assuredly helped me win votes in the Italian community.

During the 1970's I became involved with the Cayuga Speedway and, as its press officer, I ended up becoming the press officer for the Export "A" Stock Car Series, one of this country's first major national racing series.

At that time I also became involved with a new racing club known as the Can Am Midget Racing Club and for many seasons announce their events held at Cayuga. In the 1980's an opportunity opened for me to purchase one of the race cars. I campaigned as a car-owner for a number of seasons. One year I fielded a two-car team. Drivers for my team included Andy Mackereth, who is well known to many area residents as owner of Crown Brake and Steering garage on Dundas, east of Dixie Road.

In 1988, when I retired from political life, I was offered the job as general manager for Mosport's new track, a half-mile, clay-surfaced oval speedway to be known as Mosport's Ascot North. This track was planned to be a major player in North American sprint car racing. Unfortunately problems with the clay surface ended that plan. The track was paved over becoming an asphalt circuit. Interestingly, I became the organizer of the first race events held at both tracks, Mosport, the road course, in 1961 and the oval in 1989. The track was then leased to a local promoter and my employer suggested I make a lateral move to the road course. However, I felt I really wanted to stay with sprint cars and in 1999 I became the press and media officer for the Southern Ontario Sprints. I was subsequently elected Vice President in 2000. I decided to retire from all motor sport activities at the end of 2003 season.

15 Hurricanes and Trains

The evening of October 15, 1954 started out like many other Friday nights in what was still a growing subdivision west of Toronto. People were, however, a little delayed in returning home from work by rains that had fallen steadily during the day.

For those who had to travel from the heart of Toronto to the west, it was a little slower than usual, but, in the main, people went about their Friday routines. Some firms did send their people home a little early, but that was the exception rather than the rule.

Carol (Rose) Beaune, 825 Melton Drive, who, like so many others had returned to live in the community where she grew up, remembers life on Russett Road as a youngster.

"Our family moved onto Russett Road when Applewood was in its infancy, My mom still lives in that house at the age of 89. It seems an eternity ago that I was uprooted from my established life in the west end of Toronto with its numerous amenities to be plunked in the "sticks" with nothing of interest for a young teen.

It took our family a while to adjust to the peace and quiet. How could it be otherwise with a farm in our backyard, orchards and country on all sides? Even the Queen Elizabeth Highway was as silent as a whisper and few planes passed overhead. Malton Airport was an oversized bungalow of sorts.

We had a creek (Applewood Creek) behind us on Russett Road which was a delightful 'water feature' in today's parlance. What a difference a hurricane makes. That hurricane turned that innocuous streamlet into a raging river, rising up over two terraces, sending my mother and grandparents to the second storey as flood water entered the basement, igniting their fears. Major damage to homes at Russett's north end occurred. For many years we could pinpoint the water line at its highest level," said Carol.

Almost a half-century later, Carol Beaune would note that her link to the Shipps would go beyond residing in two Shipp-built homes. *"When I taught Grade One at Riverside Public School in Port Credit, I had the pleasure of having Victoria Shipp as a pupil."* Victoria, is now President of the Shipp Corporation.

Applewood Creek, which seemingly started life in the early days as a swale collecting water runoff, eventually becomes a creek emptying into Lake Ontario. This watercourse is not a branch of any other watercourse in the region.

At left is the starting point at Fred Halliday Park, at right is at the south side of the QEW, showing the actual size of the creek's encasements. The creek continues southerly under Dixie Plaza. On December 31, 1959 Township Council estimated the project cost would be $367,618.20. Nine firms bid on the job with quotes ranging from $140,889.03 to $256,397.00. Photos by Dave Cook

Today the creek remains between the homes along Russett Road and Harvest Drive, but it has been encased in a large concrete box and buried for all time. Planning for the project began in November 1958 and the box was constructed the following year (plan D-5528). The size of the box can be realized by observing the screened channeling where it enters under the parking lot of Dixie Plaza, on the south side of the South Service Road, opposite the foot of Harvest Drive. The creek started its life north of The Queensway, and meandered its way south crossing the QEW at the foot of Harvest Drive. During the construction of the homes on Stir and Meander (Plan 936 by Edrich Construction in 1972), the drainage of Applewood Creek formed an integral part of the Plan of Subdivision. When the Copperthwaites purchased their home at 2024 Harvest Drive in 1959, the real estate agent boasted that this was the only home not flooded at the time of the hurricane.

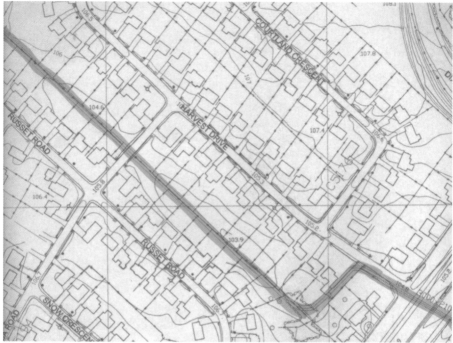

The solid line shows the location of where the creek has been buried and its course behind the homes along Russet Road and Harvest Drive (note the correct spelling of the road name Russet on the map).Floodline mapping courtesy of the Credit Valley Conservation Authority

The large encasement actually makes a 90-degree turn eastward behind 2024 Harvest, then comes along the south side of the home to Harvest Drive where it again makes a 90-degree turn and goes south under the QEW. Applewood Creek today acts as a storm drainage system for a very large area. Basically all the lands between Dixie Road and Cawthra Road, and from Dundas Street south to the Lake, drain into this system.

Ernie and Elva S. Dodd moved into 2125 Russett in 1952 and Elva remembers the time of the flooding as if it was yesterday. Many area residents were attending a concert at T.L. Kennedy High School on the Thursday night and when they arrived home they could see the water was starting to come up its banks from the little creek behind their homes. At the storm's peak, the water crested the banks and filled the Dodds' basement to the roof. In fact, the water made it as far as the road. Elva recalls that the ditches were not put in yet and, as a result, the water flowed across Russett Road. Residents were also horrified to see black oil slicks moving downstream during the peak of the flooding. As it turned out, two tank cars were overturned on the rail tracks north of Applewood and the oil from the tanks had leaked into the system.

The devastation of Hurricane Hazel has been well documented. As a result of the hurricane, the Provincial Government established conservation authorities to regulate wetlands and flood sensitive areas. Mississauga is well served with the Credit Valley Conservation Authority (CVCA) responsible for western areas of the City and Metropolitan Toronto and Region Conservation Authority (MTRCA) responsible for areas in the east.

Twenty-five years later, almost to the month, Applewood residents would be involved in what has been hailed as North America's largest peacetime evacuation attracting world media attention.

A few minutes before midnight on Saturday, November 10, 1979, Train 54 on CP Rail from London, destined for the Toronto yards at Agincourt, derailed at Mavis Road. The first derailed car was the 33rd car in the 106-car train and it was loaded with Toluene, a clear, colorless liquid with a distinctive smell. It is produced in the process of making gasoline and other fuels from crude oil and making coke from coal.

In total, 24 cars left the tracks, 19 of which were carrying what was classified as dangerous commodities. Fire spread quickly through most of the derailed cars and the eighth, 12th and 13th cars, which were loaded with propane, exploded and caused considerable damage to neighbouring property. The City's Recreation and Parks building and yard were totally destroyed.

The seventh car, which was loaded with chlorine, a deadly gas, suffered a hole in its shell 2.5 feet (.76 metres) in diameter and, because of the fear of the escape of chlorine, almost a quarter of a million people were evacuated from their homes and businesses for periods of up to five days.

Three of the cars exploded within one-half hour of the accident and as a result, three great fireballs erupted into the sky and the larger parts of the bodies of cars eight, 12 and 13 were sent flying. Interestingly, a very large part of car 13 was thrown 2,222 feet (677metres) and when one considers that if this derailment had taken place minutes later, the train, which was traveling at 50 mph (90 kph), would have been within striking distance of Applewood Acres.

The CPR line runs south of Dundas, north of The Queensway, between Cawthra and Dixie Roads and, had that derailment occurred at Stanfield Road, the chances of massive destruction would have been likely. To bring it into perspective, the CPR crossing at Stanfield Road is at mile 13.10 of the CPR Galt Subdivision. Mavis Road is at mile 16.6, therefore, the distance from Stanfield Road to Mavis Road is 3.5 miles (5.6 km), which means that the train would have been within striking distance of the homes along Melton Drive just four minutes later than the actual time of the accident at Mavis Road.

Miraculously, there were no casualties and the reason is simple and most fortunate. Notwithstanding that the train had entered one of the most concentrated population centres in the country, at the precise point of the derailment, there was to the immediate south only industrial property, and to the north and northeast, except on the strip of Mavis Road itself, there existed one of the few large areas of undeveloped land remaining in the area.

As it was, the residents of Applewood Acres, like so many thousands of others in the City of Mississauga, were evacuated. But for Applewood Acres resident Margaret Leslie the derailment meant she was about to do what she did best all of her life,-delve headfirst into service for the community. Margaret was honoured in 1980 as Mississauga's Citizen of The Year. Applewood resident Doug Read writes about Margaret in Chapter Nine. Margaret Leslie, who was the Red Cross Emergency Chairman, received the call to duty at 12:45 a.m. and it turned out to be the start of three sleepless days and nights for her.

There was also an immediate response from the Province of Ontario. The Honourable Roy McMurtry, the Attorney General., was also the Solicitor General, and it was in that capacity as Chairman of the Cabinet Committee on Emergencies, that he attended and took command of the emergency measures in the City. Mr. McMurtry's method of command was to discuss and obtain agreement, not to issue orders. Among those advising the Attorney General included the Mayor and members of both Provincial and Federal governments, the chiefs of fire and police, Canadian Transport Commission members, a representative of Superior Propane and two university professors.

•When Hugh Graham Gammell and his wife Josephine (Jo) along with their sons, John, age 22, and Robin, age 17, moved into their home at 2103 Primate Road in the early 1950s, they were finally going to have a garden to enjoy.

But little did anyone realize that 17-year old Robin's interest in theatre was about to bloom into a career that would take him from the stage at the Clarke Hall in Port Credit to stages around the world such as the Stratford Festival, the Guthrie Theatre in Minneapolis, Pennsylvania's Hedgerow Theatre, New York's Festival Theatre, the Crucible Theatre in the U.K and the Matrix Theatre in Los Angeles. Later in his career he would take his skills to television studios and the silver screens of major motion picture studios. **Robin Gammell** made his mark and continues to do so to this day.

But before Robin went on to an outstanding theatrical career and before John went on to become a Provincial Court Judge, Family Division, living in Applewood was a very exciting era. Just a few years after WW11 Canadians were enjoying this new phenomenon of subdivisions. People were excited about the fact they could purchase a home on larger lots, do landscaping and plantings, fencing and grass seeding or sod laying.

Hugh was a banker, employed by the Bank of Canada. They had lived in Montreal, where their children were born, and later in Ottawa. Hugh had encountered heart problems and was transferred to Toronto, appointed to a posting requiring a little less stress. He was to become the Bank of Canada's financial representative to Toronto's 'Financial Street'. In his position he knew William Pope, a lawyer in Toronto. Mr. Pope had been the Assistant Regional Supervisor for Ontario with the Central Mortgage and Housing Corporation before joining G.S. Shipp and Son as General Manager. It was through his association with Mr. Pope, and also a business associate, a Mr. Lilly, who already had moved into Applewood, that Hugh Gammell became aware of this exciting new subdivision located just west of Toronto.

Because of their father's heart problem, John and Robin spent a great deal of their time landscaping and building around the house. John said that everyone became 'domesticated in a subdivision sort of way'. Robin recalled fondly constructing the culverts out of stones located in the nearby Applewood Creek.

While the family was settling into a new lifestyle, Josephine continued to participate in an artistic interest she had started years earlier. She was accomplished in the art of puppetry and became a member of the Toronto Guild of Puppetry. Jo has 10 puppets in the collection at the Canadian Museum of Civilization in Ottawa. While they are not always on display, they can be seen on request during a visit. The puppets came into play at Halloween every year as the Gammell residence was always a favourite 'haunt' for the neighbourhood children.

Robin attended Port Credit High School as Gordon Graydon was still four years away from its opening. All the students from Applewood had to make the trek to Port Credit High School or to Thomas L. Kennedy, which had just opened. Neither school, however, had anything to offer in the way of theatre for Robin and as he recalled in an interview more than a half-century later, he sought out the Credit Valley Dramatic Society, which presented its productions at the Clarke Hall in Port Credit. His interest in theatre was sparked when he was attending Fisher Park High School in Ottawa. He then joined the Julia Murphy's Theatre, also the Saturday Players. While with the Credit Valley group Robin had lead roles in such productions as *Bell, Book and Candle* and *The Night Must Fall.* Often Robin would be the guest speaker at various gatherings in Applewood to talk about Shakespeare. In November, 1955, he was the guest speaker at the Home and School Association's monthly meeting.

While his family stayed in Applewood until 1956, Robin was soon off to pursue his love for the stage. Robin found himself at the Caravan Theatre in Sarnia, and then he got his big break at Stratford as a 'child' actor. Stratford was about to enter its third season when Robin joined in 1955 and was influenced by Tyrone Guthrie, a well-known British director.

Mr. Guthrie was the first artistic director at Stratford and as such directed the who's who of Canadian theatre. He directed Sir Alex Guiness, who played the title role in *Shakespeare's Richard 111* when Stratford opened on July 13, 1953, along with other greats such as Bruno Gerussi, Robert Goulet, Don Harron, James Mason, Jason Robarts, William Shatner and Christopher Plummer.

Tyrone Guthrie, whose original approach to Shakespearean and modern drama greatly influenced the 20th-century revival of interest in traditional theatre, he was highly regarded in the UK and was knighted in 1961.

It didn't take long for Robin's talents to show. His first speaking role was the Boy in the Langham-Plummer production of *Henry V*. This was one of the few times this role had been played by an under-age actor rather than a younger man. When the Stratford Festival company was invited to perform *Henry V* at the Edinburgh Festival in August 1956, Robin was included.

While in the UK, Robin was awarded the Tyrone Guthrie Scholarship along with fellow actors William Shatner and David Gardner. He studied in London until he returned to Stratford in 1961 to play the lead role in *Romeo and Juliet*. It would be nine more years before Robin would again play Stratford and, this time, he returned as a mature actor, a comedian and leading man. He spent one more season at Stratford in the production *An Italian Straw Hat*.

Like so many talented actors whose acting career has a solid Shakespearean foundation, Robin easily moved into other media. He has played leading roles in more than one dozen movies and guest-starred in more than 60 movies and 35 television major drama series, including well-known TV productions such as *Star Trek, Hill Street Blues, Lou Grant and The Rockford Files*. While on the set of *The Rockford Files* he met a young lady and was soon blessed with a daughter, Winslow Corbett. She has since become an actress in her own right

Robin would often be called on to play the role of a judge. His brother John recalls fondly that Robin got even more press than he ever did in a lawyer's newspaper called *Law Times*. Robin starred in the CBC production *Scales of Justice* and when the *Law Times* reviewed the production for its members, Robin was featured and pictured in a full-page critique.

Robin was nominated in the category *Best Performance by an Actor in a Leading Role* for the 1980 Genie Awards, the first year the awards were presented by the Academy of Canadian Cinema and Television to honour outstanding achievements in the Canadian film industry.

He was nominated for his performance in Jack London's *Klondike Fever*, a story about Jack London's epic journey from San Francisco to the Klondike gold fields in the gold rush of 1898. Robin was edged out for the Genie Award by no less a talent than Christopher Plummer in his performance *Murder by Decree*.

When I spoke with Robin Gammell about his memories of Applewood Acres, it didn't take long for events to spring back to mind. Robin, who at the time of the interview was playing the lead role in the production of *Julius Caesar* at the outdoor festival stage at the Old Globe Theatre in San Diego, California, recalled with obvious great delight living in Applewood. He remembered getting his father's car stuck in the mud of the Applewood Creek and having the farmer (presumably Mr. Death, whose farm was located between Primate Road and Dixie Road) pull the car out. Indicative of the affinity Robin has for the area is the fact that recently, while attending a performance at Stage West on Dixie Road, he made a point to travel south on Dixie. He just had to once again drive past his former Primate Road home.

•CBC Television was still in its infancy when students from Westacres Public School were featured on the 'Dominion- wide' network. According to an article in the Toronto Telegram in 1957.

"Creative activities play a big part in the physical-education program at Westacres School. Encouraged by physical training instructor Douglas Read to think out stunts and various other athletic endeavours for themselves, 20 students have become so adept that they are appearing on CBC-TV Children's Program tomorrow night. It will be seen on the Dominion-wide network.

Without expensive equipment and with only the barest of necessities the students, 10 boys and 10 girls are able to put on a program of an hour's endurance.

English trained and a holder of a three-year certificate in physical education, Mr. Read believes the only way to have children actively participate in sports is to encourage them to "dream up" their own ideas. The program has proven a huge success.

166

Composed of pupils from grade five to eight, the children have been busy practising during the past two weeks to iron out a few wrinkles in their exhibition.

Westacres School is the only school in the greater Toronto area to be selected to put on the sports display. Time of the program is 5.15 p.m. and it is a certain bet every child and teacher of the school will be glued to their television sets to see their fellow classmates perform."

•Television continued to grow and broaden in its presentations and in 1972 **Bob Gibbons**, who was an established staff producer/director in television with the Canadian Broadcasting Corporation (CBC), moved into 1202 Greening Avenue.

By his own admission Bob's best known productions would have to be the popular children's shows, *The Friendly Giant and Mr. Dressup.*

You would be hard pressed to meet anyone who grew up in the era of the 1960's to 1990's who didn't watch the two shows as a youngster. Casey and Finnegan's old pal, Mr. Dressup (the late Ernie Coombs) was saluted in September 2001 on a timely *Life and Times* episode on CBC. Featured in the one-hour special were interviews with many of Ernie's closest TV friends and colleagues. One of them was Fred Rogers (*Mr. Rogers Neighborhood*), who brought Ernie to Canada in 1962.

Ernie Coombs debuted on *Butternut Square* in the 1960's as Mr. Dressup. He was the man with the never-ending supply of costumes. The character was a hit from the start and three years later the CBC gave him his own show.

Ernie Coombs and Mr. Dressup were both a staple of CBC's morning schedule for an amazing 32 years. His final show was February 14, 1996. That same year he was awarded the Order of Canada for his many years of bringing quality programming to Canadian children. He passed away September 18, 2001 at age 73.

The Friendly Giant, played by Bob Homme, was beloved by Canadian children for more than a quarter of a century. In the 15-minute show which ran until 1985, the good-natured giant introduced children to books and music. 'Friendly' played the recorder and clarinet; Rod Coneybeare, of early CBC radio fame, was the voice of both Jerome the Giraffe (who also

167

sang) and Rusty the Rooster (who played the harp with the assistance of John Duncan).

Bob Gibbons said that he never realized at the time just how he was shaping the minds of children. It was an awesome responsibility and he came to realize that many years later.

During his 35-year tenure with CBC he produced numerous other television documentaries and shows, along with many specials such as the Grey Cup Parade and gala productions during the visits by the Royal Family.

In 1980 Bob enlisted the talent of seven children from the Applewood area to play a background role in the television drama documentary "The Donnelly's of the Biddulph". This was the story of Canada's notorious Irish family that was massacred in 1880 in Lucan, Ontario, near London. The movie was shot at Black Creek Pioneer Village.

Another documentary with a little 'local' touch was the true story of Alvin "Creepy" Karpis, 1934 public enemy number one in the United States, who Federal Bureau of Investigation (FBI) Director J. Edgar Hoover said was the leader of the toughest gang of hoodlums (the Ma Barker Gang) the FBI had ever been called upon to eliminate. In fact, Karpis was the only criminal ever arrested personally by Hoover.

Karpis, whose real name was Karpawicz, was born in Montreal in 1907. He ended up one of the first people to be incarcerated at the infamous Alcatraz Island Prison and was also one of the last to leave it just before it closed in 1962. In all he spent just over 26 years in prison.

On his release, Karpis was deported back to Canada where he settled for a short time in Cooksville living above a little pizza shop in a strip plaza on the north side of Dundas Street, west of Hurontario Street.

When Bob Gibbons was making the documentary on Karpis, he invited him to supper at his Greening Avenue home. According to Bob, Karpis was certainly a person he will never forget.

Alvin 'Creepy' Karpis, center, talks to reporters from the Mississauga News. Editor Rob MacCormick, left, Karpis center, and John Rutherford, right, Photo courtesy of John Rutherford and The Mississauga News

Bob met his wife Nancy (Simmons) while filming the show *All About Toronto*. Nancy lived on Primate Road , next to the Gammells. The family purchased their home in 1953 and Nancy was one of the first students to attend Applewood Public School. She also was one of the first to enroll at Allan A. Martin School just before she went on to Gordon Graydon Secondary, where she was chosen one year as Miss Graydon. Nancy pursued her artistic interests and became a drama student at York University. She was part of a group doing drama in parks and outdoor venues. Bob did a production on the group and says that it was then and there he met his 'Cinderella'. They were soon married and in 1972 moved into their home on Greening Avenue.

Nancy managed to continue with her musical interests and, as part of a choral group, The Toronto Concert Singers, Nancy once sang a duet with Sesame Street's Bob McGrath during a special Christmas concert with the Toronto Symphony Orchestra at Massey Hall. Nancy also performed in *The Popcorn Man*, a children's special produced by her husband singing a number of background vocals.

Community residents are blessed with such a talented person who is active in the community. Nancy was a founding member of a musical group which grew out of the choir at St. Luke's Church. Known as "Joy in The Morning", the group has recorded two CD's for which Nancy composed the music and also wrote the lyrics.

•Few people have had the impact that **Michael Burgess** has had in the 1990's in Canadian entertainment. As a young boy, born in Regina, Saskatchewan, Michael spent part of his youth growing up at 2033

Courtland Crescent in Applewood Acres. Michael went on to become a household name in the world of Canadian show business.

Probably best known for his role as Jean Valjean in *Les Miserables*, Michael has performed a variety of roles on stage from Shakespeare to O'Neill and Cole Porter to Stephen Sondheim. He has been dubbed a national treasure by the Toronto Star and a Canadian musical icon by the Calgary Herald. He also starred as Don Quixote in *Man of La Mancha*, and the narrator in *Blood Brothers*, all performed at the Royal Alexandra Theatre in Toronto.

Michael crossed into the arena of recording artist and is accomplished in virtually every entertainment medium: television, film, recording and performance.

On television he has starred in *Friday the 13th*, *Top Cops, Bordertown, ENG, PSI Factor, Earth Conflict,* as well as his own Gemini Award winning television special *Michael Burgess at Massey Hall*. He starred in the feature film *Entry in a Diary* which garnered the Roberto Rosselini Award at the 43rd Film Festival in Salerno, Italy. Michael also had a starring role in *The Original Sin*, directed by Geoff Rayes, which qualified in the short film category for the 1999 Academy Awards, and his was one of the celebrity guest voices in the Famous People Players production of *Leave the Porch Light On.*

His stunning voice, passionate performance and natural charisma have now been captured on a CD release, "A Place in the Sun". He followed with a Christmas album, *Angels in the Snow.*

In February 1999, Michael performed to sold-out audiences with the Calgary Philharmonic at the Jack Singer Concert Hall in Calgary. He also performed in a new production of *Jacques Brel is Alive and Well and Living in Paris,* that toured to Ottawa and Vancouver and to Toronto's Winter Garden Theatre.

Among the perks a Canadian musical icon receives is to open sports events with his rendition of *O Canada.* Michael has sung at the world championships for figure skating, tennis, baseball, basketball, Canadian football, the Molson Indy automobile race, and NHL hockey. He holds the distinction of being the first person to sing Canada's national anthem at a World Series Baseball game in 1992 and again in 1993.

170

Michael began his musical career at St. Michael's Choir School and obviously learned well. In a quick conversation with Michael, he told me he has warm memories of living in Applewood and recalls the fun he had when his father would take him to the Dixie Road overpass and toboggan down the slopes. Like others who have gone on to fame and fortune, Michael still has affection for this area and recently returned to have another look at his childhood home on Courtland Crescent.

•**Jim McNulty** may not have been a Canadian musical icon, but he was certainly very popular with audiences across Canada whenever and wherever he would appear with his Chromatic Button Accordion and his Scottish kilt.

This colourful and talented musician moved to Canada in 1954 and, while he wasn't a full-time professional musician, he certainly kept busy entertaining people at all kinds of events.

When Jim moved into his home on the North Service Road in 1977 he had already become well established having played at Expo 67. Following his Expo 67 appearance he played with such stars as Count Basie, The Four Aces, Joan Fairfax and Juliette. He retired in 1994 after a performance at Toronto's Roy Thomson Hall.

•For three glorious summers area residents lived on the edge of what was at the time billed as Canada's "Broadway". While not exactly situated within the physical boundaries of Applewood Acres, **Music Fair**, Canada's first musical theatre-in-the-round, raised its curtain June 23, 1958 just south of Dixie Plaza on the west side of Dixie Road and north of the golf course.

James Garner, Roddy McDowall, Red Buttons, Dorothy Collins, Eve Arden, Gail Gordon, Hans Conreid and Gretchen Wyler, all Hollywood and Broadway icons, played summer stock in this theatre.

Music Fair, owned and operated by the Buffalo, N.Y. based Melody Fair, opened with considerable fanfare. The media claimed Canada had stepped into the lead with the most lavish and complete musical theatre in the world.

The structure, a circular tent, was engineered for the visual convenience of the 2,000 patrons, with seats surrounding a lowered round stage. Each row of seats were set on a six-inch raised tier.

Toronto dancers and singers were employed for the chorus line as well as apprentice actors. Many youngsters from Applewood Acres were employed as stage-hands or general summer stock workers.

Among the stars featured in its final season were Eve Arden in *Goodbye Charlie*; Hans Conreid in *South Pacific*; Red Buttons in *Teahouse of the August Moon*; Gretchen Wyler in *Redhead*; Roddy McDowall in *Meet Me in St. Louis*; and James Garner in *John Loves Mary*.

Music Fair's first two seasons failed to turn a profit, but despite the successful 1960 season, the owner, Melody Fair, decided to fold its tent and leave.

•Gordon Graydon Secondary School student **Bill McLean** turned a  passion for music into a solid career as a member of a popular Canadian folk/rock music group known as Edward, Harding and McLean.

Originally called Edward and Harding, the group was started in 1968 by Graydon students Bill Harding Candy and Don Edward Owen, both Orchard Heights residents. The duo first performed at Graydon as a folk group and then eventually at other area schools. Meanwhile, Bill McLean was the resident rock musician at Graydon and was carving out his own following.

When Bill Candy graduated in 1970 he decided to take a year off and pursue his music. The folk group, Edward and Harding, had by this time secured a recording contract with Quality Records and was fast becoming established in coffee houses. They would perform two months in the spring and two months in the fall. In all, the duo performed as a group for three years.

In 1973 they asked Bill McLean to join them. They were playing coffee houses in the United States and felt that they could bring their talents to a more upscale market if they changed from a folk format to a 'swing' style of music. The trio, Edward, Harding and McLean, was born.

Many nights and afternoon rehearsals were held in the little room in the rear of St. Luke's Anglican Church where Bill Candy's father was the minister and at the McLean house on Melton Drive.

The first swing vocal they performed was the *Boogie Woogie Bugle Boy of Company B,* written in 1941 by Don Raye and Hughie Prince and popularized by The Andrew Sisters. The song was nominated for Best Song in the 1941 Academy Awards. This song characterized their singing style and the trio was on its way to becoming a very successful Canadian swing group during the 1970's and 1980's. In all they recorded four 'vinyl' recordings during their career.

Appearances on radio and television followed as did a CBC Radio recording *Now and Then* which featured songs such as Mack the Knife and Java Jive. The group would hire additional musicians as needed for various performances. They were a favourite among many radio and TV producers as they built a reputation on being able to do their performance in 'one take'.

They were featured by many of the top CBC program hosts, including numerous appearances on the *Bob McLean Show*, a lunch-time network magazine program and also as regulars with radio personality Peter Gzowski. Soon the group found themselves hosting their own 13 part musical series on CBC known as *Whose New.* They would introduce new talent from across the country.

The trio went their separate ways in the 1990's but Bill Candy recorded two CD's. The first, in 1995, *Closer to the Music* and in 2002 *Common Ground.*

•It's amazing how professional an amateur can be when they are driven by passion. **Margaret McCuaig** is quick to point out how lucky she is that she has a hobby that is a passion. As a base singer with the North Metro Chapter of the Sweet Adelines, a 175-member four-part harmony group who sings a cappella, Margaret has taken her hobby to international heights and recognition.

A resident of 2143 Russett Road since 1967, she first became involved in this style of music when she joined the Mississauga Chorus in 1979. In 1983 she became a member of The Sweet Adelines who sing in competitions.

The Sweet Adelines International is a highly respected worldwide organization of women singers committed to advancing the musical art form of barbershop harmony. The international membership exceeds 30,000 women in chapters across North America as well as in Australia, England, Finland, Germany, Japan, New Zealand, Scotland, Sweden and The Netherlands. There are more than 1,200 registered quartets and 600 choruses.

During Margaret's years with the group the Chapter has won every one of its regional competitions and capped that off with three International Championships. The group injects dancing into its presentation and does its own choreography.

After winning the Regional title in 1996 in Syracuse, N.Y. the group set out for Ft. Lauderdale, Florida in October and, in a convincing style the chorus took top honours to win the gold medal.

Like many other international champion choruses, North Metro visited the international stage many times before earning a gold medal. In fact, it was on its 10th attempt, at the 1996 international contest, that North Metro presented a performance package that was said to have changed the face of barbershop contest performances forever.

Thanks to the creativity of Director June Dale, who has been the North Metro Master Director for more than 25 years, the group became the first chorus from outside the United States to win the international chorus competition since its inception in 1973.

North Metro Chapter began in 1967 and has grown from a modest 17 members to an astounding 182 members. The chorus has been eligible to compete at the international level 10 times and has placed in the top 10 nine of those times.

Rules for these competitions do not allow gold medal winners to defend their title the following year, but do permit the World Championship winners to be the headline entertainment at the next year's competitions. The group traveled to Salt Lake City, Utah in 1997 to headline the show there. Unfortunately the group did not get a chance to sing with the Mormon Tabernacle Choir, which at one point was going to happen.

They gained success again in 1999 as they were back in Syracuse, N.Y. to win their regional event and then on to Atlanta, Georgia to capture their second gold medal.

In 2002 the group repeated with a regional victory and gold again, this time in Nashville, Tennessee to become the 2003 championship winners. North Metro beat out groups from Ohio, Arizona, California, Washington, Colorado, Sweden, Georgia, Oklahoma and Texas. For the Nashville competition North Metro placed 175 singers on stage and won singing 'Gold Minin' Gang' and 'All of My Life'.

Involvement in the Sweet Adeline Chorus by Applewood Acres residents actually dates back to 1956. In April of that year, Mrs. **Mary Boddington** and her daughter **Patricia**, competed in a Sweet Adeline Regional Competition held in Detroit: and placed second. The following year they again traveled to Detroit, this time they took top honours. The Boddingtons, who lived at 943 North Service Road, owned and operated one of Toronto's best known music and publishing stores. It was not unusual for Fred and Mary to host the Sweet Adelines at their summer cottage at Morrison Lake in the Muskokas. Both Boddingtons held executive positions with music groups, Fred with the Toronto Barbershoppers and Mary with the Sweet Adelines.

•While not yet on the international stage, it may not be too long before a marquee boasts the name of **Mike Ferguson**. Born in 1966, Mike grew up with two brothers and two sisters at 1008 Hedge Drive. His father and mother, John and Bonny Ferguson, moved into Applewood in 1968. Mike attended Westacres Public School, Allan A. Martin Senior Public and then Gordon Graydon Secondary School. He began singing in the late 1990s and, in a short period of time, started to receive voice training from Kristina Marie Guiget, a principal vocalist with the Toronto cast of *The Phantom of the Opera* in 1995, 96 and 97. Mike was offered a position with the Mississauga Opera but declined as he felt he didn't have enough time to learn the score. He did, however, accept invitations to sing the National Anthem for the Mississauga Ice Dog hockey games, and an international Polo Tournament. He also has signed to sing at a Toronto Blue Jay baseball game as well as a Toronto Raptor basketball game.

•No other Canadian orchestra enjoyed greater exposure than did Mart Kenney's Western Gentlemen. In addition to their dance engagements, the distinctive sounds of their music were broadcast from coast to coast into every Canadian home through the magic of radio. 'Sweet and Low', a phrase that became the identifiable name of Mart Kenney, could almost describe the natural voice of one of his singers, **Lea James**. Lea (Leona) married James Laverty, who was active in sports. (I write about James in chapter 14).

Lea and James Laverty lived at 1163 Greening Avenue, having purchased their home in 1952. At the time Lea had pretty much set her professional singing career aside to concentrate on raising a growing family and attending the new social activities people in Applewood were thrust into in those very early years.

Kenney, who is well into his 90's, is still blowing his horn, big band style. His latest CD, Celebration 2000, a swinging musical showcase, was released in the year 2000. His music has been heard over five generations, but it was in the 1950's that he became a household name and it was at about that time that Lea was at the peak of her career as a singer. Lea sang popular songs. She had absolutely no formal training and, at this writing at age 82, she says she can still sing as beautifully as she ever did. A 'natural' singing voice lasts much longer than a 'trained' voice she will quickly tell you. Lea sang with Kenney in special events. When the big band would play at the King Edward and Royal York Hotels in Toronto, Lea would be there with Mart Kenney.

She actually started her singing career with the Norm Harris Band in Hamilton, Ontario and during WW II, Lea found herself singing with the United Services Board (USO) while in British Columbia. The USO was formed in 1941 when U.S. President Frankin D. Roosevelt determined it would be best for private organizations to handle the on-leave recreation of the armed forces. The USO was formed by six groups, the YMCA, YWCA, Salvation Army, National Catholic Community Services, National Travelers Aid Association and the National Jewish Welfare Board.

After WW II ended, Lea returned to the Toronto area where she began singing with Kenney and at many other special events including stints with local bands for performances at Centre Island. She was the pre-game singer at Maple Leaf Gardens and when she decided to slow down in the early 1950's, she was replaced at the Gardens by a young rising star from the west by the name of 'Juliette'. Few performers achieve such stature that they are known by a first name only. But Juliette arrived in Toronto in 1954 and by 1956 she had her own television show, which became a staple of Saturday night broadcasting from coast to coast. At this point Lea was well into a settled lifestyle here in Applewood and on her husband's urging she joined with a number of others at Applewood United Church as part of the Applewood Church Choir.

●Actress **Lisa Jakub** began her career at age seven with a small role in the 1985 film adaptation of Nicholas Gage's dramatic autobiography *Eleni*. Lisa was born in Toronto on December 27, 1978. While living in Applewood Acres at 2139 Courtland Crescent she attended Westacres and Kenollie Public Schools in the 'mode 3' program for gifted students. She launched her career in *Eleni* playing Katis' granddaughter. This was followed by roles in such movies as *Rambling Rose* and *Matinee*. Lisa then played Lydia Hilliard in *Mrs. Doubtfire* starring Robin Williams and Sally Field. She then acted in numerous other movies including *The Beautician and The Beast*, *Painted Angels*, *A Walk On The Moon* and *George Lucas In Love*. She also played Alicia in *Independence Day* starring Will Smith. Lisa also has considerable television exposure -*Night Court* which starred John Larroquette and *ER* which starred Anthony Edwards, as well as a role in the NBC television movie *Blue Heaven* where she played Ally Withrop. In all, by the year 2000, Lisa has played in 27 feature films and made-for-TV movies.

•**Don Borisenko** lived at 2193 Rambo Road with his parents, three brothers and three sisters. Nicholas and Dena Borisenko purchased their home from Peter Langer in 1959. (I write about Peter in Chapter 13). Don had an interest in the arts and had just started to take part in the Long Branch Little Theatre group. When his girl friend, who worked for a talent agency in Toronto, informed him that there was an 'Open Call' for actors to apply for parts in Canada's first all-Canadian feature film, he was on his way.

Having just been hired as a Fuller Brush Man and after one week of work, and feeling down in the dumps, the Open Call was just what the doctor ordered. Despite the more than 300 people in the waiting area, Don was not daunted. He was so enthusiastic about being there, that when it came time for him to be interviewed, all he could do was tell one fabrication after another about his acting experience. Eventually he was caught up in his elaborations. The director smiled and said that he had the job. After all, anyone who could live that fantasy so convincingly was perfect for the part. The director told him to walk out and tell those in the waiting room that the lead had been cast for what was Canada's first all-Canadian feature movie, *Now That April's Here*. Years later that movie became the centerpiece of the Toronto International Film Festival. The film was based on four short stories by Morley Callaghan and was introduced and narrated by Raymond Massey.

Don's career moved along rapidly, with one movie a year for the next seven years. His second movie was *Ivy League Killers* (a.k.a. *The Fast Ones*) and his third was *The Last Gunfighter* (a.k.a. *Hired Gun* and also *Devil's Spawn*), both Canadian productions. The director for *The Last Gunfighter* was Sidney J. Furie, an accomplished writer, director and producer, who had left for England to write *During One Night*. He had been so impressed with Don's ability he wrote this movie with Don in mind. After the movie was completed Don remained in the U.K. to perform in a number of BBC 90-minute live television productions and it was there that he was 'discovered' by Hollywood. He was signed by 20th Century Fox and he was off to India to co-star in the film *Nine Hours to Rama*. The story was about the nine hours in the life of Naturam Godse leading up to the assassination of Mahatma Gandhi. The film starred Horst Buchholz, Jose Ferrer, Robert Morely, Valerie Gearon and Don Borisenko.

Don Borisenko played Jebai in the 1965 *Genghis Khan* movie with such stars as Omar Sharif, James Mason, Eli Wallach, Telly Savalas and Robert Morely. Photo courtesy of the Borisenko family album.

By 1965 Don found himself in the company of Omar Sharif, James Mason, Eli Wallach and Telly Savalas in the movie *Genghis Khan*. It was during this period of his life that he was being pressured to change his acting name to something 'easier' and after his 1966 movie *The Psychopath*, he caved in to the idea and Donald Borisenko became Jonas Wolfe.

As Jonas Wolfe, he did two more movies, the first in 1972 with Martin Landau, *Black Gunn* and his final movie, *The Laughing Policeman in 1973* with Walter Mathau and Cathy Lee Crosby.

It was time to change direction in life and he opened Boomers, a rock and roll night club in Venice, California. Before they became world-famous headline groups, Van Halen, Canned Heat and the popular all-girl group

Runaways, appeared on a regular basis over the two years that Jonas owned and operated Boomers.

Another change in career direction to fulfill a lifelong artistic desire followed. This change resulted from a very tragic accident that happened before Jonas started his acting career. When he was just 16, and driving a dump truck for a living, a renown artist-illustrator had driven his car into the path of his dump truck. It was learned later that the artist was depressed and had actually committed suicide. This incident left Jonas with a need to bring out his own artistic abilities. Always artistic, he now felt the need to concentrate strictly on art. He lives today in Oregon where he works with unusual art media, more along the lines of Japanese Zen art. Although most Zen art focuses on nature, the art is not limited to any specific mediums. The introduction of nature, irregular patterns and tones, and unpredictable topics has made Zen art one of the most easily identified and revered existing art forms. He admits quickly that he is always on 'the edge', always experimenting. Surrounded by family, Aaron, a son from his first marriage, is a water biologist for the State of Oregon and lives nearby while Rebecca and Joshua, children of his second marriage, also live nearby. All the children are very artistic.

•**Robert Aitken** C.M., M.Mus. is one of three people who have lived in Applewood Acres and who have been made Members of the Order of Canada. Robert was appointed October 27, 1993. His investiture was held October 19, 1994. Robert, a renowned flutist, composer and conductor is a highly sought after teacher. He is one of the original Westacres residents having moved here as a teenager with his parents Herbert and Hannah, in 1954.

Herbert and Hannah Aitken didn't know what they were getting into the night they were due to arrive at their new home in Westacres. That was the evening of October 15, 1954. They had driven to Toronto from Nova Scotia, and with no radio in their car, they had no idea that Hurricane Hazel had beat them to it. They got as far as the Humber River and were turned back. Fortunately, they had relatives in Toronto to stay with. Three days later the Aitkens and their children, 16 year old Robert and 12 year old Linda, took up residence in their new home at 861 Melton Drive. Robert was enrolled at T.L. Kennedy Secondary School. He became very involved with area scouting and became a Queen's Scout. In 1956 Robert won the solo amateur and professional class at the Kiwanis Music Festival with a 92, the highest score of the day. With the victory he was given the Loblaws Grocerteria Wind Instrument Scholarship.

Robert was born in Kentville, Nova Scotia in 1939 and, by the time his family had settled here in Applewood Acres, he had developed into such an outstanding musical talent that, by age 19, he became the youngest principal flute in the history of the Vancouver Symphony and at the same time studied composition. He left the orchestra the following year to continue his composition studies and also electronic music. Two years later he received his Bachelor of Music Degree at the University of Toronto.

Sharing a rare moment together at his niece's wedding. Robert Aitken, second on right, between his sister Linda (Aitken) Johnston, right, and his wife Marion,. at left Gordon Johnston. Photo courtesy of the Johnston family.

He continued with post graduate studies and during that period became a member of the CBC Symphony performing under such noted conductors as Karl Bohm, Hermann Scherchen, Hector Villa-Lobos and Igor Stravinsky. In 1964, a Canada Council grant enabled Robert to study in Europe. At age 25 he returned to Toronto as co-principal flute of the Toronto Symphony Orchestra. Conductor Seiji Ozawa selected his *Concerto for 12 Soloists and Orchestra* for performance on the main subscription series. Robert left the Toronto Symphony Orchestra in 1970 to devote himself to composing as well as to developing a solo career. He was the founder/director of the Music Today Festival at Niagara-on-the-Lake (1970-1972) and in 1971 he joined composer Norma Beecroft to co-found the New Music Concerts in Toronto. He taught from 1960 to 1975 at the University of Toronto and 1972 to 1982 at the Shawnigan Summer School of the Arts in British Columbia. In 1981 he founded Music at Shawnigan, a three week festival devoted to advanced chamber music study. From 1986 to 1989 he was the artistic director of the Advanced Studies in Music Program at the Banff Centre. He then accepted the position of Professor of Flute at the Staatliche Hochschule fur Musik (University of Music and Performing Arts) in Freiburg im Breisgau, Germany.

While the Order of Canada is without doubt a most prestigious award, Robert has been the recipient of numerous awards throughout his colourful career. He received the Canada Music Citation, the Wm. Harold Moon Award, the Canadian Music Medal, the Jean A. Chalmers National Music Award and the Chevalier de l'ordre des Arts et des Lettres (France). His most recent award came in Las Vegas when he was presented with the 2003 National Flute Association Lifetime Achievement Award. The Governor General, The Right Honourable John Hnatyshyn's comments about Robert Aitken may express it best, "This internationally acclaimed flutist has brought music of every idiom, baroque, classical, modern, and experimental, to a wide audience. His virtuosity as a performer, conductor, and teacher, has had a great impact on the Canadian music scene."

•Applewood Acres residents can boast having many outstanding journalists living in their midst over the years. Without a doubt the greatest of them all was **Peter C. Newman**. He only lived in Applewood a short while, a little more than one year. He purchased his home at 825 Melton Drive in 1954 and, in late 1955, he moved to Ottawa to take up duties as editor of MacLean's Magazine.

Peter Charles Newman was born in Vienna, Austria, on May 10, 1929. He arrived in Canada as a refugee in 1940. Eve Spafford, who resided at 2182 Wedgewood Drive, was one of many scribes over the years to write the Community Activities column for the Port Credit Weekly. She reported in the December 3, 1959 issue that Peter had just released his first book, *Flame of Power*, and in her column she wrote the following:

"Mr. Newman speaks and thinks in four languages and has lived in six countries," she wrote. *"He grew up in Czechoslovakia, where his father's*

beet sugar refinery holdings ranked his family among Central Europe's pre-war business dynasties. Following Hitler's invasion, his family spent 18 months dodging Nazi troops and agents, finally escaping to England in a small boat from Bordeaux. After arriving in this country in the 1940s he attended Upper Canada College and later the University of Toronto and McGill. He has worked underground as a gold miner, been a department store magician, and served as a Lieutenant in the Royal Canadian Navy."

His journalism career has continued with amazing energies and in the course of five decades, he has authored 20 books which boast sales in excess of two million copies.

He is the recipient of five honorary doctorates. He was awarded a Lifetime Achievement Award by the Canadian Journalism Foundation (1998), elected to the Canadian News Hall of Fame (1992), awarded the Book of the Year Award (1987), National Business Writing Award (1986), Best Television Program of The Year, ACTRA Award (1981), Quill Award, Journalist of The Year (1977), President's Medal, University of Western Ontario (1974), Michener Award for CBC TV Series, The Tenth Decade (1971), CBC's Wilderness Award for Best Television Documentary (1967), and the National Newspaper Award for Feature Writing (1966).

Mr. Newman was recognized for his notable contribution in the field of journalism on April 25, 1979 when the Right Honourable Edward Schreyer made him an Officer of the Order of Canada. He was promoted to Companion on October 24, 1990 by the Right Honourable Ray Hnatyshyn. Although Mr. Newman was an Officer, his title returns to the Chancellery of Honours with his Investiture as a Companion of the Order of Canada, which takes precedence.

Coincidently, Peter C. Newman lived just four doors down the road from the Aitken family, who in turn lived across the road from the Archibald's. Rare indeed to think three people living so close to one another would one day be recipients of the Order of Canada.

183

17 The Queensway

Like water, development often takes the route of least resistance and if the truth be known, the location of The Queensway is probably an excellent example.

It has been said that the route of The Queensway out of Toronto was originally going to align with Melton Drive. According to Dorothy Clarke, at 2240 Dixie Road, discussions took place about the purchase of their house, which aligns with Melton Drive. But as time went on, more development started to take place just south of the hydro right-of-way, east of Dixie Road in Sherway, and also, in 1972, Edrich Construction built along Melton east of Stanfield Road. The cost to the plan to use Melton as The Queensway would not have been practical.

According to Sheldon Nablo, an Applewood Acres resident who was employed by Toronto Township Hydro, the utility had earlier acquired property on Stanfield Road for its Greening Sub Station, which effectively put a nail on the lid of the plan to connect Melton Drive with the Queensway out of Toronto. This property was actually blocking any suggested alignment. To this day that property remains without its intended station on site.

The Queensway finally found its home under the high-tension wires of the massive hydro towers and instantly became a major corridor for traffic in and out of Mississauga and Toronto.

According to the minutes of the Annual General Meeting of the North Applewood Homeowners' Association, held March 18, 1975, the then member of Council Ron Searle, spoke briefly on the plans for the extension of The Queensway and the need for some form of sound abatement measures. Councillor Searle spoke in favour of using 'berms'. Regardless of what form of sound abatement was selected, the Association voted to support the plans for the extension of The Queensway.

A meeting, sponsored by The Region of Peel, was held at Applewood Public School on June 3, 1975. Only those living along Melton Drive were invited and about 55 people attended. Concern was expressed that there was no provision for sound abatement measures or a fence, and secondly, that Haines Road (later changed to Cody Lane) would be open to The

184

Queensway from both sides. Residents demanded that some form of sound abatement be undertaken and that also Haines be closed to Melton Drive. The residents learned at that meeting that The Queensway was planned to begin in August 1975 and to be completed within one year. A petition was then drawn up and sent to Council. Also, it was agreed that a newsletter would be prepared and delivered to the community.

Later that same evening, a homeowner representative, Arnold Tremere, of 2252 Haltrye Court, who had held the position the year before as President of the North Applewood Homeowners' Association, raised these issues to Councillor Searle at an Official Plan meeting held at Cawthra Park School.

At the October 22, 1975 meeting of the Homeowners' Association, a very interesting development took place. It was learned that a group of residents west of Highway 10 were forming in opposition to The Queensway. A motion was passed that the Association agree to support other homeowner groups west of Cawthra to stop The Queensway from going any further than Cawthra Road.

When The Queensway did open, Haines Road was closed and a solid concrete sound barrier was constructed to the western limits of Applewood North Park. Haines Road was legally closed by way of the proper municipal instruments at City Hall but it was never completely taken up out of the ground. To this day asphalt remains under a layer of top soil there. The southern tip of that road which leads onto Melton Drive was renamed Cody Lane.

It wasn't until 1977 that more homes adjacent to the hydro right-of-way would be built by Cape Developments. Eight years later, The Queensway opened from Cawthra Road to Hurontario (Hwy. 10).

Applewood Acres residents had every right to be concerned about the impact The Queensway would have not only in terms of noise levels but also in traffic flows throughout this very quiet community.

According to the City of Mississauga's 2002 Employment Survey, Mississauga saw its employment increase 193 percent, from 132,000 in 1977 to 387,000. Population kept pace increasing from 250,000 in 1976 to 628,250 in 2002, an increase of 151 percent. The Queensway handles its share of the traffic generated by the work force and population.

The Apple Press headline in its Summer 1995 issue reads " A Nightmare On Annapolis Drive," but in fact it was more of a nightmare for residents along Annapolis, Whitney, Breezy Brae, Johnathan, Candish Lane, Melton and Stanfield Road.

It was a long dusty and noisy summer in Westacres thanks to a project known as the Hanlan Feedermain.

This massive project called for the installation of a new, high pressure, seven-foot diameter (2.1 meter) water main running from the Lakeview Water Treatment Plant to service new developments in the City of Mississauga, Brampton and Caledon up to the year 2031. The contract administrator and consultant for the construction of the feedermain were Ontario Clean Water Agency (OCWA) and KMK Construction respectively.

On May 16,1995 contract No. 3, Project Number 5-0020-53 sprang to life and the residents of Applewood Acres endured a summer long construction project of massive proportions.

The feedermain starts at the Lakeview Water Treatment Plant and runs northward entering Applewood Acres at The North Service Road and Annapolis Road. From there it continues north to Whitney Drive, east to Breezy Brae and then north to Johnathan Drive. It then swings north along Candish Lane and then east on Melton Drive to Stanfield Road and continues north from there.

As you drive along the route in Applewood Acres you will notice that a number of homes have boulders on the front lawns. These boulders were removed during the excavation and offered to the residents.

The total cost of the project exceeded $32 million and required some fascinating construction techniques. As an example, when the water main route crossed the QEW the contractors had to use hard-rock tunnel boring equipment and actually tunneled under the highway at a depth of 95 feet (28.9 metres). Once across the highway, the water main enters Applewood at a depth of 20 feet (6 metres). The depth under the roads in Applewood would vary between 10 feet and 20 feet (3 to 6 metres) depending on what utilities had to be accommodated.

The Stanfield Road portion, north from Melton and under The Queensway, was tunneled at a depth of 65 feet (19.8 metres).

The contract was awarded on May 16, 1995 and work started on June 7th with a scheduled completion date of December 15th. The actual date of what they called 'substantial performance' was November 21, 1995. The final reinstatement of the roads with asphalt was July 31, 1996. The final certificate for the project was issued September 29, 1997.

This project was, without a doubt, the largest single works project ever undertaken through Applewood Acres. While there have been several works projects done over the years, some of which seemed to drag on and on endlessly, this one was the most spectacular and probably will never be topped.

The impact of this project was not limited to the roads on which the construction was taking place. As you can imagine, an excavation of this size did from time to time close off other roads in the area.

The Hanlan Feedermain was originally owned by the Ontario Clean Water Agency but was downloaded to the Regional Municipality of Peel in 1998 by the Ministry of Environment (MOE).

People have wondered why the water main couldn't have taken a route along Cawthra Road north. The water main route actually had a great deal of open space south of the QEW with little or no disruption for the area residents. A Cawthra Road route could have had a major traffic impact causing massive disruption to surrounding industry not to mention commuters. As it was, when the route passed through Applewood Acres, particularly on Breezy Brae, the project proved to be difficult for many of the homeowners and tempers among the residents, municipality and contractors were often heated.

To illustrate just how massive in size these water pipes are, Breezy Brae Drive resident Jean Grassie took these photographs. These pipes were on the lawn of the Broderick home at the southwest corner of Breezy Brae and Whitney Drive and were there for about a week before being laid in place. Below the pipes were being delivered by large trucks.

•**Jack Goddard** was one of three rhubarb growers in what we know as Applewood Acres. The Leaverleigh Farms (Leaver's) and a small market gardener Frank Verbonham were the others. Mr. Verbonham, who owned property in the area east of Stanfield, had a small operation and sold roots for twenty-five cents. He grew Sutton Seedless, which has a large green stalk with broad pink petioles. Leaverleigh Farms, in contrast, was a larger market garden farm operation.

Evenutally mushrooms would replace rhubarb as the crop of choice. Around 1939 Goddard Farms switched and operated four mushroom houses each with 7,000 square feet (650 square metres). The houses would be five beds high. Because mushrooms would not grow in hot conditions, The ideal growing temperature is 60 degrees F (15.5 degrees C), only two crops would be grown each year.

According to Jack Goddard, there was always a market and if a grower could produce three crops it would sell with no problem. But as it was, growing two and a half pounds to the foot (1.13 kg to 0.3 m) was about the best to be expected. Air conditioning would allow this figure to triple and of course, that's where larger firms such as Leaver's would produce such yields.

Mushroom growing is labour intensive and the Goddard farm employed four families. All that was needed to go to work was a small knife to tend to the mushrooms every day.

In the early days mushrooms would be grown largely by greenhouse growers. They would grow the mushrooms under their plants in greenhouses. About one in 10 would have a successful crop.

It wasn't until the pure culture spawn from Pennsylvania came into the marketplace that the success rate became sufficiently profitable for growers to concentrate on mushrooms as a main crop.

Goddard Farms sold wholesale mainly to Lester's in Toronto and to Agro Brothers from Hamilton. The surplus would be taken by Campbell Soups. The Goddard operation marketed mushrooms for 25 years and ended their operation when The Queensway went through in 1974.

It was a tough business with crop failures running as much as 90 per cent and, according to Jack Goddard, it was very much a hit and miss type of business. So to have marketed successfully for 25 years was quite a feat.

• "Avon calling"…. that familiar greeting can be traced back to the earliest of days in Applewood thanks to the entrepreneurship of **Dora Inns**, Applewood Acres' first Avon Lady. Dora moved to her Hedge Road house in November 1953 and on her doctor's orders, had to take up an activity that would get her out of the house for something to do.

"Applewood was a lonely place in those days. There were no telephones, and my husband was away all day at work. People were just lonely," she would say in an interview 50 years later. After a successful 13 year career Dora gave her Avon assignment to Harcourt Road resident Donna Cooper who held it for a year before a short break when her first child was born. Less than a year later Donna started back again and has been the Avon Lady ever since.

•Harcourt Crescent resident **Ken Rowe** served as the Town of Mississauga's Industrial Commissioner from 1967 through 1973, just prior to the establishment of the City of Mississauga and Region of Peel. Mr. Rowe came to the post with seven years background as a member of the Planning Board of the Toronto Township.

When he was hired by the municipality he was responsible for the task of convincing industry to locate in this growing community-a hard task in those days as anything west of Etobicoke was considered by Torontonians as the 'country'.

Mr. Rowe realized that he could reach his target audience with an intensive advertising campaign on CFRB Radio. He developed a $9,000 advertising program with ads being aired during prime time. CFRB was the most popular radio station among the decision-makers of the day. The ads would be aired three days each week and every second ad was different. Some of the old-timers in the City will remember Ken as the architect of the concept of placing obnoxious industry in an area by itself, away from other less offensive business operations. That planning principal has served this city well over the years.

•That beautiful 'canopy' of maple trees along Johnathan Drive was not planted as a condition of approval for the 1960 Plan of Subdivision by Lawsmith Holdings when that part of Applewood was developed, but rather was the work of **Jim Dalipes**.

Mr. Dalipes, who owned a florist business and lived on Johnathan Drive, decided to involve his neighbours in a project that has and will continue to live for years to come. In 1967 he convinced everyone on the street to donate $5 toward a fund to purchase maple trees. In all, there are more than 30 trees now standing soaring above the roof lines of the homes. This provides a beautiful canopy effect giving shade in the summer and, of course, when in full bloom, affording the area brilliant foliage.

•Four people have been memorialized with plaques placed on the grounds at Westacres Public School and adjacent Westacres Park.

A plaque, located at the base of a tree near the playground equipment, is in memory of Westfield Drive resident **Deborah Delo**, a young mother who, while standing on a sidewalk waiting to cross the street, became a victim of a traffic accident and tragically lost her life. Deborah was a mother at Westacres Public School and also active at the Applewood Co-Operative Preschool, which operates at the Applewood United Church. Deborah's preschool colleagues placed the plaque which reads "In Memory of Deborah Delo, 1952-1990. Applewood Co-Operative Preschool". A memorial fund has been established in Deborah's name to benefit families who come to the school who may have some financial concerns.

The second plaque was placed at the tree just at the end of the garden section off Breezy Brae at the north-west end of the park. The plaque reads "In Memory of **Ted Vanderstarren**, March 1994. Remembered by his colleagues at the City of Mississauga Parks Department". Ted, who died of a heart attack at age 57, was the horticulturist responsible for Westacres Park. He was instrumental in the design and development of the park's floral garden and spent 14 years with the department at this location.

The third plaque is to remember the passing of **Mrs. Moxam**, a teacher at Westacres Public School. The school staff and students dedicated a tree in her memory and a framed picture taken to mark the ceremony hangs in the hall outside of the school office. The story with the photo is titled, "A Tree for Mrs. Moxam," and reads as follows:

"After the untimely and unexpected passing of our friend and teacher Mrs. Moxam, we thought long and hard about a fitting tribute to the memory of one who was so much a part of the life at Westacres School. After much deliberation, staff decided that a tree would enrich the life of our school with the longevity that will only be surpassed by the special memories we all have of Mrs Moxam.

The tree is symbolic of a strength, deep-rooted and unyielding in the face of trials and storms. Mrs. Moxam spent her lifetime in the defence and support of children's needs, large and small.

A tree offers shelter and enjoyment in the beauty of its changing colours, especially at this time of year. Mrs. Moxam always looked out for us, staff and students alike, with a smile of encouragement, or a joke and hearty laughter when we most needed it. Her beauty was deep rooted from within, in her care and concern for others. All of us who had the privilege to know Mrs. Moxam professionally or personally, carry memories of a very special woman, who loved and laughed, and gave of herself tirelessly to the needs of others.

May this tree continue to kindle day to day remembrances of her strength and beauty, her caring and generous sharing of her many gifts, her steadfast commitment both professionally and personally to students, parents, staff, friends and family. We dedicate this tree to her honour and memory with our love and thanks for her life."

The fourth plaque has been placed for **John William Lawrence** who was sadly killed in an automobile accident. John, a young teacher, was in Japan teaching English as a Second Language at the time of his death. John's family, Fred and Joan Lawrence placed a plaque at the foot of a tree which reads "In Memory of John William Lawrence, Lovingly Remembered by Your Family, November 14, 2000." A memorial service was held at Applewood United Church on November 24, 2000 and conducted by The Reverend Ron Hunt. To celebrate the life of John Lawrence, a new 'Vail' bed was donated to the Trillium Hospital's Neurology Unit. Funding came from the friends and family, both in Canada and Japan. John's mother, Joan, works at Trillium's Peel Infant Development and she wanted to use the funds collected in her son's memory in a way that would benefit future patients. The bed allows patients who are restless or in danger of harm from a fall to be cared for without the use of restraints.

•Road names have origins and usually people can figure out why a particular road is given its name. However, the name Bloomfield Road remains a mystery. The name Bloomfield Road does, however, show up on maps predating the establishment of Applewood Acres and the name Bloomfield Road was placed in brackets on the Plan of Subdivision 439, which was Applewood's first registered plan. It also was the address shown on the Dedication and Opening Services calendar for Applewood United Church dated March 17, 1957.

Many people interviewed during my research had little or no knowledge of the origins of the name Bloomfield. Probably the best answer given was that it was a suitable name for the area given the beautiful blooms of apple blossoms that blanketed the community. When **Jack and Marian Bloomfield** arrived in Applewood Acres and purchased their home north of Applewood United Church in late 1957, some automatically thought the road was named after them. That certainly was the case when a young Ed Woodland started to court his future wife Eileen Bloomfield. According to daughter Cindy, who still lives in the house today, her father thought the object of his affection may have come from a prominent area family.

•In the five or so years leading up to the 50th anniversary of Applewood as a community, the Applewood Acres Homeowners' Association has sponsored Community Spirit Awards to recognize those who either decorate their homes at festive times of the year, or in the summer show the Canadian flag, wear Applewood 'T' shirts or hats.

Possibly the first ever award, however, can be traced back to December 1956 when the Port Credit Weekly Newspaper reported that it was an impossible task to select the "best" outdoor display in the Applewood district.

Homeowners there had put on a grand display. **Mr. And Mrs. George Southwell,** 1277 Harvest Drive, were singled out by the newspaper. A picture showing their decorative home was published.

•One of Mississauga's most prolific builders, **Iggy Kaneff**, actually got his start in Applewood Acres, as a "hammer and saw man". According to Harold Shipp, Iggy arrived from Hungary and applied for a job as a labourer.

"He didn't have any tools at all with him, so he was given a hammer and saw and his job was to put down sub floors. He worked for us for about two and a half years," said Harold Shipp.

• The Westacres area of Applewood was one of the very first subdivisions in the country that featured buried distribution cables for hydro and Bell Telephone. The distribution cables were buried along the street and then were fed to the backyard utility poles for service to the individual homes. Russett Road resident Bill Bowyer said he made a lot of overtime money when he worked for Bell Telephone. "When Westacres residents first purchased their homes and started to erect fences along their lot lines, it was a weekend ritual for the Bell and Hydro crews to make weekend calls to repair cut cables." With the new concepts for delivering the service came a totally new way of using the telephones. The era ushered in the 'telephone exchange' with catchy names and a 'dial' service. The numbering for phones, as an example, went from the rural listings such as 65R13 to AT9-1983 (the AT stood for Atwater). The Atwater exchange went into service on February 1, 1954. Other area exchanges included CR-8 for Crescent, which went into service in May, 1952. Then years later the exchanges gave way to all numeric listings such as 905-277-1893. The 1951 Toronto Suburban West telephone book listed 124,000 names and numbers and covered the areas of Bronte, Clarkson, Cooksville, Port Credit and Streetsville. Long distance rates applied for calls between Port Credit and Oakville (10-cents for anyone calls to 20-cents for person to person calls).

Wood wall phone. To place a call you would lift the receiver, wind the handle on the side of the box to 'ring' the operator, and then ask her to connect you. Of course, there were up to a dozen or so people sharing your party line.

•While the Bell cables were buried providing an aesthetic landscape, almost overnight television antennae sprouted atop the rooflines of the houses. On September 8, 1952 CBLT Toronto started its broadcasting service and the Applewood Acres area was in the heart of television country. A smattering of American channels were received but basically the Canadian Broadcasting Corporation had a monopoly on television. CHCH Television in Hamilton went on air in June of 1954 as a CBC affiliate. Years later, in 1961, CFTO Channel Nine in Toronto became the first privately licensed television operation in this area. It was only a few years earlier, June 3, 1947 to be exact, that Canadian General Electric engineers in Windsor, Ontario, received the first official electronic television broadcast in Canada. The signal was transmitted from the new US station WWDT in Detroit. One year later television manufacturing began in Canada and grew rapidly. The antennae started to disappear in the early 1970's when colour televisions became popular.

Television antennae dotted the landscape eventually giving way to cable and then to satellite dishes; Photo by Dave Cook

According to Clarkson's Merle Zoerb, who really was one of the pioneers in cable broadcasting, a very effective marketing campaign was launched to convince people to switch to cable because the colour reception was dependent upon a strong signal, which the antennae just wouldn't provide.

In 1971 the Town of Mississauga was divided into six areas by the CRTC and licenses were granted to operators for cable television in each of the areas.

•At one time Hedge Drive laid claim to having the most number of Ward 7 members of Council holding office at the same time. In an oddity of sorts, when I held office for Ward 7 and lived on Hedge Drive, my neighbour **Stuart Martin**, who lived on the corner of Ribston Road and Hedge Drive and **Don Gastmeier**, who lived on the corner of Westfield Road and Hedge Drive, all held office as an elected member of council at the same time. Don Gastmeier held office in Ward 7 in the Georgian Bay area while Stu Martin held office in Ward 7 in Muskoka Lakes. Stuart owned and operated Martin's Camera Store which was located in the Applewood Village Shopping Centre, while Don was a lawyer and part time Crown Attorney for the Province of Ontario.

• **Russ Hull**, a Melton Drive resident in Westacres, may well have been the person who impressed Ontario Hydro enough to actually change its province-wide policy on garden plots in hydro corridors. In 1982 the electricity giant plowed under small garden plots placed in its right-of-way by residents living adjacent to the corridors across Ontario.

As the representative for Applewood Acres area, I immediately called a public meeting inviting City residents and Ontario Hydro to discuss the issue. Russ articulated his concerns to representatives of Ontario Hydro and, by the end of the meeting, it was obvious that Hydro was willing to listen to suggestions that would allow residents to have garden space. However, they made it clear that any such change would have to be approved by senior management of Ontario Hydro and applied uniformly across the Province. I had placed a suggestion on the floor that residents be allowed to rent plots up to a maximum of 60 feet by 25 feet (18.2 m by 7.6 m) provided they remove all produce by the end of each October and agree to cut the grass in a one yard (one metre strip) around their plot along with not allowing fencing or small sheds to be erected. In October I received a letter from Jim Dunn, Corporate Relations Officer, Central Region, Ontario Hydro, advising that Ontario Hydro's senior management had met and approved the plan.

Many years later Hydro One, as the utility became known, worked closely with residents of the community in what was known as the Trial Right-of-Way Naturalization Plan. The signs erected at both ends of the corridor at Harvest and Dixie Roads read, *"Hydro One Inc. in partnership with the Applewood Acres community, its elected government representatives and the City of Mississauga developed this right-of-way naturalization project. This three-year trial period will create an ecologically sound and*

197

aesthetically pleasing greenway between Harvest and Dixie Roads." Crests of both the Applewood Acres Homeowners' Association and Hydro One are displayed on the signs. The signs also list the species of the 74 trees and 21 wildflowers planted.

•Ontario Premier **William Grenville Davis** (Premier from 1971 to 1985) changed his name to Bill Davis and many people really don't know just how it happened. The fact of the matter is, it was so that the electorate would see his name in the top position on the ballot, which is considered to be worth an extra 10 per cent of the vote. This political move actually had an Applewood Acres connection. As it turned out, Ann Davis, the mother of Neil Davis, who was the New Democratic Party's candidate in the Premier's riding in 1971, worked at Chreston's Restaurant at Applewood Village Shopping Centre back in 1958. Neil also worked there when he was a student. I am sure that Neil didn't expect to win that election. William Grenville Davis didn't expect it either, but then again, he did change his name. Actually, William Grenville Davis often referred to himself as 'Bill'. In the 1959 June election when he first ran for office, he placed several advertisements in the newspapers showing his name as Bill. The media, however, would report his name as William. The ballot listed him as William Grenville Davis as well.

•In a very unique gesture to celebrate Canada's 1967 Centennial, students of **Westacres Public School** embarked on a project which unfortunately became lost in time. It seems that the students of the school, under the guidance of principal George Wright, contacted authorities in each province requesting that a small quantity of soil be sent to Westacres School. This soil was then placed in a plot in which a tree was planted to commemorate each of the 10 provinces. The trees were planted along the driveway on the north side. However, over time, and with the construction of the bus loop, the trees are no longer there. This project was brought back to light when, on January 7, 2003, a fax was sent to school principal Linda Kenny from the librarian of Alberta's Assembly Offices asking for information on the project. A letter had been sent to Premier Ernest C. Manning from G.F. Wright advising the Premier that the students had dedicated one square yard parcel of land to the Province of Alberta. The letter was subsequently read into the minutes of the Legislative Assembly on Monday, February 27th, 1967. When I started to read through some of the school's archives Mrs. Kenny presented me with a copy of the fax. I contacted the Chair of the School Board, Janet MacDougall, and together, traced down George Wright. Now we know the rest of the story.

198

• Famous people seemed to have moved into our area right from the day the first houses were sold. While I have been concentrating on Applewood Acres, I should make mention of a few who didn't live within the actual boundaries but still are part of the Applewood story.

Newspaper writers **Bruce West** and **Jim Coleman** both were early purchasers of homes on Applewood Road. Bruce West was a feature writer with the Toronto Telegram while Jim Coleman was the sports editor with the Toronto Globe and Mail. They both had lots to write about as one of their neighbours was **Annis Stukus**, a football standout who had played for the Toronto Argos and had won Grey Cups in 1937 and 1938. He later went on to assist in developing new football franchises in Edmonton and Vancouver.

Another neighbour who was a familiar name in the news was **Albert Steen**, who held the position of City of Toronto Fire Chief for one year before he retired. In those days the City had a policy that senior employees must live in Toronto, therefore Albert had to wait a short while until he actually retired before taking possession of his home.

Dean and Margaret Henderson purchased their home at 1559 Applewood Road in October 1951 and moved into their new home in June of 1952. Dean Henderson was appointed Treasurer of the Township of Toronto (bylaw 1544) on May 2, 1952. On May 2, 1960 he was appointed Chief Administrative Officer (bylaw 3114). When the Town of Mississauga was created in 1969, Dean became its manager. He retired from the municipality in 1974 to pursue a partnership in an accounting firm but he never really left the service of his community as he was appointed to the Ontario Municipal Board in 1978. He also served as President and later Past President of the Ontario Municipal Administrators Association. A park was named to honour Dean and is located at 2909 Hammond Road, just east of Erin Mills Parkway. The park was acquired by the City of Mississauga in 1987 and is 3.55 acres (1.43ha) in size.

•**Ted and Norma Wildgoose** arrived from Winnipeg in the early 1950's and immediately purchased their new home on Russett Road. Ted was a salesman with Canadian Liquid Air while his wife Norma, from Wales, was a teacher. She met her husband during WW11 and came to Canada as a war-bride. She taught mathematics and sciences in a Winnipeg area school. Toward the end of her stay in Winnipeg Norma

199

began a modeling career and it was her interest in fashion that would see her pursue a new and exciting career when she arrived in Ontario.

She was hired by CIL, a major paint and textile manufacturing company, to model clothing fabricated with CIL's new Terylene fabric. Soon Norma was involved in cross-Canada tours. Twice she did fashion shows across Canada as a model and a third time as the show commentator. Fashion was big business ranging from haute couture to everyday fashions. Haute couture was available from major department stores in Toronto at Eatons, Simpsons, and Holt Renfrew and was worn by Toronto socialites in their roles as social and cultural volunteers. The 1950's were considered the Golden Age of fashion and from November, 2002 to May, 2003, the Royal Ontario Museum presented *Elite Elegance: Couture Fashion in the 1950's*. The show illustrated just what impact haute couture had in its day. But haute couture was not what Norma presented in the fashion shows she produced as fund-raisers for the Applewood United Church. Norma would produce shows featuring affordable clothing and would involve area clothing stores from the Applewood Village Shopping Centre. Also, she would call on a few of her professional model friends to complement residents of Applewood who were selected as models for each show. Norma's talents were soon in demand, as Torontonians in the 1950's were fashion conscious. Yorkdale Shopping Centre hired Norma as its fashion coordinator, a position she held for 25 years. All during the early years when Norma was building a successful modeling and fashion show business, she continued to involve her self in the community and also surrounded herself with family. Her father and mother, William and Catharine Lotwick, came from Wales to live with Ted and Norma until William's passing in 1959. William was very active with the church as was Ted who served on the Committee of Stewarts in the early 1950's at Applewood United.

•Major industry in the area was limited to a few companies which settled in what really was rural farm lands and small villages spread along the shores of Lake Ontario. Ontario Hydro, as an example, established North America's largest coal-fired power station in 1958 with the Lakeview Thermal Generating Station. To the west, also along the waterfront, was Gulf Canada Ltd., which was established in 1943 to supply fuel during wartime. A little closer to Applewood Acres was the AMI Steego plant, a division of McKerlie-Millen Inc., on Haines Road. This plant took over the Dixie Steel Company in the 1960's.

The arrival of Applewood Acres might well mark the start of the decline in the farming industry. Certainly it was for those who farmed in what became Applewood Acres. But also as more and more people settled in new establishments in Toronto Township, the lands used for development were prime farming lands. Industry quickly followed.

One of the first to arrive was Devereux Produce, which eventually became Cardinal Meats. Founded by Jack Devereux and his son Bryan in 1953, the firm settled on Second Line (Stanfield Road) and Middlegate Road and specialized in fresh butter, eggs, chicken and frozen turkeys, ducks and geese. The firm was sold to Cardinal in 1966. Cardinal Meats eventually moved its main offices to Caravelle Drive in the Malton area, but the firm continues to operate its factory outlet store in the original location at Stanfield and Middlegate Roads, and has served the residents of Applewood Acres well over the many years. Cardinal has been one of the main supporters of the annual Homeowners' Association BBQ and Free Swim at Westacres Park.

Astra Zeneca arrived in 1954 and built a modest plant on Middlegate Road. The firm, which continues to grow and expand, has become one of the world's leading pharmaceutical companies with a world-wide portfolio. Astra continues to prosper with its Canadian head office on Middlegate Road.

By the mid-1950s, Middlegate Road blossomed with Whitehall–Robbins starting its operations in 1956. East of Dixie Road companies like Caterpiller of Canada, Excide-Willard, and Cryovac (W.R. Grace) began, while a little north of Middlegate, on Stanfield Road, Revlon and Mother Parkers moved in. Mercury Marine started its operations on Dundas Street at about this time. In 1955 there were plans announced by Canada Safeway to develop a 400,000 square foot (37,169 sq.m) warehouse. However, those plans were never completed. Fruehauf Trailer Company purchased the lands to supplant the Safeway warehouse project and started to build in 1957. Tonolli Canada Ltd., located just south of the tracks on the west side of Dixie Road, arrived in 1959. Tonolli is the only approved recycler of used car and truck batteries in Ontario. The recycled products Tonolli manufactures are returned to the battery manufacturing industry.

By the 1960s, Wedlock Paper Converters Limited had become established in the area. Wedlock Paper Converters is an independent family-owned business established more than 70 years ago. It is a major supplier of flexible packaging materials to retail manufacturers. Founder Alan Wedlock remembers the opening day at what is now Stanfield Road and The Queensway. January 1, 1960 Reeve Mary Fix broke ground in a ceremony held on a very cold day. Other firms opening in the 1960s were Province Cartage Systems, which became Sureline Transportation and in June 1960, Samuel and Son, located at Dixie Road and The Queensway, opened its doors.

Dixie Growers Limited, located south of the rail tracks on the west side of Dixie Road, was probably one of the earliest commercial concerns and is still doing business today in what became the Applewood Acres area. Photo by Dave Cook

With all this growth, one small local farming-based operation flourished over the years. Dixie Growers Limited, a cold storage warehouse located on the west side of Dixie Road and snuggled up on the south side of the rail tracks, opened in 1943 to serve as a co-op among members, eventually becoming a limited company. The names of those who served on the Board of Directors reads like the who's who of early Toronto Township. Fred W. Scriven (1943-44), James McCarthy (1943-88), Arthur Stanfield (1943-56), Eric Chudleigh (1943-52), Lindsey Death (1943-52), Don Pallett (1943), I. J. Clarkson (1943-75), Ken Pallett (1946-52), Garnet Goddard (1944-50), Alfred Conder (1951-78), Grant Clarkson (1951-88),

Leslie Hughes (1951-54), Leslie Pallett (1948-50), J.O. Pallett (1952-92), Jack Goddard (1952) and Quint Ferri (1961).

•Home-based businesses are not at all unusual and there has been a countless number of residents operating small businesses from their homes in Applewood Acres over the years. During my interview with Shakespearean actor Robin Gammell and his brother John, mention was made about their next door neighbour, **Albert Simmons**, whose family had moved into their home at 2107 Primate Road in 1953. Mr. Simmons was employed by a German industrial/commercial film manufacturer and as a sideline business, he imported electronic 'flashguns' for cameras. This was the start of a company called Braun of Canada. When Albert arranged with Braun of Germany to handle products in North America, his German partners said they would be surprised if a dozen items would be sold the first year. Several thousand items actually were sold and the success followed with Braun of Canada handling a wide range of home appliances including the famous Braun Shaver. Later, Albert had great success as North America's Hasselblad Camera distributor as well as distributor of Arriflex motion picture cameras. Braun of Canada was purchased by Gillette Canada in December 1967. In a little touch of irony, Gillette is headquartered at The Mississauga Executive Centre, 4 Robert Speck Parkway, Mississauga, built by The Shipp Corporation. Many years later, Albert's son, Robert, continued with the entrepreneurial talent of the Simmons family and invented a home security timer for lights. The product was featured in the book "Inventing Canada" by Roy Mayer. The product is sold at major stores across the country. Sister Penny also is not to be left out. Penny has a chain of shoe shine stores called Penny Loafers Shoe Shine and writes a weekly newspaper column in the Toronto Financial Post.

Another small home-based business which grew to a major concern was the Bottle Green Drinks Company started in Canada in 1995 by **Andrew and Corrie James**. The James' live on Russett Road and operated Bottle Green Drinks from their home. They had obtained a license to operate Bottle Green in North America from Andrew's relatives in the U.K. who started the business there in 1989. The garage became the warehouse and the offices were located inside with the bottling being done in Grimsby, Ontario. Their first customer was Tiveron Farms Apple Market on Camilla Road.

When 21 year-old Lloyd Leaver persuaded his father George to purchase 48 acres (19.4 ha) on the Second Line East, what is now Stanfield Road, back in 1922 to start Leaverleigh Farms, growers of fine garden vegetables, the move didn't sit too well with the rest of his family.

But Lloyd, who had just graduated from the Ontario Agricultural College (OAC), knew that the light sandy soil only required fertilizer and humus to produce profitable crops. Little did he realize that he had just planted the seed for what was to become one of Canada's most recognizable names in mushroom producers.

George Leaver was born on Henley On Thames, England in 1863 and when he was just 19 years of age he emigrated to Canada on a cattle boat. He arrived penniless but found his way to Toronto where relatives helped him start a grocery store.

By the turn of the century George Leaver was married and he owned and operated two grocery stores. He had two sons and one daughter, Charles, Frank and Grace. Lloyd was born in 1901 while Ross was yet to be born.

The birth of Leaverleigh Farms, some 20 years later, necessitated the use of manure and in his brand new 1922 Rainier truck, Lloyd started calling on bread and dairy stables to pick up the much needed manure.

It was at this time that Lloyd was to meet his future wife Amy Clarkson, whose family owned a dairy farm on the south side of Dundas Street in Summerville, located just west of what is now Highway 27. There were a number of Clarksons who farmed in Summerville. The courting began and Lloyd made frequent visits to the Clarkson farm.

Amy's father, George Clarkson, had a very interesting hobby. He was growing mushrooms in his barn. He had become interested in mushrooms while visiting the Canadian National Exhibition where he had seen mushroom brick spawn from England and decided to try growing them.

Spawns are used to grow mushrooms the same way seeds are used to grow plants The quality of spawns determines the quality of the mushrooms produced. So even if growth conditions are exactly as they should be, the product won't be good if the spawns are poor in quality.

Dry spawns were first produced in sheets, but later, spawns were produced in the form of clay bricks. To produce these bricks, compost and clay were formed into brick blocks 1.9 inches (five cm.) wide. Then a small hole was made in the corner of the bricks and some spawn was placed inside. When the spawn covered the whole surface of the brick, it was dried and made ready to use.

In another method, used earlier, farmers used the soil where the mushrooms grew naturally to produce spawns. They spread the soil over a prepared surface and allowed it to cover the whole surface. Then they used some to grow mushrooms, and dried up the rest for later use.

Because in both methods the spawns were not sterile, disease spread with the spawn and infected the products. Today, common table salt is used to help kill crop-threatening bacteria.

By 1924 Leaverleigh Farms prospered. George and Lloyd built rhubarb sheds and a boiler plant on the east side of Stanfield Road and planted apple, cherry and pear trees on the west side.

In 1928 Lloyd and his father tried to grow mushrooms by using one side of a rhubarb shed. Their first attempt ended in failure as the few mushrooms produced did not pay for the cost of the imported spawn.

The following year Lloyd and Amy were married and the first profitable mushroom crop was produced. However, it all happened just as the stock market crashed and everyone was about to face the inevitable hard times.

Leaverleigh Farms, however, managed to survive because they were producing a line of food products which could be traded for other goods and services when cash was in short supply.

The period 1930-1934 saw a change in that the business became more tree fruit and less vegetables. Lloyd, however, continued to experiment with growing mushrooms and, by 1936 the first block of mushroom houses was built in place of the rhubarb winter forcing shed. A garage for composting was built, which later became part of the maintenance shop.

A large cold storage plant was built in 1938 and above the building were employee rooms. During the construction of this facility, Lloyd fell and fractured his skull. It would be a year before he was fully recovered and by this time Canada was sending troops overseas in World War 11.

During this period there was once again a shortage of cash and also there wasn't a labour force but there was a big demand for food. It was at this time that Lloyd would arrange to have expelled Japanese from British Columbia come and work the farm and, by 1947, Leaverleigh Farms was doing less market gardening and producing more mushrooms.

Between 1947 to 1950 Leaverleigh Farms would see expansion. A dormitory and kitchen were built to house the increasing staff, mostly Japanese and Portuguese with some mid-Europeans. Leaverleigh Farms purchased 450 acres (182 ha) of land on Hurontario Street which would become a large turkey growing and processing plant. It would also be a source of clay for casing and a cash-crop farm department.

By 1952 the Stanfield operation was being surrounded by G.S. Shipp and Son's first plan of subdivision with homes and new roads opening up to the south and east. Greening, Melba, Tolman, Russett, and MacIntosh roads were developed while Stanfield south of the Leaver's farm was also being developed.

In 1955 the Leavers were faced with relocating their composting operations and by 1958 composting for the Stanfield plant would begin at a site in Campbellville on 453 acres (183 ha).

It was in the late 50's and early 60's that Leavers would see the switch from fresh market production, including bulk sales to Campbell Soups (the largest buyer), to more and more canning. The turkey operation was less profitable and it was discontinued, the plant being converted to a mushroom cannery only.

Business would continue to grow and by 1968 a major expansion was necessary to meet the demand as Leavers could not cope with the financial burden. A sale or merger was pursued in order to build a modern farm at Campbellville which would utilize the tray method of growing. This method differed in that mushrooms were grown in trays stacked from floor to ceiling and could be grown in bright cool rooms.

The sale was proposed to many firms including Labatt's, Molson's, Canada Malting and Campbells. Sixty percent of Leaver's interest in the company was subsequently sold to Canada Malting Co. Limited and by 1975, Leavers was wholly owned by Canada Malting.

Lloyd Leaver died in 1977, 19 years after his father George Leaver had passed away. The operations on the east side of Stanfield were then closed. In 1982, the entire Leaver operation in Applewood Acres came to an end. Interestingly enough, it was Leaver Mushrooms' best year in its 60-year history on Stanfield Road.

The former main plant office for Leaver's operations is still in use as an office building. Photo by Dave Cook

21 Events and Organizations

Young families moving into Applewood Acres quickly found a need to 'meet their neighbours'. While it was a new and exciting time living in the first major subdivision west of Toronto, there was a void created by living this far from the centre of the 'big city' of Toronto.

Organizations, clubs and social groups sprouted quickly. There were bowling leagues, music groups, card clubs, and service organizations, such as the Dixie Lions Club, which was established here in Applewood Acres. Another group, the Applewood Acres Chapter of the Imperial Order of the Daughters of the Empire (IODE) got its start in May 1955 when Mrs. T. Teddler of 2080 Russet Road was elected Regent. In 1956 Mrs. G.S. Shipp was appointed as Honorary Regent.

•The major social activity on most weekends in the very early days would be chatting across property lines with your neighbours. Then, fences started to develop rapidly. One group in the Johnathan Drive area, got together to 'pool' their money and co-operatively build their fences. Mrs. Storen, at 945 Johnathan Drive , recalls those early days when a group on her street got together to build their fences. Everyone knew someone who could supply materials at a reasonable discount. In all, about $170 was raised to complete the fencing job. That was for paint, wood, nails and other bits of needed hardware.

Mrs. Storen recalls how the fence-building project turned into a social club known as 'Club 50' which became the social highlight for many area families for several years. Club 50 provided the young families with their social outing without having to travel to Toronto. The members would be close to home and the baby sitters all knew where everyone was. Club 50 organized about eight dances every year from the mid 1950's to the early 1960's.

The dances would be organized by a committee of four couples drawn from the membership list. Everyone would take a turn. The events were all held in the banquet hall above Chreston's Restaurant in the Applewood Village Shopping Centre.

•The first Home and School Association was established November 5, 1953 when 55 members elected Ken Creber as President. Alan Boyd of 1351 Primate Road and William Cochrane were elected Vice Presidents, K.A. Grant of 2093 Bloomfield (Stanfield Road) was elected Corresponding Secretary while Alf Houston of 2070 Harvest Drive was elected Secretary. Doug Appleton of 2119 Primate Road was elected Treasurer. Both Mr. Creber and Mr. Cochrane lived on Glenwatson Road in Orchard Heights.

Seven months later, on May 20, 1954, outgoing President Ken Creber welcomed Mr. Appleton as its newly-elected President. The significant thing about this meeting was that the principals of two new schools were first introduced to the community. Mr. Eric N. Trewin, Principal of Orchard Heights was introduced as was Mr. G.W. Finlayson, Principal of Westacres Public School. Since the children from Orchard Heights and Applewood areas first went north to Dixie Public School, the association executive included residents from both areas. The Home and School Association in Applewood flourished and is, in fact, the only community group to be continuously active since its inception.

•June 11, 1955 was a day that kicked off an event destined to become one of the most popular and longest standing events in the history of the Applewood Acres community, The June Fair.

Originally known as the Westacres June Fair and Field Day, the event was held in conjunction with a fair sponsored by the Home and School Association. Exhibitions of volleyball, skill and stick gymnastics and track and field events were billed as the main athletic program while the day's fun fair started off with folk dancing. There were fish ponds, pony rides and a miniature train ride for the children.

The school's classes were divided into three 'house' sections for the athletic competitions. Each section chose one of three names, Stewart, Graham or Kennedy, which were all prominent family names from this area of Toronto Township. The idea was that each team would carry its own colours and at the end of the day, the victorious 'house' would be named. One of the Stewarts actually was on hand to present one of the trophies. The opening ceremonies were performed by R.E. Cole, recently elected Chairman of the South Peel Board of Education.

209

Kennedy House took top place for the day with 570.5 points, Stewart House was second with 535 points while Graham House placed third with 499.5 points. Dick Runstedler was named the most outstanding boy in competition while Gaye Hall was top girl.

Trophies were presented to the school for house champions, given by W.L.A. Pope; boys' relay trophy given by John H. Aiken; girls' relay trophy given by Max Smith. The girls' field day champion trophy was awarded by H.B. Stewart while the boys' trophy was awarded by J. M. Milne.

Citizenship awards, given by the Home and School Association, were presented to the boy and girl chosen by their classmates as best exemplifying good citizenship. These were presented to Linda Austin, grade seven, and Carol Elliott, grade eight.

While the first Fair was held the second weekend of the month, the June Fair started its traditional first weekend of June format on June 2, 1956. The June Fair has become very much a part of the culture of the school and involves many volunteer hours for staff, parents and teachers. Planning of the event starts in September to culminate on the first Saturday in June.

The Fair is the major fundraiser for the school and over the years money raised has been used for such things as resources for the library, theatrical presentations in the school, subsidies for educational field trips, replacement of school textbooks and the purchase of computers.

•The Applewood Acres Homeowners' Association origins can be traced to August 15, 1952 when it was reported in the Toronto Telegram that Henry Moxon, of 2072 Toman Road, chairman of an emergency ratepayers' association, hurriedly established a group of homeowners to fight for a school closer to home than the Dixie Public School where Applewood children were being accommodated. Mr. Moxon pointed out that the plans to construct an overpass on Dixie Road over the Queen Elizabeth Highway added to those fears, and would bring even more traffic into the area during its construction phase.

The association became officially established when a meeting was held on November 26, 1953 and took the title of "North Applewood Homeowners' Association". Malcolm Nasmith, who resided at 1293

Queen Elizabeth, what is now the North Service Road, was elected President. Alan Boyd was elected Vice President, Bob Rankin of 1221 Greening, Treasurer and Reg Johnstone of 2048 Snow Crescent was elected Secretary.

What was probably the most important single battle this community has ever seen was in 1954 when those who had mortgages might well have been placed in an impossible financial bind. According to Deputy Reeve Mary Fix, some could end up losing their homes if the Township was forced into bankruptcy. The ratepayers' group never really fought the issue but rather was a side-party to it. On March 18th, 1954, Peel County Council passed a motion for a 27-day postponement on the matter of an application by the Village of Malton to separate from the County. This move would have pushed Toronto Township into bankruptcy, 104 years after its formal incorporation.

By a vote of 15-4 council approved an amendment to the original bylaw, calling for a delay on its final readings until April 14. It was expected that Royal Assent would be given to a Bill in the Legislature of Ontario making the Ontario Municipal Board the arbiter in the dispute. A petition signed by 90 percent of Malton's 2,000 residents wanted the Province to enact legislation that would incorporate Malton as a town. By doing so Malton would increase its industrial tax revenues from $3,000 to $140,000 annually. Obviously Toronto Township opposed the petition.

"Reeve Adamson and I have just come from the climax of a fight that may very well have saved your homes ," Deputy Reeve Mary Fix told a packed house at the Applewood United Church where the North Applewood Homeowners' Association held its meeting. Deputy Reeve Mary Fix told the gathering that it was a hard-fought battle. "We have just had a sweeping victory in Peel County Council and everyone here with mortgages might have lost your homes had we not won," she told the residents.

The meeting at the church that night was held to discuss many things, one of which was a report about four septic beds draining onto the school and park property. Other concerns discussed at that meeting included a 'demand' that G.S. Shipp proceed immediately with the establishment of a promised shopping centre. Also on the agenda that night was a cry that postal delivery be started in this area and that hobby crafts be included in the summer playground programs.

In a study done a little later by three members of Council, it was discovered that 30 of 300 septic beds had problems. On June 8, 1954, Fred Lund of the Peel County Health Unit advised Council that the problem was resolved when an agreement was reached with G.S. Shipp and Son's to have a filter placed on the 30 septic beds.

The name "North Applewood Homeowners' Association" was first used formally on October 6, 1953 when the Association made an application for a Scout Group Charter. The organization changed its name to the North Applewood Ratepayers' Association in October 1972 and then on April 13, 1982 was named the Applewood Acres Homeowners' Association. If a constitution ever existed it was never found nor mention of one was ever made in the minutes in the archives. However, on June 3, 1998, as President of the Association, I presented the executive with a document which was accepted as its first formal Constitution. It was signed by the executive.

While there were obviously more individuals than Henry Moxon, Malcolm Nasmith of 1293 Queen Elizabeth Way, R.B. Martin of 1234 Russet Road, W. Clayton Drum, 2218 Bartlett Lane and Clare Wilson of 1089 Henley Road, who served as Presidents of the Association, the only other recorded names, with year elected, are as follows: Arden Gayman, 1065 Henley Road (1972), Nick Staples, 2196 Breezy Brae (1972), Arnold Tremere, 2252 Haltyre Court (1974 & 1975), Margaret Hamilton, 2135 Courtland Crescent (1975), John Walmark, 2098 Harvest Drive (1979 & 1986), Jane Baggetta, 1074 Baldwin Road (1981), Dave Cook 2059 Stewart Cres., (1991 & 1998), Bruce Davies, 2101 Harvest Drive (1992 &1995), Peter Daigle, 2196 Stanfield Road (1993).

Through the years the Association has been involved in numerous issues, some minor and others not so minor. The Association has also been instrumental in organizing the annual BBQ at Westacres Park every summer. The event was originally started to promote usage of the pool when the City announced it was being slated for closure. One of the features of the Association has been a newsletter, called *The Apple Press*, which is published four times each year and has been an excellent source for communications with the residents.

•A garden club was formed in January 1999 and in its first two years boasted a membership of more than 30 people. The club has been active in all aspects of gardening in the area ranging from organizing garden tours to doing plantings at the Applewood Village Shopping Centre.

•Tennis has been very much a part of life in Applewood Acres almost from the beginning. Lance Ward, of 957 Melton Drive, tells the story of the Westacres Tennis Club.

On our excursions to Westacres Park with our children during the mid-1950's we had to pass the two courts of the Westacres Tennis Club. We were not aware of how much work and negotiating had already been done in order to get those courts. At that time they didn't look very attractive, being of disintegrating asphalt on a shallow stone base with painted lines. There were back fences but no side enclosures. The local young people amused themselves riding their bikes across the courts even while play was in progress.

Some of those far-sighted early enthusiasts were Herb Aiken, Bob Speck, Doug Reed, Lois and Ernie Hyde, Clayton Drum and Bob Hartwell. Young players were encouraged to join. Initial meetings to increase membership were not well attended.

Playing conditions were difficult. Clayton Drum carried two sets of nets to the courts every Saturday, Sunday and holiday afternoons. Any attempt to leave the nets overnight immediately attracted vandalism and damage. The net posts were occasionally removed or turned ninety degrees to make the mechanism non-operative. The end fence was too low and holes were developing.

The Parks and Recreation Department of the Township of Toronto, which owned the facility, was interested in greater general use of its investment. It became apparent that a strong club would be necessary in order to build enthusiasm, develop young players, provide teaching, and generally supervise activities.

In 1964 Bill and Bev Ritchie joined the club and spearheaded an effort to widen the membership base. Fees were raised from $2 to $10 per year. Young people found that the student fee of $5 was acceptable. When membership had grown to around 200, the Parks and Recreation Department showed increased interest and the club opened discussions with elected municipal councillors, among whom were Reeve Robert Speck, and Councillor Ron Searle. Also supportive of the club's efforts *was Terry Butt who would go on to sit as a member of Council in later years.*

Parks and Recreation staff were also helpful with advice and suggestions. A flourishing tennis club began to take shape. Bake sales and social gatherings were common fundraisers. By 1974 enough funds had been assembled to permit the club to contribute toward a new playing surface, full and higher fencing, and a locked gate. The new look attracted additional members. Club championships were well attended and matches hotly contested.

In 1981 court lighting was installed extending the playing time by several hours daily. Small groups were coming together: men on Sunday mornings; women on Tuesday and Thursday mornings; a seniors' group; under 14's, 16's, 18's, and mixed youth. Group play was available almost at any time.

The opening of the refurbished courts was a gala affair. According to Jerry Love, who was a senior staff member of the City's Parks and Recreation Department, Canadian tennis legends Don Fontana and Lorne Main were on hand. They not only officiated at the opening but also gave a tennis demonstration. Also, Applewood's own Louise Brown and her son David, who went on to become legends in the sport, were also present.

•The Scouting movement, founded by Lord Baden-Powell in 1907, came to Canada in 1908 and has become very much a part of most youngsters' lives since. Scouting arrived in Applewood Acres on October 6, 1953 when the North Applewood Homeowners' Association sponsored the group's first charter. T.H. Jolley of 1165 Melba Road, who was the Vice President of the Association, submitted the application to the Boy Scouts Association for the establishment of a Group Charter. The group met at Applewood United Church.

Group Committee members were R.B. Martin of 1234 Russet Road, Albert M. Walters of 2108 Harvest Drive, and Reginald R. Wilson of 2057 Snow Crescent and the first Wolf Cub Pack leader was Mrs. Jim Wark of 2066 Tolman Road. In all, 36 children were listed on the application form with ages ranging from eight to 11 years of age.

Registration of the Wolf Cub Pack was completed on February 25, 1954 when an application was submitted by Gordon H. Spry who lived at 2225

214

Rambo Road. C.E. Whitten of 2055 Courtland Crescent was the Assistant Cubmaster. Mr. Whitten was age 30 at the time and had entered the scouting movement at age 12, making him a great asset to the Pack, which had an enrollment of 30 children at the time.

The Dixie Lions Club, which was established in Applewood in 1954, with Howard Cober of Munden Park area elected as its first president, became the sponsors of the Cubs in 1956.

The First Applewood Guide Company started October 1, 1954 and met at Applewood United Church until February 1970, when the company was renamed the 68th Mississauga Girl Guide Company and the unit moved to Westacres Public School. By 1966 there were four Packs and four Guide Companies plus a Ranger unit. In the ensuing years the age range of the girls was adjusted lower and this allowed for the establishment of two groups, Sparks, ages five to six, and Pathfinders, ages 12-15.

•Lavinia Nablo who has lived with her husband Sheldon at 795 Melton Drive since 1958, became involved immediately with the Girl Guides. Having realized when she moved into Applewood that there was a need for a Ranger leader, she organized the 1st Applewood-Orchard Heights Ranger Unit. She has been both District Guider and District Commissioner and has served on many committees over the years. Lavinia was honoured in 1988 with a Medal of Merit and in 2002 she was presented with the Queen's Medal in honour of the Queen's Coronation. She recently was honoured for her 50 years of volunteering. She was presented with a certificate by the Credit River Division Commissioner and the Provincial Commissioner, at a gathering at the Girl Guides White Oaks District office. Other groups over the years which were established for the youngsters include the Canadian Girls in Training (CGIT) and the TYRO group for boys. Both of these groups have mentions in the recently produced 50th Anniversary book of Applewood United Church.

• A story, prepared by the Executive Committee of the Applewood Co-operative Preschool, is reprinted with their permission.

"You begin with a mere $50 and a good reserve of willing parents. You end up with a thriving nursery school where mothers learn as much as the youngsters for around $10 per pupil per month." This quote was taken from the October 1957 Chatelaine magazine that highlighted the early years of what is known today as Applewood Co-operative Preschool.

The location for the first class of 15 children (age three to five years) was St. John's Anglican Church. Since that time over one thousand families have stepped into the pages of Applewood history. Applewood Preschool provides a co-operative environment that fosters a positive preschool experience for children and promotes greater understanding by parents in matters relating to early childhood education.

The original Preschool served the local Applewood neighbourhood. Today the Preschool still serves the neighbourhood and areas beyond. Many families are willing to travel a distance in order to participate in the excellent care and co-operative spirit found at Applewood Preschool. The school continues to survive due to the dedication of teachers and families alike who work together for a common goal-the children. Even within the Applewood United Church there have been members who have had their children enrolled, or in some cases, are original students of the Preschool.

Originally, the Preschool operated from October until April with one large classroom. Since then it has blossomed into two classrooms and operates from September until June. The co-operative spirit of many helping hands has given birth to some great traditions and events. Seasonal themes were and are still celebrated at the Preschool. For example, Applewood families always have a special memory of the traditional Christmas Party. Families also gather on the last day of school in June to celebrate another successful school year and to reflect back on some fond memories at the Annual Bronte Creek Picnic. During the picnic an award called the 'Golden Apple' is presented in recognition of an outstanding individual from the school year. This award was established in 1992 in honour of a former teacher, Amy Reist.

From two mothers, Betty Dales and Phyllis Beamish, in 1955, chatting over a morning coffee and initiating plans for the Preschool to modern families raising children in a busy society, Applewood Co-operative Preschool has captured the hearts and minds of both young and old in the community and at the Applewood United Church.

Phyllis Beamish and her husband Gregory lived at 861 Johnathan Drive. Gregory was a senior executive with the Ford Motor Company in Oakville, while Betty Dales and her husband John lived two doors away at 861 Johnathan Drive. John was a professor at the University of Toronto.

Gordon S. Shipp, left, with son Harold, stand in front of the Applewood Landmark and Applewood Place in 1977. Photo courtesy of the Shipp Corporation.

Roger E. Riendeau, an accomplished author, highlighted the Shipp Corporation in his book, *Mississauga, An Illustrated History* published by Windsor Publications in co-operation with the Mississauga Board of Trade in 1985. With permission of Mr. Riendeau, his story follows:

Shipp Corporation is one of the few businesses that can truly make the claim that it built Mississauga. When the late Gordon S. Shipp founded the company in 1923, the construction of custom housing in Toronto was a

217

central activity. Now, more than sixty years later, Shipp Corporation has a hand in virtually every aspect of construction. From the original single-family homes, through substantial multi unit residential buildings, to office towers and other commercial units.

Three generations of Shipp perfectionists have built an enviable reputation for quality into their work. One brick bearing the name Shipp-Built is part of every building as a signature of pride in craftsmanship.* *(see footnote)*

Chairman and Chief Executive Officer Harold G. Shipp (son of the founder) notes: "Few developers build under their own name-that's why you get companies such as ABC Developments or EG Builders. We're proud of the work we do. Why not let others know who stands behind their product?"

Shipp's first venture into what was later to become Mississauga took the form of a purchase of 200 acres of land in Toronto Township in 1951. Father and son envisioned an entire subdivision on the property at a time when the area was considered too remote in relation to the city of Toronto. Financing was difficult to obtain.

But eventually the challenges were met, and within four months plans were approved, an infrastructure was built, and the first furnished model home was completed-with an attached garage, of course, for it was assumed that anyone venturing to live that far out of Toronto would need to commute by car.

Today this Applewood Acres area is still known as one of the largest and most successful residential areas constructed by a single builder. Homes that originally sold for $12,800 are now on the market at well over $100,000.

"Applewood" has become a trademark for Shipp-built residences. No longer limited to communities of single-family homes, the name appears on apartment buildings, condominiums, townhouses, and even an automobile dealership, Applewood Chevrolet Oldsmobile.

The latter part of the 1970s witnessed a surge of new activities for the company. An initial venture was made into the United States with construction of Shipp's Landing, a luxury resort condominium complex on the Gulf Coast at Marco Island, Florida.

At the same time, Shipp was kept busy on a local level, as Mississauga became the fastest-growing suburb of Toronto. The Mississauga Executive Centre, opened in 1979, proved to be a focal point for the area with four office towers, a hotel, and three high-rise apartments.

Shipp has also been active in neighbouring Etobicoke with its landmark construction of the Shipp Centre office tower/shopping concourse in 1981. Negotiations are in progress for another similar Etobicoke commercial project, to be known as Shipp Centre West.

*(Author's note: the single Shipp-Built brick was not installed in Shipp homes in Applewood Acres. It first appeared when the firm moved north of Dundas where more than one builder was constructing homes. I once quipped to Harold Shipp that he didn't put any in the Applewood Acres homes. Harold came to me one Christmas and presented me with two bricks. One was s installed in my home at 860 Hedge Drive. Some 18 years after we moved to 2059 Stewart, I had the opportunity to have the second brick placed.)

In 1953 Gordon S. Shipp was elected President of the National House Builders Association of Canada. Mr. Shipp, who was born in Kent, Ontario, some 61 years earlier, began his career as a builder in East York Township and had practically built his way across Canada.

He served as President of the Toronto Metropolitan Home Builders' Association, an organization with which he had been associated for more than 28 years. Mr. Shipp was active in the community where he lived as a member of the United Church and a member of the Toronto West Progressive Club. He became the first person outside of the United States to be named to the National Homebuilders' Association Hall of Fame.

Gordon Stanley Shipp was in his late twenties before he began to think about leaving his 100-acre (40 ha) farm and entering the building trade.

By the time he was 30 his mind was fully made up. "My wife was having to work too hard on a farm and, in any case, building had always appealed to me," Mr. Shipp was quoted in a magazine interview in 1953. "So my cousin and I went into partnership, bought some land, and started to build," he said.

Little by little his knowledge grew. The partnership was dissolved and Mr. Shipp struck out on his own, putting up houses in East York, Forest Hill and New Toronto.

It was reported in the Canadian Home Builder magazine in October 1953 that Mr. Shipp learned every one of the intricate jobs that go into the building of a house, and that he could lay a floor, plaster a wall or tile a roof as well as any of the more than 150 men working for him.

He built his own seven-room home in about four months, which is, like most Shipp homes, well below the national average time of six to seven months. Weekends, Mr. Shipp would drive to his summer cottage in Bobcaygeon, to relax in a Shipp-Built cottage.

Gordon S. Shipp died February 9, 1981 at the age of 89. He was a big man with a soft voice, a reserved, almost shy manner, and a serious preoccupation with his job. He was not without a sense of humour. He was quoted by the media one time responding to the problem facing many builders of having to fill out more than 40 forms to complete the mortgaging process, saying "If it gets any worse, some builders will never find the time to build."

Gordon's son Harold is probably the member of the Shipp family most recognized by those living in Applewood Acres. Over the years Harold has visited the area several times. He has been the guest speaker at the Homeowners' Association annual meeting and he has also attended several functions in Applewood including the annual BBQ and Picnic and the renaming of the Don McLean Westacres Pool.

He was born in East York, as one would expect, in a Shipp-built home. One might say that he was involved with his father's business from the start. There would be many nights that a young Harold would stoke the burners to keep the wood dry on cold winter nights at his father's house building sites.

Being exposed to the industry and helping his father as a youngster, and having been brought up through the depression period, Harold soon had an understanding of all the trades needed to build a house.

After graduating from Etobicoke College Institute in 1945, Harold decided to build homes himself. His father 'staked' him with a $1,000 bond. Harold had not only built four homes, but he had paid back the loan in full.

He became a full partner in his father's business on April 1, 1946 and one year later to the day, a new name, G.S. Shipp and Son was incorporated. By 1952 the offices of the company would be temporarily located in a house at 1177 North Service Road. Later, the offices would be situated in the upper level of the Applewood Village Shopping Centre, above Mainprize Drug Store.

In 1966 Gordon S. Shipp became Chairman of the Board allowing Harold to take the position of President and Chief Executive Officer.

Five years later Harold would be elected President of the National Homebuilders' Association and also President of the Housing and Urban Development Association of Canada. In rapid succession, new honours and titles would follow.

In 1974 he was named to the Board of Counsellors, Oxford College of Emory University, Oxford, Georgia. In 1982 he was elected President of the Mississauga Board of Trade and in 1986 he was named Mississauga Business Person of the Year.

One of the crowning moments in the career of Harold Shipp came when he acted as the Chairman of the Royal Visit to Mississauga for the official opening of City Hall on July 18, 1987.

The arrival of Their Royal Highnesses The Duke and Duchess of York was a grand affair with members of Council and dignitaries assembled in the courtyard to greet them. This was followed by a luncheon a little later with a fairly small gathering attended by a few special guests and members of Council. My wife and I had the pleasure of being present. This was the first major event to be held in the Great Hall. A humourous little story must be told about this luncheon. Harold had summoned The mai-tre d' and asked quietly if he would bring an empty wine bottle to the head table with the cork pushed all the way inside. Of course his request was granted and, when the bottle arrived, Harold placed the bottle on the floor by his feet, out of sight to all in attendance. June, Harold's wife, whispered, "Harold, you're not going to do that trick here are you?" she asked disapprovingly.

Harold, who was seated next to Prince Andrew, quietly said to the Prince that he knew the Royals do not carry Coin of The Realm in person, "but, if you did, would you wager that I can extract that cork from the bottle without breaking the bottle or the cork?" The Prince, being a sport, was most intrigued and said he would. Picking up the bottle, keeping it out of sight of the luncheon guests, Harold started to stuff the silk table napkin into the bottle. He then moved the bottle just enough to flip the cork onto the napkin and then started to pull the napkin out, which carried the cork along with it.

Many years later Harold, who is a director of the Jockey Club, was attending a reception for the Queen's Plate. He was introduced to Princess Margaret Rose and it became known to her Highness that Harold was the chairman of the Royal Visit of the Duke and Duchess of York for the official opening of the Mississauga Civic Centre. At this point, Harold had quipped that he had taught Prince Andrew a trick with a wine bottle. The Princess remarked that she was very aware of this trick as her nephew had shown that trick many times over the years.

The year 1988 was also a very special one for Harold. He was inducted into the Hall of Fame of the Canadian Homebuilders' Association and also, that year, was named as Mississauga's Citizen of The Year, an award that carries his father's name. The event is sponsored annually by the Mississauga Real Estate Board and The Mississauga News. All recipients of the Gordon S. Shipp Memorial Award have their photos on display at Mississauga City Hall. The next year Harold was elected to the post of Honorary Trustee in the U.S.-based Urban Land Institute. In 1991 he was given the City of Etobicoke Corporate Award. He was presented with the Silver Jubilee Medallion in 1992, which is a commemorative medal for the 125th anniversary of Canadian Confederation. Harold had served as President of the Mississauga Hospital Foundation and celebrated 25 years' involvement.

In 1955, G.S. Shipp and Son purchased 165 acres (66.7 ha) of land owned by Col. Kennedy for $500,000, which began the development north of Dundas Street at Tomken Road. Tomken Road, of course, was named after Col. Kennedy. Two years later Col. Kennedy paid a visit to Harold's office and suggested he consider running for office to replace him when he retired.

According to Harold, Col. Kennedy was about 80 years of age at the time and had explained he was becoming too old to sit in the Legislature and it was time to step down. He then gave Harold an endorsement if he ran for office as his replacement. In the political arena of the day, that was equivalent to an anointment. Harold gave it his full consideration but decided not to take the Col. up on his offer. Instead, Harold paid a visit to a friend in Brampton, a bright young lawyer named William Grenville Davis. It's well documented how Mr. Davis went on to became The Honourable William Grenville Davis QC, M.P.P., LL.D, Premier of Ontario. He was first elected in June 1959, became Minister of Education in 1962 and then Premier in 1971, holding the office until his retirement in 1985. Harold said he had a little joke with Mr. Davis, that he would stay out of politics if Mr. Davis would stay out of the development industry.

With all of the developments both domestic and also offshore, and through the years, the name "Applewood" has remained not onlyrespected with the thousands of residents who have called this area their home, but also highly regarded by the Shipp family. To this day, the logo for the Shipp Corporation is an "Apple" and under it is a single word "Applewood."

Harold was the guest speaker at the Applewood Acres Homeowners' Association annual meeting held September 23, 1992 and was asked how the name Applewood Acres was selected. After all these years Harold's eyes became bright and a smile crossed his face, "I was thinking about apple tree, apple farm, apple land and one morning at 6 a.m. the name Applewood Acres came to me. I will always remember the time in the morning the name came to me. I was excited about it and just couldn't wait any longer. I called my dad at 6:15 a.m. to suggest the name "Applewood Acres."

"It would have sounded just as good at half-past seven, " came a quiet reply.

Acknowledgements:

-The Shipp Corporation: Harold Shipp, Victoria Shipp, Lloyd Gunby
-Hydro Mississauga
-Tricon Restaurants International (KFC)
-Applewood United Church
-John Court, MA, Centre for Addiction and Mental Health
-Dufferin Peel Catholic District School Board,
-Peel District School Board
-City of Mississauga: Councillor Carman Corbasson, Paulina Mikicich,
    Planner, Rosa Salandra, Planning Records, Jerry Love (retired)
    Director of Recreation and Parks, Barbara Zapf, Transportation and
    Works, Art Leonard, Building Department, Linda Mailer, Council
    Secretary, Joan LeFeuvre, City Clerk, Joe Hamilton, Engineering
-Lavinia Nablo, Girl Guides, Phil Frost, Scouts Canada
-Mississauga Library Systems: Ted Sharpe, Manager, Marian Kutarna,
Senior Librarian, Dorthy Kew, Senior Librarian
-City of Toronto Reference Library
-The Stanfield Family, Howard, Jim and Anna (Carr)
-Canadian Amateur Diving Association-Bev Hugenholz
-Westacres Public School: Linda Kenny, Principal, George Wright,
    Principal (retired)
-Stewart Petrie and the Stewart Family
-Frank Martins, QEW Senior Engineer MTO
-George (Bulldog) Hansen, Calgary Stampeder Alumni
-Bill Small, Edward Small & Sons Construction
-Valerie Cowton, Gillette Canada (Braun of Canada)
-Mary Bracken, Credit Valley Conservation Authority
-Mr. T. Molyneux, National Rifle Association, U.K. and Mr. D. Vamplew,
Dominion of Canada Rifle Association

BIBLIOGRAPHY

The Port Credit Weekly, The Mississauga News, The Toronto Star, The
Toronto Telegram, Toronto Globe and Mail.
Reflections From Yesterday/ Frederick M. Ketchen/ The Anglican
Church of St. John The Baptist, Dixie.
Windsor Publications/ Author, Mississauga, Roger Riendeau.
The Report of The Mississauga Railway Accident-The Honourable
        Mr. Justice Samuel G.M. Grange
National Library of Canada
The Apple Press